Editorial Introduction: Charting Our Course Here and Forward

Zachary Beare and Jacob Babb

How many PhDs does it take to write an editorial introduction? This question sounds like the start of a bad joke, but what would it mean to ask it seriously? Presently, there are two of us in the editing history for this document, each of us with our own working habits and sensibilities—Jacob, the disciplined early worker, and Zach, the procrastinator. (Jacob rarely disagrees with his co-editor, but he objects to this description of our work habits. Not enough to remove it, but enough to hope that Zach doesn't notice this insertion. Reader, quiet please.) But the two of us would never have entered into this editorial partnership and started writing together if it wasn't for another PhD, Zach's former doctoral student, Melissa Stone, who is Jacob's colleague at Appalachian State University. A conversation between Melissa and Jacob led to Jacob sending Zach an email. Email exchanges were followed by a zoom meeting, countless text message exchanges, and an application. A letter of recommendation from another PhD-holding colleague was required, which our mutual friend and Zach's NC State colleague Casie Fedukovich graciously wrote for us. Our candidacy was reviewed by the previous editorial team (three PhDs) and the journal's Advisory Board (thirteen PhDs). It took twenty PhDs just for us to get access to the Google Drive folder to write this.

Of course, that is just the beginning. We might name the members of our own dissertation committees and the faculty members we worked with throughout our educational careers. We might name the faculty across institutions who mentored us and helped us reach points in our respective careers where we felt comfortable applying to be editors. There are also the folks we have encountered at academic conferences or followed on social media who have influenced our ways of thinking, often without us being able to trace back to those original encounters. Then there are the countless writers of other editorial introductions whose approaches over time have coalesced into the genre of the editorial introduction with what Carolyn R. Miller might describe as its "typified rhetorical actions based in recurrent situations" (159) like this one. Asking how many PhDs it takes to write an editorial introduction invites us to think about the complex stories behind the texts we compose, the sources of knowledge we draw upon, and the people who have intervened, sometimes deliberately and sometimes serendipitously, in our lives. While writing is often represented, at least in popular depictions, as a largely solitary enterprise, our field has long been invested in representing the social and interconnected nature of composing practices. Asking how many PhDs it takes to write an editorial introduction helps us to chart that, to highlight the elements along our journeys to this moment.

In our last editorial introduction, we described our desire to "keep the ship afloat," an admirable goal that probably also evidenced our great anxiety that we might somehow harm a journal that means so much to the both of us and, as we have learned, means so much to so many of you. The urgency of keeping the ship afloat has been brought into sharper focus because of conversations with colleagues across the field who have shared their own stories about *Composition Studies*, its previous editorial teams, and what this journal has meant to them at various points in their careers. We feel the incredible privilege and responsibility associated with our roles.

To open this issue, and to continue our deployment of slightly awkward nautical metaphors, we want to talk about charting our own course with the journal. The language of "charting a course" simultaneously directs attention toward the future (destinations planned) and toward the past (a recording of where one has been and how one got there). Charting a course is about the relationship between the past and the future.

Our decision to enter into an editorial partnership and our visions for the journal's future are outgrowths of our past work. Both of us have long-standing scholarly interests in disciplinary knowledge making, in the composing processes of composition scholars, and in the emotional dimensions of writing for publication and processing reviewer feedback, requests for revision, and rejection. These shared scholarly interests are shaping our approaches to editorial work and our visions for the journal's future and what might be possible. We are interested in the ways that a journal called *Composition Studies* is especially well suited for, well, studying composition. We see our editorial work as scholarly, as a continual inquiry into the dynamics and nature of composing and recording the work of composing. The journal's name and its aims and scopes, we argue, should not only shape the content of the articles we publish; they should also provide us direction for thinking about the practices of the journal, the ways that we engage with writers and reviewers, and the ways that we might explore new genres for sharing the complex histories behind the texts that we publish.

Some of the ways that our backgrounds and scholarly investments in these topics have impacted our practice are relatively simple. As a small example, we decided that we won't send out decision letters on Fridays, or on holidays. Both of us have experienced weekends derailed by a rejection, and we imagine many of you have as well. Even good news like a positive revise and resubmit can rob one of a restful weekend sometimes. We have decided we don't do that. We are also actively trying to incorporate what we have learned through our own qualitative research into the experiences of writing for publication to write decision letters that better support the authors who put so much time

composition STUDIES

Volume 53, Number 1

Spring 2025

SUBSCRIPTIONS

Composition Studies is published twice each year (Spring and Fall). Annual subscription rates: Individuals $50 (Domestic), $80 (International), and $25 (Students). To subscribe online, please visit https://compstudiesjournal.com/subscriptions/.

BACK ISSUES

Back issues, five years prior to the present, are freely accessible on our website: https://comp studiesjournal.com/archive/. If you don't see what you're looking for, contact us. Also, recent back issues are now available through Amazon.com. To find issues, use the advanced search feature and search on "Composition Studies" (title) and "Parlor Press" (publisher).

BOOK REVIEWS

Assignments are made from a file of potential book reviewers. If you are interested in writing a review, please contact our Book Review editor at wcui9@jh.edu.

JOURNAL SCOPE

The oldest independent periodical in the field, *Composition Studies* publishes original articles relevant to rhetoric and composition, including those that address teaching college writing; theorizing rhetoric and composing; administering writing programs; and, among other topics, preparing the field's future teacher-scholars. All perspectives and topics of general interest to the profession are welcome. We also publish Course Designs, which contextualize, theorize, and reflect on the content and pedagogy of a course. CFPs, announcements, and letters to the editor are most welcome. *Composition Studies* does not consider previously published manuscripts, unrevised conference papers, or unrevised dissertation chapters.

SUBMISSIONS

For submission information and guidelines, see https://compstudiesjournal.com/submissions/.

Direct all correspondence to:

Zachary Beare, Co-Editor
2211 Hillsborough Street
Campus Box 8105
Raleigh, NC 27695-8105
compstudiesjournal@gmail.com

Composition Studies is grateful for the support of the North Carolina State University and Appalachian State University.

©2025 by Jacob Babb and Zachary Beare, Co-Editors

Production and distribution is managed by Parlor Press, www.parlorpress.com.

ISSN 1534–9322.

Cover art by Susanna Crum.

https://compstudiesjournal.com/

composition STUDIES

Volume 53, Number 1
Spring 2025

Contents

and energy into producing manuscripts and submitting them for our consideration. The nature of editing a journal like *Composition Studies* is that we will have to reject a large percentage (nearly 90%) of what we read. So much good work is included in that 90%. Projects we would like to see in print are often included in that group. We do not take pleasure in that rejection rate. Instead, as responsible stewards of the journal, we have to consider not only the quality of scholarship we publish but also the very real financial challenge of limiting the size of each issue.

While we can't publish everything, what we can do is demonstrate that we have carefully read the manuscripts we receive. We can help writers see how we read their work, share thoughts we had about it, and offer suggestions towards the future. We want our decision letters, even rejections, to offer writers directions forward (whether that might be a recommendation for revisions or recommendations for a more fitting venue for the work). We recognize the vulnerability that comes with submitting a manuscript and want to honor that. In practice, this means we divide lead authorship of letters between us, basing our feedback in those letters on our discussions of each manuscript in addition to reviewer responses, and then we prompt the other, usually through a quick text, to ask them to read the draft and make revisions as needed. Now that we are almost a year into responding to authors' work, we are getting better at producing these letters in the initial draft, but we still hold firm to this practice because we believe it not only makes our feedback better—it makes our responses more empathetic.

Our shared research interests have not only impacted our current practice; they also shape our imagination for what the journal might do in the future. As WPA nerds, we can't help but question how we might assess our journal's practices, how we might study our letters, the peer review reports we share, and the manuscripts we publish. We feel strongly that assessment is necessary to see whether the journal is enacting (or failing to enact) the values we have committed ourselves to. As two people interested in the complex underlives and hidden histories behind compositions, we are also considering ways to use both the journal and other modes and communication channels to share stories of revision and experiences with the editorial process. These are important parts of the process that end up erased once a piece goes to print. We are in a position to think about how we might better surface them. And we think doing so could have benefits for the field, perhaps especially for early-career faculty and graduate students.

We are so excited about the future of this journal and so grateful to the countless people in our own lives and in the field who have helped us chart our way here and are helping us imagine the future forward. At this point, we want to thank several of our Advisory Board members, who are rotating off of the board to make room for new voices. All five of these board members have served the journal for several years beyond the intended three-year cycle, and we are grateful to all of them. Advisory Board members provide us with a group of people with whom we can consult when we are discussing different kinds of issues or challenges. Board members also sometimes step in to complete manuscript reviews for us when we have difficulties getting a second review. In other words, their service is crucial to the ongoing success of the journal, and we are so grateful for their willingness to serve. Following the publication of this issue, we are saying goodbye to these board members: Sheila Carter-Tod, Michael McCamley, Jessica Nastal-Dema, Annette Harris Powell, and Darci Thoune. Thanks to each of you for your dedication to *Composition Studies*.

We will welcome our new Advisory Board members in the fall issue, but in the meantime, we want to welcome our newest content editor, Carina Jiaxing Shi, a PhD student at the University of Maryland. Carina has already demonstrated her keen eye as we prepared this issue for print. Finally, we want to say thank you and goodbye to Mikala Jones-Wall, one of our social media editors. When we applied to edit the journal, we noted in particular how impressed we were with the journal's social media presence, and Mikala is one of the social media editors responsible for that. She has served in this capacity since 2022, and while we are sad to see her go, we are grateful that she has done so much to help the journal reach new readers. As always, departing colleagues leave big shoes to fill.

In This Issue

Issue Cover

We hope that readers will remember to open this issue rather than simply gazing at the gorgeous cover, although we understand the temptation. The cover art is "Attention," created by Susanna Crum, a former colleague of Jacob's. As someone who is fascinated with spatial rhetorics, Jacob always enjoyed seeing her work when they were colleagues; he still has a print of hers on his office wall. We are so thrilled and grateful Susanna agreed to contribute this beautiful work for the cover of this issue.

Susanna is an artist and teacher based in Louisville, Kentucky, where she co-founded the shared print media workspace, Calliope Arts. Her drawings, prints, and sculptures investigate printed artifacts and maps as messages to the future. Her artwork has been exhibited throughout the United States and internationally, and she has been artist-in-residence at studios in California, New York, Scotland, and Norway. Visit www.susanna-crum.com to see more of her work.

Susanna offers the following statement about her work:

"Attention," 2025
Cyanotype and ink on paper
18" x 12"

I recently heard a therapist describe frustrations with attention as walking through a maze with fog obscuring one's path. With a surprising urgency and certainty, I responded, "Which path? And aren't there trapdoors and tunnels that take you to another place entirely?"
I often work with found and archival imagery, but this image flowed right out with a sense of urgency and unusual focus in these times. Using the ancient drawing method of axonometric perspective and the early photographic process of cyanotype, I explored a model of what this mental architecture could look like.

At a Glance

Jaclyn Fiscus-Cannaday's contribution for this section provides an overview of her new book, *Reflection-in-Motion: Reimagining Reflection in the Writing Classroom*, recently published by Utah State University Press. We invited Fiscus-Cannaday to produce this contribution for "At a Glance" because we were intrigued by her work to introduce new methodologies for conducting research about reflection. Reflection is one of the pillars of our discipline, the kind of metacognitive activity that just about everyone incorporates into their writing courses. Fiscus-Cannaday's work calls for readers to pay attention to what she calls reflection-in-motion, which she defines as "how practitioners define, identify, and practice reflection in real time through everyday activities in the writing classroom." We hope readers will enjoy Fiscus-Cannaday's contribution as an *amuse-bouche* and seek out the full course in her new book.

Articles

The articles in this issue cover an array of topics-contract grading and how it is enacted and received in various contexts, the perennial WPA challenge of articulating (of agreeing on) outcomes, how disciplinary expertise is defined and contested, and the political and ethical implications of our pedagogical approaches. The articles also represent a diversity of methodological approaches-classroom-based inquiry, corpus analysis, actor-network theory, and survey and interview-based research. One of the exciting elements of editing a journal like *Composition Studies,* with its broad aims and scopes, is that we receive submissions that represent our field's diversity of research interests.

Course Designs

The course designs presented in the issue (and the supplementary materials shared on our website) showcase curricular responses to student needs at their respective institutions. Casie J. Fedukovich and Brooke Mulhollem discuss their approach to reconfiguring a first year writing course to attend to the needs of students following the COVID-19 pandemic. As they detail, these students have experienced various forms of learning loss, and, perhaps even more significantly, they have experienced a collective trauma. Fedukovich and Mulhollem share how their development and employment of an "ACT Model" is designed to support students and help facilitate metacognition and learning transfer. Megan J. Busch reports on the development of a credited corequisite course for students placed into her campus's bridge program for students whose GPAs and/or test scores are below typical admissions levels. The description of this corequisite model is likely relevant to faculty and WPAs at many campuses who are adjusting to the elimination of traditional developmental writing programs. Finally, Meghan A. Sweeney shares her approach to developing a "Writing for Nonprofits" course offered at Saint Mary's College of California, an Hispanic Serving and Asian American and Native American Pacific Islander Serving Institution. Sweeney reflects on the ways that a course focused on writing for nonprofits connects to the Lasallian spirit of her institution and its mission to foster social justice and inclusive communities.

Where We Are

In her call for proposals for the 2026 Conference on College Composition and Communication, incoming program chair Melissa Ianetta asks

> Why go to the conference? What does being together in real time afford that print, digital, and asynchronous online interactions cannot? What do conferences offer that recent "un-conferences" cannot or do not?

Ianetta's questions urge the field to ask the kinds of questions that we have posed to conference planners across the discipline, and we are glad to see the field taking up these questions as we all reflect on what conferences can be.

Academic conferences serve numerous purposes: They provide spaces for scholars and professionals in specific disciplines and organizations to gather and share ideas with one another. They offer opportunities for professional organizations to hold meetings for officers, executive bodies, and committees that complete the numerous tasks associated with organizational business. They present the chance for longterm friends to catch up with one another and for participants to build new connections and relationships with others. They create opportunities to build special interest groups that create micro-communities within the larger community of the organization. They make space for authors, editors, and publishers to meet with each other to discuss in-progress or future publications.

Conferences also present different challenges: They are often prohibitively expensive due to the high costs of booking spaces in conference hotels, air travel, and hotel accommodations for multiple nights, a barrier that can prevent faculty members from institutions with fewer available travel resources from attending. They are often not accessible for participants with physical or mental disabilities, although organizations work consistently to make conferences more accessible. They can be overwhelming for new members of the field, who can find the sheer size of our larger conferences daunting or find the intimacy of smaller conferences to feel cliquish. All of these challenges have been intensified by institutional and governmental austerity, as well as the global disruption of COVID-19, which made attending conferences in person a major public health risk, a risk many are no longer willing to take.

We hope that the contributions in this section will prove helpful for those organization leaders and conference planners, but we also hope that all readers will benefit from these inside looks at how conferences happen. This section includes reflections written by leaders and planners from the Conference on College Composition and Communication (CCCC), the Two-Year College Association (TYCA), Feminisms and Rhetoric, the Global Society of Online Literacy Educators (GSOLE), the Council of Writing Program Administrators (CWPA), the International Writing Across the Curriculum Conference (IWAC), the Northeast Writing Centers Association (NEWCA) and the Thomas R. Watson Conference. We are grateful to all of these authors for giving their time and energy to crafting reflections that take seriously the question of what academic conferences may look like in the future.

Here is the brief prompt we sent to this section's contributors: We want to take this moment to take the pulse, as it were, from several different organizations that hold conferences, particularly as we increasingly consider accessibility and inclusion for academic conferences and in the aftermath of a global pandemic. In short, this seems like a good time for us to ask: where are academic conferences going? How might they change to accommodate the needs of individuals who cannot travel to attend, or who may not have sufficient funding from institutions that take austerity as the new governing budgetary logic? What kinds of challenges are organizations facing that they can address through changes to how academic conferences work?

Book Reviews

Finally, the issue includes four reviews for books that each address hot-button issues of our current cultural moment. Kimberly A. Bain reviews Henry Louis Gates Jr.'s *The Black Box: Writing the Race*, Katie Silvester reviews Cruz Medina's *Sanctuary: Exclusion, Violence, and Indigenous Migrants in the East Bay*. Gideon Kwashie Kwawukumey reviews Staci M. Perryman-Clark's *The New Work of Writing Across the Curriculum: Diversity and Inclusion, Collaborative Partnerships, and Faculty Development*, and Sean Murray reviews *Rhetoric and Guns*, edited by Lydia Wilkes, Nate Kreuter, and Ryan Skinnell.

Work Cited

"2026 Call for Proposals." Conference on College Composition and Communication, https://cccc.ncte.org/cccc/call-2026?utm_source=National+Council+of+Teachers+of+English. Accessed 15 April 2025.

Miller, Carolyn R. "Genre as Social Action." *Quarterly Journal of Speech*, vol. 70, no. 2, 1984, pp. 151–167. doi.org/10.1080/00335638409383686.

At a Glance

New Methodologies for Researching Reflection: Reflection-in-Motion in the Writing Classroom

Jaclyn Fiscus-Cannaday

In Asao Inoue's 2019 CCCC Chair address, Inoue called the field to reconsider its deep-rooted white habitus, asking: "Is the Framework being used as method to get students to write White, but not used to attend to an ever-widening universe of reflective discourses?" (14). Inoue encourages us to be wary of research that privileges (White) mainstream understandings of reflection. This At A Glance contribution offers an overview of my recently published book, *Reflection-in-Motion: Reimagining Reflection in the Writing Classroom* (2025)—a book that offers new methodologies for researching reflection, and thus provides exciting new pedagogical implications for reflection in the writing classroom.

In *Reflection-in-Motion*, I begin with a review of reflection scholarship, suggesting that the field has often relied on John Dewey and Daniel Schön's understandings of reflection as a starting point for what reflection might mean in our writing classrooms. Researchers have used those theoretical underpinnings to imagine where reflection might be taken up in specific genres. In doing so, reflection researchers have ignored what participants might identify as reflection, perhaps ignoring the rich histories of reflection in non-Western traditions—and their associated definitions and practices.

Figure 1: Cover of *Reflection-in-Motion: Reimagining Reflection with Reflective Practitioners in the Writing Classroom.*

OFFERING NEW METHODS AND METHODOLOGIES FOR RESEARCHING REFLECTION

Reflection-in-Motion argues that we should pay more attention to what I call "reflection-in-motion," or how practitioners define, identify, and practice reflection in real time through everyday activities in the writing classroom. To better attend to reflection-in-motion, I offer new methodologies for researching reflection. I adopt Venus Evans-Winter's Black Feminist qualitative mixed-method of "mosaic": gathering traditional and nontraditional texts to explore a complex research problem (24). The project purposefully centers the experiences of students and teachers at Minority Serving Institutions (MSIs) listening to them with feminist ears, so we can learn best practices for serving our marginalized students.

I then use storytelling as feminist methodology to explore how students and teachers take up and enact reflection in the everyday moments within the writing classroom. In relaying these stories, I illuminate the complex entanglements of contextual factors that affect how reflection is taken up: the timing, materials, spatial layouts, emotions, relationships, histories, affect, and more. Research participants reported reflection as resulting in five different rhetorical actions: awareness, introspection, learning, mindfulness, and perspective.

VENUS EVANS-WINTERS AND A "BLACK FEMINIST MOSAIC"

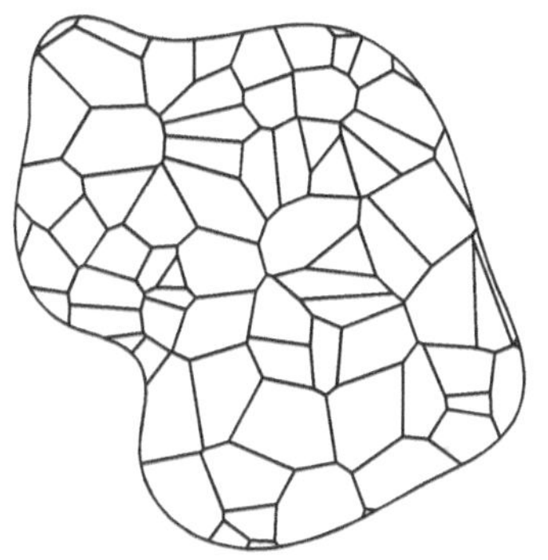

DATA FROM

3 — MSIs
6 — FYW Classrooms
5 — Focal Teachers
20 — Focal Students
63 — Surveys

STORYTELLING AS FEMINSIT METHODOLOGY

REFLECTION AND ITS RHETORICAL EFFECTS

reflection-for-awareness: analyzing thought process(es)

reflection-for-introspection: exploring internal state of being

reflection-for-learning: considering action to revise or adapt

reflection-for-mindfulness: prioritizing acute present-ness

reflection-for-perspective: reconsidering a belief or ideology

FINDINGS

Reflection was never as simple as teacher asks students to reflect and then students reflect—nor student decides to reflect so they reflect. In fact, many students took up reflection in ways unexpected by teachers: perhaps discounting an intended reflective activity as busy work, while manipulating another activity (unintended by the teacher as reflective) to do the rhetorical action the student associated with reflection. Put simply: whether students decided to take up, refuse, or subvert their instructor's reflection request was, in large part, due to the contextual factors within the rhetorical situation and the rhetorical action that followed.

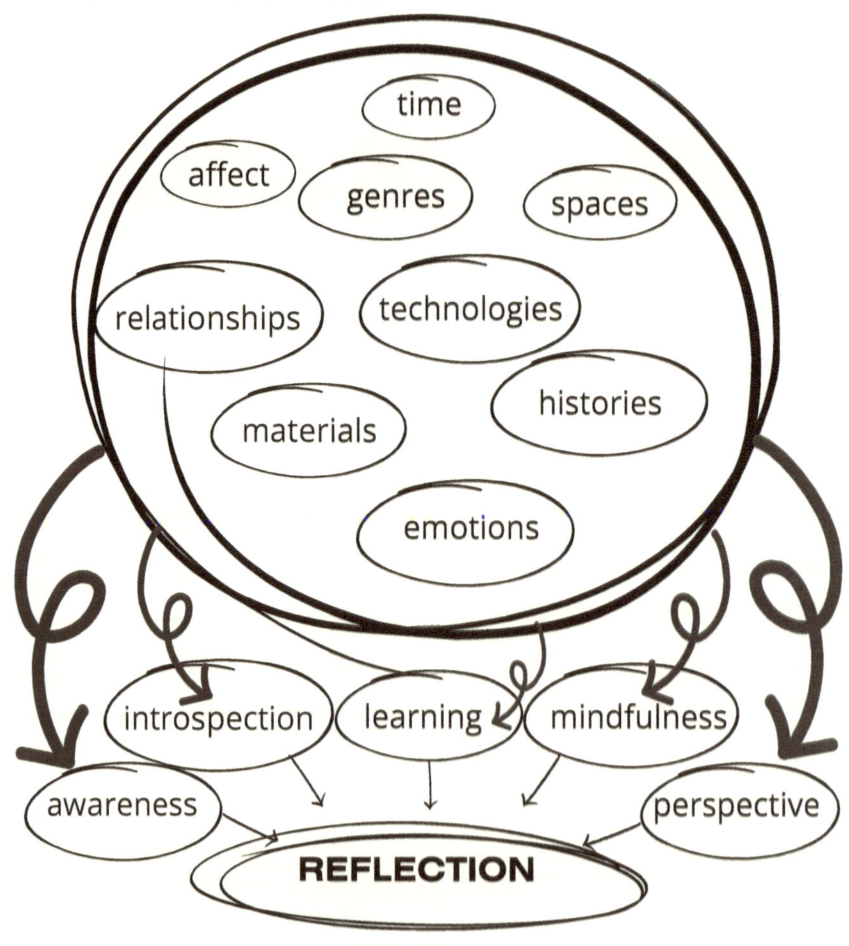

Though the practice of reflection was subject to contextual factors, it was identified as "reflection" (or not) because of the rhetorical action associated with reflection. Their associated action was based on past experiences—like familial relationships, religious practices, journaling activities, sports, and more—and those experiences shaped what students and teachers saw as their definitions of reflection. Students and teachers' definitions of reflection were instrumental, then, in their identification of reflective activity. Yet, participants were still willing to consider alternative definitions of reflection—and could use those definitions to imagine new possibilities for what might count as reflective activity, too. This indicates that definitions of reflection are important in identifying and practicing reflection, but definitions can also be used as a tool for finding new avenues for reflective activity (perhaps even outside the students' or teachers' original ideas about what reflection is and can be).

Reflection was embedded in the daily happenings of the course. Students and teachers reported activities like:

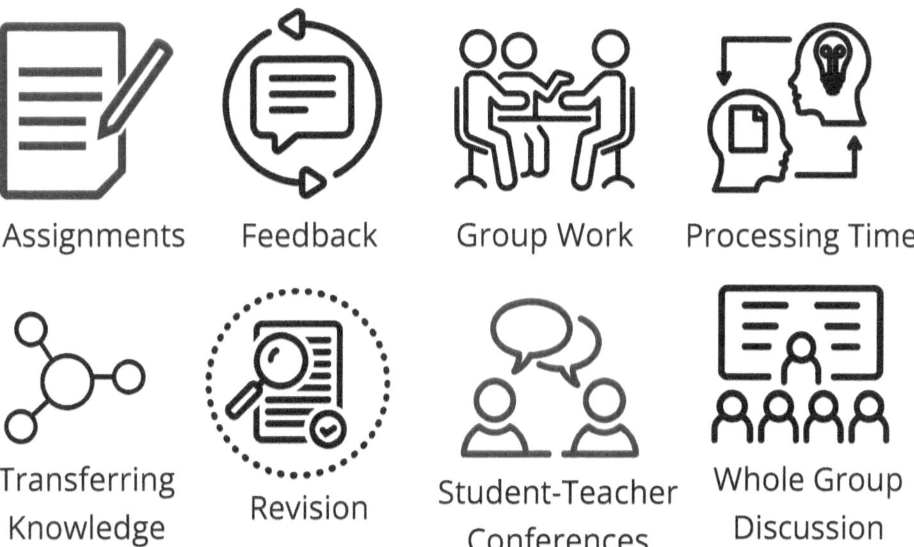

Just because reflection *could* be identified in these activities (among others), did not mean that reflection always happened whenever these activities occurred. Instead, participants saw potential for the rhetorical actions they associated with reflection to occur. The participants definitions of reflection and their potential genres for reflection are just some of the many different actions I anticipate that reflective practitioners might associate with reflection in other contexts. Yet, they already suggest an important broadening of what we think of as reflection in the writing classroom. Upon talking to participants in my research study, I define the reflection as follows:

 Reflection is the intentional consideration (of activity, perspectives, or ideologies) that emerges from a rhetorical context and results in rhetorical action(s). 

I am careful in this definition to leave open the modalities, mediums, timeliness, genres, technologies, and materials that reflection might take up. Reflection is not isolated to static, written, or retrospective texts. It is instead, always and already, interwoven in the everyday fabric of writing classrooms. My findings suggest that reflection is multimodal and dynamic, happening throughout the writing process in relationship to complicated rhetorical contexts for rich rhetorical effects. In what follows, I present a pedagogical activity inspired by these findings.

PEDAGOGICAL ACTIVITY

Ask yourself: How do I define reflection? Where does that definition come from? How does that definition effect what kinds of activities I intend for my students to take up as reflection?

Ask your students: How do you define reflection? Where does that definition come from? How does that definition effect what kinds of activities you use to do reflection?

Notice the overlaps, the mismatches, and the complications.

Make room for negotiation, and use the opportunity to brainstorm with students.

Consider: What do they already do to practice reflection? What contextual factors play a role in their reflective practice? And, how can you help them curate a context conducive to the conditions necessary for reflective activity?

Depending on desired rhetorical actions, modalities, materials, affect, time, and emotions, consider what genres might be appropriate. These might include activities like:

WORKS CITED

Evans-Winters, Venus E. *Black Feminism in Qualitative Inquiry: A Mosaic for Writing Our Daughter's Body*. Routledge, 2019.

Fiscus-Cannaday, Jaclyn. *Reflection-in-Motion Reimagining Reflection in the Writing Classroom.* Utah State University Press, 2025.

Inoue, Asao B. "2019 CCCC Chair's Address: How Do We Language So People Stop Killing Each Other, or What Do We Do about White Language Supremacy?" *College Composition and Communication*, vol. 71, no. 2, 2019, pp. 352–69.

Jaclyn Fiscus-Cannaday is assistant professor at the University of Minnesota, Twin Cities. She specializes in critical composition theories and pedagogies—including feminist, accessible, antiracist, queer, and linguistically informed strategies for teaching writing. Her research explores how teaching writing works, how people think teaching writing should work, and how we might learn from classrooms, communities, and writing programs that support and welcome all writers.

Articles

Risk-Taking in Labor-Based Grading Contracts for Collaborative Multimodal Composing

Daniel Libertz

In this study, I examine how six students in an honors section of first-year writing at a predominantly working-class public university in the northeast experienced the impact of a labor-based grading contract (LBGC) on their practice of collaborative multimodal composing (i.e., a class podcast assignment). After analyzing survey and interview data, results suggest that the LBGC helped these students take risks in their learning in different ways (i.e., collaboration, multimodal composing, and selecting a group role). However, students also indicated that they felt the LBGC may have had negative effects on motivation and their perception of the "quality" of the podcast. I conclude by considering the tension between motivation/ quality and risk-taking in learning in the context of collaborative multimodal composition.

Introduction

Taking risks in learning can be a valuable undertaking for college students, as it increases the likelihood they might try something different and learn something new. Alexis Teagarden, Carolyn Commer, Ana Cooke, and Justin Mando have identified traditions in composition and allied fields of scholarship where "the concept of intellectual risk [is] a pedagogical term that typically describes when a student attempts a new way to learn" where in doing so they risk "being perceived as less competent," "facing public criticism by peers," or "losing a personal belief or coherent sense of social identity"(117). Teagarden et al. surveyed students and instructors for their own definitions of risk and their thoughts on when and how risks should be taken. One of Teagarden et al.'s findings for students was a stated tension between seeing value in trying new things in learning and perceptions of how risk would negatively affect grades.

One of the theorized benefits of many alternative grading approaches is that, by removing the punitive element of grades, students may be more willing to take risks. For instance, Asao Inoue has argued that labor-based grading contracts (LBGCs) "open a space for practices that can fail or miss the mark, allowing students the freedom to take risks, and try new things in their writing without the fear of losing points or failing the course" (*Labor-Based Grading* 138). Additionally, Jane Danielewicz and Peter Elbow argue that students are more "open to radical changes . . . since they have a solid cushion of safety" of contract grading (255). Beyond contract grading, others have made similar claims. In specifications grading—a type of grading where pass/fail specifications are aligned to tiered levels of assessment—Linda Nilson has argued that "specs grading augments motivation" leading to a "learning orientation" rather than a "performance orientation," where learning-oriented students will be more likely to take risks and be okay with making errors (107–08). Others have claimed that ungrading also encourages risk-taking. For instance, Laura Gibbs has argued that "[n]ot putting grades on [students'] work is the key to encouraging them to take that risk and try something new" (99).

Unlike most writing assignments students complete in school, collaborative and multimodal composing might be particularly risky due to its novelty. Both forms of writing can be difficult to evaluate and students may be afraid to take chances, clinging to models or rubrics that might better guide them toward a desired grade outcome. In terms of collaborative projects, evaluation can be difficult due to balancing an evaluation of the overall group, formative learning of the group, and individual learning (Fittipaldi 1787). From the perspective of students, they may be frustrated by differing conceptions of "fairness" in terms of workload distribution and intellectual credit now that they are depending on students other than themselves—all of which threaten graded outcomes (Isaac; Sutton). For multimodal composing, Shane A. Wood claims that contract grading may be particularly well suited as it "complements the affordances of multimodal pedagogy: student choice/agency; an emphasis on processes, genre, and pedagogical flexibility; and public audiences" ("Multimodal" 260). Furthermore, Julia Voss highlights how digital collaborative projects can exacerbate divides of race, gender, and class by distributing learning outcomes inequitably (e.g., leadership and technical roles being dominated by privileged students). Perhaps, then, alternative grading practices like LBGCs can be advantageous for risk-taking in collaborative multimodal composing for all students.

Because, ultimately, "all grading and assessment exist within systems that uphold singular, dominant standards that are racist, and white supremacist when used uniformly," judging by any singular standard can create barriers to students of color and others who don't "naturally" fit that standard (Inoue, *Labor-Based Grading* 3). Inoue's solution—tying labor to grading—is an elegant one. If traditional grading systems based on quality too easily reward and encourage students who are closer to a White racial habitus, then the LBGC sidesteps (at least some of) this issue. Inoue writes that when "no grades are circulating" but only "documents and judgments, then labor and its value become more prominent and important, and more obvious" (Inoue, *Labor--Based Grading* 80). For Inoue, "one *habitus* is not privileged as the standard, instead amount or quantity of labor determines grades" (*Labor-Based Grading* 83). However, there are limitations to using an LBGC. For instance, there is a danger in promising too much in terms of racial justice or benefits for students that can only be addressed through activism and organizing (Craig; Fernandes, Brier, and McIntyre). There can also be shortcomings in terms of considering disability and access. For instance, not considering how neurodivergent students have learned to adapt in other classes (Kryger and Zimmerman) or universalizing how time for labor is conceptualized in assignments (Carillo, *Hidden Inequalities*; Wood, "Book Review") can create accessibility issues related to disability or other contextual factors like socioeconomic considerations (e.g., care-taking responsibilities). While these criticisms point to the need for continual and further adaptations (e.g., Carillo's "engagement-based grading" in *Hidden Inequalities*, Inoue's *Cripping Labor-Based Grading*), I find value in alternative grading practices like LBGCs in how they shift focus away from tying judgment to the grade as a commodity, and I was curious about how an LBGC specifically could be beneficial for untraditional writing assignments like collaborative multimodal projects.

In this article, I explore a pilot study using Inoue's LBGC grading model by tracing how it affected student learning in collaborative multimodal composing.[1] Namely, I was most interested to see if the LBGC helped students get comfortable taking risks in this kind of writing—in this case, a class podcast. In survey and interview results of six students in a first-year writing course at a large, public university in the northeast, participants emphasized that they were indeed more willing to take risks and further their learning during the collaborative multimodal project. However, several participants also noted that they felt they would have produced a better quality podcast and students would have been more motivated under conditions of traditional grading. I conclude by considering how we might live with this tension between risk-taking and motivation/quality.

Study Design

I teach at a large, public university in the northeast where students are primarily working-class, recent immigrants or children of immigrants, slightly more female than male, and predominantly Asian and Pacific Islander (AAPI) at just over 40% of our student population (with White students at about a quarter of the student population, followed by Latinx at about 20%, and then Black students at about 11%) ("Baruch College Fact Sheet: Fall 2021"). There were fifteen students who remained enrolled in the class, six of whom completed the study. Students took an anonymous pre-survey in the second week of class so I could get a sense of their history with grading and then an anonymous post-survey in the penultimate week of class about the effects of the LBGC. During the following semester, I asked all six students if they would be willing to participate in an interview of approximately thirty minutes. All six students agreed and I conducted semi-structured interviews. I also asked about the following demographic information: race, gender, and whether they were a first-generation college student. In future studies of LB-GCs and other alternative grading practices, researchers should consider asking about disability given the work of scholars like Kryger and Zimmerman and Carillo.

Participant Background

It is important to note a few things about this class section. First, it was hybrid, meaning that students met on campus once a week while the second "course meeting" was composed of asynchronous coursework. This may have affected how students could work on a collaborative project, producing challenges with fewer on-campus class meetings which had a structure for collaborating that the asynchronous aspect of the course lacked. Second, this was an honors section and the sample is small. In this institution, there is an honors college where students get certain advantages (e.g., specialized advisors). Additionally, honors students are less likely to be first-generation students (18%) at the City University of New York ("About Macaulay") compared to the general student population (60%) at the City University of New York ("Spotlight: CUNY and the New York City Economy"). From one perspective, these students know how to "do school," and thus, can probably handle just about any grading system thrown their way. They are also a group of students more likely to have privileges or come from advantageous backgrounds compared to their peers at this institution, which might limit how we can interpret their survey and interview responses (e.g., less likely to be first-generation students, some students came from better-resourced high schools relative to their peers). However, these students are also under pressure to obtain good grades. In this institutional context, if their GPA drops below 3.5, they jeopardize losing scholarship money. Since many of these students are working-class, this can have a huge financial impact on them, which, in turn, can create the kinds of pressures that high-achieving students at other schools may be less likely to encounter. As one student put it in the anonymous pre-survey, "I feel more pressure now" as an honors student and feel like they are "not allowed to make mistakes."

Participants were split on how they felt about traditional grading in the pre-survey: one felt positively, three felt mixed, and two felt negatively. When identifying positive elements of traditional grading, they found it a useful tool for motivation and discipline as well as providing some external marker of progress. When viewing traditional grading negatively, these students found it damaging to self-esteem, alienating, and a deterrent to learning.

Participants were also asked what they worry about regarding grades for collaborative multimodal projects. Participants said they worried about there being a fair distribution of workload (*n*=4) and about being graded fairly (*n*=4). However, one student mentioned that their concerns are lowered for an "honors class where students are willing to split up work evenly." Another student felt like there is just "never a good way to determine how to grade people fairly," and, thus, there isn't a perfect system for grading anything.

The post-survey data results were very consistent with the interview data results. Because the survey data has less nuance, I center my analysis on the interview data in this article. However, the consistency between post-survey and interview data is notable since the post-survey was anonymous, which indicates the students may have been fairly honest with me in our interviews despite my relation to them as their former instructor (e.g., students were critical of the LBGC even though they may have felt a need to suppress criticism since they were talking to their teacher).

Below are participant pseudonyms and demographic information they provided during interviews:

Table 1

Demographic Information of Participants

Pseudonym	Gender	Race and Ethnicity	First-Generation College Student
Aarya	Female	Southeast Asian	No
Carolina	Female	Latina, Ecuadorian	Yes
Erica	Female	White-Hispanic; half-Irish and half Argentinian	No
Kevin	Male	Indian-American	No
Linda	Female	Latina	Didn't answer
Nate	Male	White	No

Approach to Coding

I followed Cheryl Geisler and Jason Swarts's guidance on systematic coding of language to segment and code the interview data. I analyzed the codes to see what themes tended to emerge, using a grounded theory approach (Corbin and Strauss) where a theory is constructed by the analyst from an iterative process of coding the data where I began with open coding and worked with a second coder to create a reliable coding scheme. After finalizing the coding scheme, here were the codes I applied to all interview data with abbreviated definitions:

- Risk, Growth, and/or Motivation: any mention of learning, growth, feelings of motivation, or elements of risk-taking as a result of the LBGC.
- Stress and Workload: any mention of feelings of stress, pressure, or mention of the amount or type of workload done as a result of the LBGC.
- Students: any mention of other students or the general status of being a student without reference to the LBGC.
- Class Design: any mention of how the design of the class (e.g., assignments) impacted stress, learning, etc. without reference to the LBGC.
- Preference: any mention of general preferences for learning without relation to other codes.

Course and Grading Contract Design

For the first-year writing class I taught during Fall 2021, students listened to the podcast *Nice White Parents* (a podcast about the influence of White, upper-class parents on gentrifying public schools in New York City) as our "course text" while writing a rhetorical analysis paper and a research-driven paper. These assignments helped students learn about the genre of podcast episodes and helped them dig deeper into potential topics to work on during the final major project: a collaborative podcast assignment. For their podcast, students chose to create a guide for students and families who are choosing high schools in New York City. There were four episodes (one for each group): traditional public, private, public charter, and public specialized.

Throughout the semester, I mostly followed Inoue's model (e.g., negotiating and drafting a contract, having students log information on tasks, weekly labor journal entries). There were two primary adaptations I made: adjustments to reflections on labor and to labor instructions. For the reflections on labor, I introduced labor journal entries about reflecting on collaborative labor as well as something called a "podcast post" that did similar work. I agree with William Duffy that "coauthors must invent their own processes as they write," but that there are still practices we can encourage that can help students discover those processes (127). One of these practices is the "risky account" of "parallel composition" (Duffy 114). Duffy defines these accounts of parallel composition as not "a *process narrative*," but instead something that has a "coterminous emergence alongside the primary text of the collaboration" and is written without an explicit, deliberate end to achieve (114). Quite like Inoue's triumvirate of the labor log, labor post, and labor journal, Duffy aims with parallel compositions for mindfulness about the work being done, but with collaboration specifically in mind (116). Duffy writes that "coauthors are better positioned to understand the labor of coauthorship the more attuned they are to the 'task at hand' of their writing together . . . [and] the more cowriters pay attention to their work, the more they recognize what they are doing" (116). Concretely, Duffy advocates for "literal accounts, or accounting, of what co-authors experience as they write together" (116). Because collaborative writing is slow writing, having such a record helps to create "a jumping-off point for inquiries into the labor of coauthorship" and make visible these "*resistances and discontinuities*" in collaborative work that can help enrich a collaborative project (119).

In two labor journal entries during the podcast unit, students wrote a parallel composition as they worked on their podcast, writing about some combination of the following: excitements/breakthroughs they had while working with others on the project; frustrations they had while working with others on the podcast; what had been working well with their group work; more generally what wasn't working well in group work; and/or ideas on ways to best further the work of the podcast. These labor journal entries both helped students be mindful about the labor they had been completing that week as Inoue advocates while also creating a record of "resistances and discontinuities" to help pay attention to the work of collaboration in parallel to the ongoing work for their podcast, as Duffy recommends. Additionally, students were re-quired to complete one "podcast post" on our class Discord server where they were prompted to think about their ongoing collaborative labor but in more specific ways (e.g., how interviews could be completed, what work the narra-tors could do) and, importantly, in public ways. Posting on Discord helped students think about the way they were working collaboratively and use more public writing to work out further how they might do things going forward.

Another key difference was that unlike other work in the course that followed detailed labor instructions with time estimates and procedures for completing work as Inoue recommends in his original book on LBGCs, the podcast itself had no such instructions. After giving them space to see models and learn more about how to write scripts, complete interviews, edit audio, etc., I wanted to leave it up to the students to come up with their own processes and workload distributions for completing the podcast. This move has some resonance with what Carillo proposes in her "engagement-based contract" (EBC). Carillo writes that EBCs "offer a range of ways that students might engage with the course" without a "series of assignments and an estimated amount of time to spend on each assignment" (*Hidden Inequalities* 56). Students instead can "choose their forms of engagement and are assessed on those" to help create multiple ways to access the course, which is important when considering multiple needs and ways of learning for a range of disability as well as socioeconomic factors (*Hidden Inequalities* 56).

In the case of the podcast assignment in my class, students were able to choose their roles in the project (i.e., project manager or "producer," narrator, scriptwriter, audio editor) and after that, it was up to the groups to form the podcast and commit to whatever amount and form of work they wished to do. There were perhaps more constraints here than Carillo advocates for—it is not maximally flexible since students have to fulfill some base level of meeting the duties of their roles (e.g., the scriptwriter must produce a script, the audio editor must edit the episode)—but none of the role responsibilities were meant to rest entirely on any individual. The script writer would receive input and also could have co-writers. The project manager could help complete interviews. The audio editor could do additional research. Someone had to work on the cover art for the podcast. Someone had to help complete transcripts for the episodes. And so on. There were a lot of different kinds of work that had to be completed, and it was up to the groups and the class to choose what worked best for them. Students could lean on others if they were too busy in a given week and there was not a "normative student and a normative sense of time" embedded in things like labor instructions with time estimates (Carillo, *Hidden Inequalities* 16).

Findings

In the following five subsections, I examine the main findings: the LBGC helped reduce stress for the podcast assignment, the LBGC placed limitations on the quality of and/or motivation to work on the podcast, the LBGC helped some students take risks in role selection, the LBGC helped some students take risks in collaboration, and the LBGC helped some students take risks in multimodal composing.

Reducing Stress

All six students, in one way or another, reflected on a reduction of stress. However, one student, Kevin, offered a detailed portrait of writing-in-the-moment, which helps to show how the LBGC helped him focus his energy toward the podcast. Kevin explained that because of the financial implications of dropping below a 3.5 GPA as an honors student (i.e., losing his scholarship), that there is "always pressure on [him]" and that "there's always that thing in the back of [his] head" on every assignment he works on. He felt that he has to "spend every second of [his] free time studying towards something." This perpetual stress leads him to avoidance coping: "watching YouTube for a great period of time . . . going on my phone for a long period of time, just getting nothing very productive done." Under conditions of traditional grading, writing is stressful and he had trouble finding value in it. He also said he was more likely to avoid getting started on assignments due to nerves surrounding academic and financial penalties. For Kevin, the experience of being in a state of constant stress leads to a feedback loop of YouTube, phone-scrolling, and a frozen state of not knowing where to begin.

But with the LBGC, he was "more likely to tackle this problem" the "second [he] gets it, because [he] knows there's no real bad, awful consequence" to how he decided to complete his work as long as he meets the baseline requirements. With traditional grading, Kevin explained it this way: "[if I] put 110% of my work into something and I get a C, I'm disappointed . . . that caused effects on my mental health." But, with the LBGC, if he puts "110%" into his work, he knows how he will be evaluated, he will get comments on his writing, and, as he explained: "[it] makes me more confident as a student and makes me more willing to participate in classes." Carillo argues that there is a growing consensus that ungrading practices help reduce stress ("Ungrading" 133). As Carillo mentions, this increasing scholarly consensus may point to how alternative grading practices can help students transition to college, maintain adequate mental health, assist with retention, and other possibilities. It also might open the door for having the necessary space and comfort to take intellectual risks in writing, as all six participants discussed how the LBGC helped them take risks and grow as learners—which may be especially important for collaborative multimodal composition, as something that could be more intimidating for some students.

Motivation and Quality

While appreciating the reduction in stress, all students also commented on how the LBGC negatively impacted motivation to complete the assignment and/or reduced the quality of the final product. "Quality" for these students seemed to mean something related to consistency in form and tone across episodes as well as an assumption that the podcast would have been generally "better" if students were more motivated.

One interpretation of these perspectives could be that the reduction in stress caused by the LBGC led to poorer motivation and a poorer-quality podcast. It's also possible students idealized traditional grading as something that would "force" them to make a better product so they just assumed the podcast would be better were they graded more traditionally. It is hard to say definitively, and it would be interesting to see further study of student perceptions of "quality" in various grading contexts and for different kinds of writing.

One thing that might contribute to the idea that the podcast could have been "better," though, is that the episodes produced by each group did not all cohere as much as "professional" podcasts often do (e.g., episodes had different lengths, they opened with cold opens from interviews or with exposition from narrator, they had more and less formal tones, some were more humorous and some imitated investigative reporting genres). Perhaps, with a traditional grading approach, students may have felt more urgency to create more coherence among the four episodes.

But it is also true that experimenting with cold opens, weaving in interviews, using music in different ways, etc. may simply not have happened. Thinking about having a podcast that was maybe just a little too tonally consistent, or a little too NPR-polished, or a little too consistent in length might have meant paying too much attention to what Nate had meant when he said that if he were graded traditionally, he would have approached script writing by doing something to some standard "on Google or a format on what it's supposed to be" rather than following writing that had his "own . . . uniqueness" that he was allowed to play with. It is entirely possible students may have utilized the pressure of traditional grading to create a different and maybe even "better" product, but it is hard to say that the same kind of learning would have occurred.

That said, issues with motivation are intriguing. Several students noted that they had trouble getting started on the podcast assignment (Nate) or felt traditional grading can motivate with "positive" stress (Linda). Some students (Erica, Kevin, Carolina) also felt other groups or group members were not as motivated to work on the podcast assignment (e.g., Erica noted that some people said things like "Oh, well we're not being graded anyways, so whatever" or "It doesn't matter, because I'm still going to get a decent grade"; Kevin felt that the "lack of . . . punishment" from grades led to lower motivation of students and quality of product). This was especially true at the end of the semester when students were stressed about work in other classes. Other research has supported the idea that students' relationships with grades are complex. For instance, Joyce Olewski Inman and Rebecca A. Powell found that grades were desired by writing students as "markers . . . used to communicate progress or lack of progress" (45) and Hannah T. Davis's preliminary findings on motivation point to the possibility that "positioning grades as antithetical to learning" may alienate students who may benefit from the extrinsic motivation that grades provide for them (146). As much as the LBGC may have helped reduce stress, it is an open question if it impacted motivation and quality of writing in a negative way for some students, especially for collaborative multimodal work that could be more intimidating for some writers.

Selecting Roles

Five of the six participants felt the LBGC helped them take risks in selecting their roles. For instance, Erica points out that she was more "motivated to take on a challenge" with the role she selected due to the LBGC, while in a traditional grading environment, she would have "felt a little too scared to mess up, too scared to take on something new, something that might be a little challenging, because I'd be scared to mess up my grade, mess up other people's grades" in the podcast assignment. Erica was eager to take on a leadership role (i.e., project manager), whereas normally she might try to take on more of a background role.

Notably, Linda mentioned her Latina identity in relation to selecting a role. Linda chose the audio editor role instead of something more in her comfort zone like the narrator role. Following Voss's advice about having students reflect on "the participation gap context in which role uptake decisions are made" regarding how people of color and women are less likely to take on leadership and technological roles in society and in group projects (73), I asked students to talk about whether an activity we did in class related to this participation gap affected their selection process for their group role in a labor journal entry. In the interview, Linda explained further:

> I remember . . . I wasn't really surprised or shocked [reading] that most of the kind of engineering or the technical roles in industry go to men and White people. So I think I was just kind of thinking about it in my head . . . [The audio editor role] is something that could be considered technical. . . . I know a lot of times, from my experiences, men usually seem to take over those sections. . . So I think as a woman of color, it would be kind of resisting, but I think resisting would be a good thing . . . to kind of be a part of minimizing it is something that's kind of important to me.

In terms of how the LBGC helped her make such a decision, to underscore its role beyond the reflective activity's influence, Linda explained that:

> Well, I've noticed a lot of the time that when it comes to grading, there's certain bias for certain students, like maybe . . . a teacher that relates more or has more in common with another student, so maybe they are more prone to give that person an easier or a better grade than another person . . . So I really think that [the LBGC] was helpful because there's no, 'Oh, I hope the teacher likes me so that way, he can give me a better grade.' There's no worrying about that . . . It's more of just kind of showing you your skills and how you can grow

from that. So I thought that's something that really helps, especially since a lot of the time, that bias that teachers have for students is based off of their gender, or if a male teacher has more in common with a male student, or if a White male teacher has more common with a White male student. So just those commonalities are kind of taken away and just peels back to the core of teaching, which is learning and growing.

Without the pressure of a grade, it's possible students feel more comfortable choosing roles that challenge and interest them, especially when they are given space to consider how racism and sexism might interfere with role selection.

Collaboration

Kevin, Nate, Erica, and Aarya talked about how the LBGC helped them take risks in their learning about collaboration. Both Kevin and Aarya felt the LBGC allowed them to give up control in positive ways. Previously, Kevin would "get [his] hand" involved in all aspects of the project, like a micromanager, to ensure the project would obtain the best grade possible. Aarya explained that she is usually "scared that [the project] is not going to get finished," so she usually "end[s] up doing like 90%" of the project. With the LBGC, they were both more open to figuring out how to work with others on the project rather than micromanage and control other group members.

The LBGC also opened up space for students to try things in collaboration they wouldn't have tried before. For instance, Kevin said he learned to start meetings without mentioning the project (e.g., talking about their major), ultimately finding that locating "a common interest with your group members" helps to make "collaboration . . . come [as] second nature." Investing time to know coauthors was something Kevin just wouldn't have spent time doing under conditions of traditional grading. But this was something valuable to learn in collaboration, as the trust built through getting to know one another can help create opportunities for more sustained collaboration. As Richard Gebhardt has argued about collaborative writing, paying attention to emotional dynamics in groups is extremely important for building trust (70–71). Furthermore, high group cohesion has been shown to decrease social loafing (i.e., someone putting in less effort in a group) in writing and communication classrooms (Lam), so efforts like Kevin's yielded useful practices (and lessons) for collaboration.

Nate also explained that the LBGC helped him to learn lessons about collaboration, where the LBGC set the conditions not just in communication "but in how we flowed." Nate elaborated: "We weren't so focused on, okay, what are the requirements? What do we need to get done? It was like, oh, what should we add? What should . . . we do? What do we think? How do we want to format this?" Furthermore, Nate said that the LBGC helped his group "work together and not put down each other's ideas when we didn't think something was the best." He recalled one example when his group was discussing something related to editing the group's episode and he explained his perspective as: "instead of shutting that idea down, you have to go at it from a place where, oh, that's a good idea, but I think maybe we should do something else." Nate felt his group, without the pressure of a grade, developed more patience for working through ideas together. He said he learned to "start with positives on what [he] like about the idea" before going into critiques. There was less of a rush to get through what Duffy would call the "procedural process" of collaborating in which students efficiently follow a "well-worn path" to adhere to guidelines for collaborative projects (101–02). Instead, there was much more room for "the emergent quality of a coauthored text as a distinct object with which collaborators interact to invent novel discourse" (102). Instead of individualizing a group project, Nate took a chance by slowing down and working together as a listener and supportive groupmate.

Erica also felt the LBGC gave her room to improve her ability to collaborate, explaining that in a traditional grading system, she would have been more concerned "about the professor and less about my groupmates." She felt, with the LBGC, she was "more focused on how to work with" her groupmates and "each other's ideas and our own creativities, and less about 'Okay, let's just follow the rubric'" to try to make the instructor happy. She also learned to choose her battles, recalling a moment when she disagreed with a creative choice a groupmate wanted to make in audio editing. Because her disapproval of the choice was only mild and the choice really made her groupmate "excited" and "happy," Erica was willing to prioritize her groupmate's happiness and creative experimentation. Like Kevin, Erica made space for prioritizing the group's emotional and social health. Because of scholarship critical of consensus in collaborative work (e.g., Trimbur, Myers), I followed up with Erica to ask her if she would have been comfortable speaking out against something she more vehemently disagreed with. Erica responded that because "this is also a project that represents my work," she would speak up if she disagreed more strongly (i.e., she felt she did not want to reach consensus just for its own sake). Notably, if the class podcast was graded traditionally, Erica's response indicated that she would have been more likely to shut down her groupmate's idea due to nerves about how it might impact her grade. For each of these students, the LBGC may have opened up space for students to challenge themselves in ways that may enhance their abilities as collaborative writers in the future.

Multimodal Composing

Nate, Aarya, and Erica all mentioned the influence of the LBGC on their multimodal composing. Unlike collaboration, these students spoke more generally about how it impacted their decisions, possibly because they had less practice in metacognitive reflection on multimodal composing compared to reflections about collaboration.

As a scriptwriter, Nate spoke about the freedom the LBGC provided him to follow his interest in writing. Nate said that rather than "a letter grade" driving him, the LBGC "helped [him] learn instead of being punished for not doing something." Occupying a space where he felt he could focus on learning rather than avoiding punishment, Nate explained he was more focused on his own and the group's vision in his role as scriptwriter rather than "what is on Google or a format on what it's supposed to be." Because he didn't specify, I can only speculate on what that creative experimentation may have been. One choice in the podcast episode Nate wrote involved having the narrator interrupt interviews several times with reflections (e.g., reflecting on a student's surprise about what she perceived as a wealthy public school lacking funding for textbooks for an Italian class). A more conventional choice would have been to save these reflections for after the interviews were completed and reflecting all at once; interrupting the interviews with the reflections were effective in how they tried to anticipate listeners' thoughts and feelings and address them immediately.

Aarya explained that because "there was less pressure" she felt "more creative control" to "experiment more with what we wanted to research and how we wanted [to] structure . . . our podcast." If traditional grading was implemented, she explained that "there would be less room for our own more creative part" of the podcast. While Aarya's primary role was project manager, the secondary role she took on was scriptwriter. Like with Nate, I can only speculate on her risks. Unlike the other episodes, this episode on charter schools did not begin with a focus on decision-making for high schools. It spent much of its opening detailing the history of segregation and integration in NYC schools, using research to connect charter schools to that history. Given the overall focus of the podcast on providing information to parents and students to help them make choices for high school applications, it was a risk to focus so much on histories of class and race as part of the story of charter schools. The episode also featured creative transitions utilizing rhetorical questions, changes in music, and long pauses between segments.

Finally, Erica, like Aarya, was a project manager who also held a secondary role assisting with scriptwriting, including final review of the script. Erica explained that the LBGC helped her "think outside of the box a little and not be so scared" of repercussions in grade outcome. Like Nate and Aarya, I can only speculate about risks. One notable feature of this episode on private schools was how the episode was organized as a group interview of two students. So, rather than isolating the interviews as two separate segments, each interviewee responded to questions in kind, which helped highlight the contrast in their responses (which were notable, as one student had a more positive experience and the other student had a more negative experience). Another notable move was to include a trigger warning with specific "music" for the trigger warning—something I knew was important to Erica—about an interviewee response about sexual harassment and racism at a private school. I wonder if Erica would have been as willing to keep that in the script along with the unconventional use of accompanying music (which does help underscore what is happening in the moment) under conditions of traditional grading. Each of these students spoke about multimodal composing as something they can be more creative with under the conditions of the LBGC, something that might be especially important to those who teach multimodal composition, where there seem to be many possibilities to explore a writer's creativity.

Conclusion: Different Students Need and Want Different Things

Ultimately, all six students felt more comfortable taking risks without a traditional grade attached to their assignment. But that meant different things to different students. Linda and Carolina explicitly said that the LBGC had no effect on their work in multimodal composing nor on collaborating. However, both Carolina and Linda claimed they took a risk in role selection. Kevin only mentioned the LBGC affecting risk-taking in collaboration, and Aarya took risks in collaboration and multimodal composing. Meanwhile, Nate and Erica took risks in selecting a role, collaborating, and in multimodal composing.

These students also saw the LBGC as negatively impacting their motivation and/or the quality of the podcast. Where motivation and quality might factor in, I feel we must consider our values and the potential trade-offs—for instance, if we truly value process over product, are we willing to make a potential trade-off of possibly "worse" or "messier" final projects from students where students took more risks and learned more than they might have learned by completing more standardized and "polished" final projects? Inoue argues that students "may be ready to listen or not, but their learning and labor should be their choice" while traditional grading "coerce[s] [students] into doing things, which we usually read as motivation" (*Labor-Based Grading* 70). Likewise, based on their study about the qualities of meaningful writing experiences and its possible connection to learning, Michele Eodice, Anne Ellen Geller, and Neal Lerner advise faculty to "set assignment parameters with enough student choice and enough encouragement of student agency that students may *choose* to take up the invitation, and, if allowed and further encouraged, will bring the power of personal connection, future relevance, and deep immersion to what they're thinking, writing, and researching" (133). Alternative grading, like LBGCs, may help give students more genuine invitations. It is hard to say what style of grading might make for the best products (and, of course, it is an open question in composition how much that matters), but this pilot study suggests students took risks in their learning that may not have been possible under conditions of traditional grading. That said, the issues with motivation are intriguing. Some advice I may offer is, for LBGCs for collaborative multimodal projects, it might be a good idea to have very regular check-ins with groups, perhaps even asking for something like "status reports" each week that provides updates on who is doing what (and, importantly, *why* they are doing it to show how they are furthering their project toward the group's satisfaction). Because taking risks can be uncomfortable, it's possible the idea that motivation is negatively impacted might be due to fear of failure once the risk is taken. In other words, perhaps alternative grading helps students "take a plunge," so to speak, in collaborative multimodal projects, but once that plunge is taken more attention needs to be given to help sustain student efforts toward their projects. Therefore, creating more intentional infrastructure than I reported on in this article may help students feel more supported while also giving instructors a better chance to monitor group progress for possible intervention. Overall, I'm left wondering how we might work together, as instructors and students, to determine what we want to gain in collaborative and multimodal composing. As researchers, we should continue to study how grades work with and against us in that enterprise.

Acknowledgments

I would like to thank Valerie Hanson, Mary McGlynn, Kamal Belmihoub, Lisa Blankenship, Brooke Schreiber, Cheryl C. Smith, and Colleen Libertz for their help with this project.

Note

1. The City University of New York granted exemption for this study, IRB File #2021-0604.

Works Cited

"About Macaulay." *Macaulay Honors College, CUNY,* The City University of New York, macaulay.cuny.edu/about-macaulay/. Accessed 26 Nov. 2024.

"Baruch College Fact Sheet: Fall 2021." *Baruch College,* Baruch College, 2022, www.baruch.cuny.edu/wp-content/uploads/sites/28/2022/04/Factsheet.Fall_2021_Rev-4_18_22.pdf.

Carillo, Ellen C. *The Hidden Inequities in Labor-Based Contract Grading.* Utah State UP, 2021.

—. "Ungrading: Where We Are and Where We Might Go." *Composition Studies,* vol. 51, no. 2, 2023, pp. 131–36.

Corbin, Juliet, and Anselm Strauss. *Basics of Qualitative Research: Techniques and Procedures for Developing Grounded Theory.* 3rd edition. SAGE Publications, 2008.

Craig, Sherri. "Your Contract Grading Ain't It." *WPA: Writing Program Administration,* vol. 44, no. 3, 2021, pp. 145–46.

Davis, Hannah T. "Ungrading: Self-Assessment, Effort, and Motivation." *Composition Studies,* vol. 51, no. 2, 2023, pp. 143–47.

Danielewicz, Jane, and Peter Elbow. "A Unilateral Grading Contract to Improve Learning and Teaching." *College Composition and Communication,* vol. 61, no. 2, 2009, pp. 244–68.

Duffy, William. *Beyond Conversation: Collaboration and the Production of Writing.* Utah State UP, 2021.

Eodice, Michele, Anne Ellen Geller, and Neal Learner. *The Meaningful Writing Project: Learning, Teaching, and Writing in Higher Education.* Utah State UP, 2016.

Fernandes, Maggie, Emily Brier, and Megan McIntyre. "We're All Still Grading: A Call for Honesty in Writing Assessment Discourse." *Composition Studies,* vol. 51, no. 2, 2023, pp. 148–54.

Fittipaldi, Diane. "Managing the Dynamics of Group Projects in Higher Education: Best Practices Suggested by Empirical Research." *Universal Journal of Educational Research,* vol. 8, no. 5, 2020, pp. 1778–96. doi.org/10.13189/ujer.2020.080515.

Gebhardt, Richard. "Teamwork and Feedback: Broadening the Base of Collaborative Writing." *College English,* vol. 42, no. 1, 1980, pp. 69–74.

Geisler, Cheryl, and Jason Swarts. *Coding Streams of Language: Techniques for the Systematic Coding of Text, Talk, and Other Verbal Data.* WAC Clearinghouse/UP of Colorado, 2019.

Gibbs, Laura. "Let's Talk about Grading." *Ungrading: Why Rating Students Undermines Learning (and What to Do Instead),* edited by Susan D. Blum, West Virginia UP, 2020, pp. 91–104.

Inoue, Asao B. *Cripping Labor-Based Grading for More Equity in Literacy Courses.* WAC Clearinghouse/UP of Colorado, 2023. www.doi.org/10.37514/PRA-B.2023.2203.

—. *Labor-Based Grading Contracts: Building Equity and Inclusion in the Compassionate Writing Classroom.* 2nd Edition, WAC Clearinghouse/UP of Colorado, 2023. www.doi.org/10.37514/PER-B.2022.1824.

Isaac, Megan Lynn. "'I Hate Group Work!' Social Loafers, Indignant Peers, and the Drama of the Classroom." *English Journal,* vol. 101, no. 4, 2012, pp. 83–89.

Kryger, Kathleen, and Griffin X. Zimmerman. "Neurodivergence and Intersectionality in Labor-Based Grading Contracts." *Journal of Writing Assessment,* vol. 13, no. 2, 2020. escholarship.org/uc/item/0934x4rm.

Lam, Chris. "The Role of Communication and Cohesion in Reducing Social Loafing in Group Projects." *Business and Professional Communication Quarterly*, vol. 78, no. 4, 2015, pp. 454–75. doi.org/10.1177/2329490615596417.

Myers, Greg. "Reality, Consensus, and Reform in the Rhetoric of Composition Teaching." *College English*, vol. 48, no. 2, 1986, p. 154–74. doi.org/10.2307/377298.

Nilson, Linda B. *Specifications Grading: Restoring Rigor, Motivating Students, and Saving Faculty Time*. Stylus Publishing, 2015.

"Spotlight: CUNY and the New York City Economy." *New York City Comptroller*, Office of the New York City Comptroller, 9 Apr. 2024, comptroller.nyc.gov/reports/spotlight-cuny-and-the-new-york-city-economy/.

Sutton, Mark. "Avoiding the Black Dot: Toward a Model of Fair Grading for Collaborative Writing." *Issues in Writing*, vol. 14, no. 2, 2004, pp. 152–74.

Teagarden, Alexis, Carolyn Commer, Ana Cooke, and Justin Mando. "Intellectual Risk in the Writing Classroom." *Composition Studies*, vol. 46, no. 2, 2018, pp. 116–36.

Trimbur, John. "Consensus and Difference in Collaborative Learning." *College English*, vol. 51, no. 6, 1989, p. 602–16. doi.org/10.2307/377955.

Voss, Julia. "Who Learns from Collaborative Digital Projects? Cultivating Critical Consciousness and Metacognition to Democratize Digital Literacy Learning." *Composition Studies*, vol. 46, no. 1, 2018, pp. 57–80.

Wood, Shane A. "Book Review: Labor-Based Grading Contracts: Building Equity and Inclusion in the Writing Classroom by Asao B. Inoue." *Journal of Writing Assessment*, vol. 13, no. 1, 2020, pp. 1–6. escholarship.org/uc/item/9hw9p7hc.

—. "Multimodal Pedagogy and Multimodal Assessment: Toward a Reconceptualization of Traditional Frameworks." *Bridging the Multimodal Gap: From Theory to Practice*, edited by Santosh Khadka and J.C. Lee, Utah State UP, 2019, pp. 244–62.

Daniel Libertz is assistant professor of English and associate director of the First-Year Writing Program at Baruch College, City University of New York. His research and teaching interests include quantitative rhetoric and literacy, public and activist rhetoric, assessment, course modalities and writing instruction, and the politics of literacy education.

Grading Contracts and the Behavioral Commonplaces of Composition Pedagogy

Mathew Gomes

This essay asks: What does contract grading scholarship suggest about behavior in composition studies? What behaviors do scholars who practice contract grading typically regulate? And what exigences motivate those regulations? Distinguishing "behavior" from "process" and "labor," I foreground the premise that behaviors are independently important to learning about writing and highlight behavioral regulations as a generic feature of grading contract pedagogies. These pedagogies illustrate common ways of regulating behaviors and motivations for regulations. Reviewing more than fifty published examples and descriptions from writing courses, I find scholars often regulate writing, participation, and metacognitive behaviors for epistemic, psychological, and social reasons. This article positions behavioral regulation as a significant responsibility of composition instructors, just as rhetorical, linguistic, and stylistic regulations are. Highlighting how regulatory tendencies support and reproduce (1) Western/European epistemologies, (2) identities and affects most available to White, able-bodied, and economically privileged individuals, and (3) identification with communities with shared values, I argue culturally sustaining pedagogies and emerging scholarship on culturally sustaining assessments furnish an alternative exigence to motivate how we regulate behavior: to "perpetuate and foster—to sustain—linguistic, literate, and cultural pluralism" (Paris 93).

In a 2016 article, Chris Gallagher argues composition studies should pay more attention to behavior. In his account, disciplinary interest in behavior peaked in the 1960s and 1970s and has waned since, alongside the academic cache of "behaviorist" philosophy and psychology. Gallagher suggests a "disciplinary allergy" to behaviorism may contribute to reticence to use the word "behavior," even while adjacent terms, like "processes, practices, and activities" flourish (258). However, we are "in the behavior business" and need to develop more productive and unproductive ideas about writing behaviors, both to push back against a "corporate reformer attempts to control the behaviors of teachers and students (and citizens)" (257) and to help students "expand their behavioral repertoires as writers" (258). Few have responded to Gallagher's article, and none have yet directly taken up his call for "more and less meaningful ways to talk about behaviors" (257). However, Gallagher's argument is compelling. Beyond his reasons, more attention to behavior also dovetails with current interest in questions about pedagogical responsibility for the equity and justice of composition instruction.

I think about my classroom assessments, where I have practiced contract grading for more than a decade. My early training was with Asao Inoue at Fresno State, where I used a "hybrid" grading contract (Danielewicz and Elbow), with a "community-based assessment" (Inoue, "Community-Based") to distinguish "A" and "B" grades. Like those Ira Shor describes in *When Students Have Power*, students and I negotiated some course expectations, usually focusing on behaviors like attendance, on-time submission, and those related to class participation. I have since moved toward "labor-based" models, though, in a small seminar course, I also tried a version of Ellen Carillo's "engagement-based" grading contract. Students in that class individually determined how to participate and the scope and nature of their larger course projects. While these models have technical differences, all also promote questions about behaviors, like: what behaviors should be required? Should everybody perform the same behaviors? Should behavioral expectations be predetermined, negotiated, or changed? What outcomes are certain behaviors supposed to lead toward?

Contract scholarship also reflects a persistent interest in behavior. Popular contract models emphasize behavior as an independent determinant of grade outcomes. Jane Danielewicz and Peter Elbow's "hybrid" grading contract credits "*behavior* and *writing quality*," (251, emphasis in original), and Inoue's "labor-based" model rewards "*behavior* and *labor*" (*Labor-based* 132; 329, emphasis in original). Ira Shor's "critical pedagogy" version asks students to collectively deliberate and negotiate common behavior expectations. Carillo's "engagement-based" model similarly invites students to individually determine the behaviors that contribute to their grades (*Hidden Inequities* 56–57; "What I Learned" 5). These prevailing models all raise questions about how behavior interacts with grade credit, and which behaviors to credit. Beyond these, others similarly position behavior as an object of assessment and as a part of writing, learning, and being in school and in professional spaces.

However, behaviors also emerge as a recurring, generic problem. Recent critiques focus on behaviors in some courses Inoue teaches with "labor-based" contracts. Kathleen Kryger and Griffin X. Zimmerman critique Inoue's "Labor Log" assignments, arguing the time-tracking components may not work well for neurodivergent students who experience time in non-normative ways. Carillo similarly argues Inoue's "labor-based" model centralizes an "able-bodied norm," that disadvantages disabled students.[1] These scholars echo Emily Stanback, who previously critiqued Danielewicz and Elbow's "hybrid" contract and Shor's model for expressing "tacit acceptance—and even elevation—of behavioral norms," which "could easily disqualify [neuroatypical students] from receiving a strong grade . . . even if their written work itself is excellent" (431). Contract scholarship therefore raises persistent questions about the accessibility of behavioral regulations for students.

Given these exigences, this essay considers what contract grading scholarship illustrates about behavior in composition pedagogy. Specifically, I ask: what behaviors do those who practice contract grading typically regulate, and what exigences typically motivate those behavioral regulations? Distinguishing "behavior" from "process" and "labor," I foreground the common premise that behaviors are independently important to learning about writing, and highlight behavioral regulations as a generic feature of grading contracts. Contract scholarship helps us see behavioral commonplaces—the common ways writing teachers regulate behavior and their motivations for doing so. Reviewing more than 50 publications about contracts, I find teachers often regulate writing, participation, and metacognitive behaviors for epistemic, psychological, and social reasons. Ultimately, this article positions behavioral regulation as a problematic of writing classrooms, just as rhetorical, linguistic, and stylistic regulations are. Contract literature indexes tendencies to regulate and require behaviors in the service of Western/European epistemologies, identities, affects, and habits most available to White,[2] able-bodied, and economically privileged individuals, and student participation in communities with shared values. This essay concludes by echoing calls for culturally sustaining assessments.

Behavior Anticipates Change: Defining and Distinguishing Behavior from Process and Labor

This essay defines "behaviors" as emplaced, embodied engagements with learning opportunities, which often involves other people, materials, or technologies. This definition highlights "what writers do" (Gallagher 238), focusing on scribal (rather than textual) aspects of student learning.

The word "behavior" is often explicit in contract scholarship and models, even while disciplinary discourse tends to center similar-sounding terms, like "process" and "labor." Behaviors, however, are distinct from "process" and "labor." Behaviors support writing processes, but writing processes usually involve multiple, (often) sequenced writing behaviors. Sometimes we treat behaviors as having benefits that transcend particular writing processes, such as with peer review. The term "process" also deflects our attention from regulations beyond writing, like attendance policies. The term "labor" also differs from behavior. While for Inoue, labor does account for "bodily labor," (*Labor-based* 75), most usages of this term focus on "labor power," or particular expressions that have exchange value within a classroom (80). Thus, the word "labor" most often surfaces economic questions, like the worth and use-value of labor, how much time a form of labor power requires, and if ideas about time limit neurodivergent and disabled student success when they can experience time differently (Carillo; Kryger and Zimmerman). Steeped in conversations about grading, most focus on how best to commodify student activity and center less on the nature or reasons for that activity.

By bracketing "behavior" from ideas about "process" and "labor," a common premise becomes apparent: that behaviors anticipate change.[3] Independent of particular writing processes or forms of labor, many attribute epistemic, psychological, social, and even physiological changes to performing behaviors (Danielewicz and Elbow 261; Inoue, *Labor-based* 112; Reichert; Hendrickson 131).

Grading contract pedagogies also allow us to better understand behaviors in composition because explicit behavioral regulations are a generic element of many contracts (Schwarz 63). Behavioral regulations include things like participation policies, word counts, specific process activities, or labor instructions. Though Joyce Inman and Rebecca Powell argue some students desire more regulation than contract pedagogies may provide, Inoue points out that contract pedagogies still regulate process, labor, and behaviors. All grading models mediate behavior in some way. Still, most published examples and descriptions of contracts include explicit behavioral standards, naming one or more specific behaviors must perform for passing credit.

Considering contracts through the lens of rhetorical genre studies (as Virginia Schwarz and Shane Wood do), the patterns of behavioral regulations across contracts represent typified responses to recurring exigences and situations (Bawarshi and Reiff). From this perspective, minimum word counts, attendance policies, compulsory writing activities, and participation guidelines mediate particular objectives, forming generic solutions to recurring classroom exigences. Asking how teachers use contracts to regulate behavior therefore points to more durable pedagogical exigences and responses.

Research Question and Method

This essay considers two questions:

1. What behaviors do teachers regulate in contract pedagogies?
2. What motivates behavioral regulations in contract pedagogies?

To answer these questions, I reviewed more than 50 examples and descriptions of contract pedagogies in composition classrooms, published between 1992 and 2024.[4] I compiled this sample by identifying literature cited in previous reviews of contract scholarship (Cowan; Inoue, *Labor-based*). I also found more than 25 examples published after these reviews by tracing the citations of previous items of scholarship, including examples published in a special issue of *The Journal of Writing Assessment* (JWA), in regular issues of *JWA*, *Assessing Writing* and *The Journal of Response to Writing*, *Composition Forum*, and in several edited collections. I included items with (1) concrete examples of grading contracts; (2) descriptions of contract grading pedagogies; and/or (3) reasons for particular behavioral requirements. The sample therefore included first-hand pedagogical accounts (Czarnecki; Santos), descriptions of programmatic efforts to implement contracts (Aryal et al.; Tinoco et al.), studies of writing programs using contracts (Inman and Powell; Stuckey et al.), and studies of teachers (Sims).

In reporting on the research questions, I separate patterns in regulation and motivations for those regulations, because the same behavior may have several motivations. For example, some regulate metacognition under the belief it develops rhetorical control over writing (Smith), while others emphasize its capacity for cultivating present-moment awareness (Consilio and Kennedy). Similarly, the same motivation may inform multiple behavioral regulations. For example, teachers who want students to demonstrate engagement may prompt students to write, participate, and practice metacognition. Thus, the following sections address these two research questions individually.

What Behaviors Do Teachers Regulate in Contract Pedagogies?

While teachers use contracts to regulate many kinds of behaviors, they usually focus on writing, participation, and metacognitive behaviors.

Writing Behaviors

Teachers often designate at least two kinds of writing: (1) "informal" writing, usually writing-to-learn or to express some idea; and (2) "formal" writing, usually involving a scaffolded process of developing writing through feedback and revision, often for a more public audience. Both kinds entail regulations, often related to the amount of writing (e.g., word counts, page length) and when writing is submitted.

"Informal" writing includes in-class writing, online responses (O'Meara; Mateo-Girona and Dean), homework assignments (Consilio and Kennedy; Potts), and keeping a "writing diary" (Luckert and McCormick). "Formal" writing is typically more processed and usually encourages or requires students to:

- draft;
- revise;
- edit; and
- format writing.

Many also regulate social dimensions of writing processes, prompting students to develop writing by:

- sharing and responding to writing;
- attending one-on-one teacher conferences; or
- presenting writing to audiences beyond the classroom.

Formal writing processes often include some additional social expectations, such as adherence to more subjective or "fuzzy" criteria (Danielewicz and Elbow; Aryal et al.), or objectives students help define (Litterio, "Blending"; Inoue, *Labor-based*; Walker, in Medina and Walker). Teachers also prompt some authorship behaviors, like writing collaboratively (Spidell and Thelin; Mallette and Hawks), or taking risks (Reichert; Bishop; Consilio and Kennedy; DasBender et al.). They may also regulate rhetorical behaviors, such as:

- conducting research;
- using sources;
- making claims; or
- following organizational schemes.

Finally, teachers sometimes regulate the technologies students write with by prompting or requiring multimodal or digital writing (Cicchino; Mateo-Girona and Dean).

Participation Behaviors

In one study, Schwarz found around 59% of teachers using contracts reported minimum attendance requirements, and 42% had additional minimum participation expectations (*DeNorming* 58). Often appearing as explicit items, participation policies frequently entail:

- attending class;
- arriving and leaving on time;
- speaking in class;
- working with peers and helping peers learn;
- visiting office hours;
- practicing classroom behaviors;
- signing or assenting to the contract.

Schwarz also found around 39% of teachers negotiated participation expectations (*DeNorming* 58). Especially in the "critical pedagogical" strand of contract scholarship, participation may entail (and sometimes require) deliberating and negotiating course expectations, including participation expectations.

Metacognitive Behaviors

Many use contracts to regulate metacognitive behaviors, like planning, monitoring cognition and effort, evaluating, and reflecting (Trimble and

Jankens; Gorzelsky et al. 226). In grading contract literature, teachers frequently regulate:

- acts of "constructive metacognition," like reflections, authors' notes, or cover letters;
- planning writing and learning activities;
- monitoring writing and learning, such as through labor logs and labor journals;
- self-evaluations of writing and learning.

Thus, regulation of metacognitive behaviors is a common, recurring feature of many grading contract pedagogies.

What Motivates Behavioral Regulations?

Epistemic, psychological, and social goals often underpin behavioral regulations. Some regulate writing behavior based on the ideas that informal writing leads to general improvement (Reichert; Hendrickson), that it represents cognition or knowledge (Gomes et al.), or that it helps form positive attitudes toward writing (Reichert). Teachers may understand writing processes as a natural focus of writing courses, and therefore regulate those processes (Danielewicz and Elbow; Litterio, "Contract"; Klotz and Whithaus). Participation regulations may promote critical consciousness and affirm a political reality where students are able to "re-make their culture" (Shor and Freire 99), foster engagement, or contribute to peer learning (Gomes et al.). Finally, metacognitive regulations may help students to learn about and gain "more control over their dispositions," and to "perhaps change some of them" (Inoue, *Labor-based* 265–267), develop "willingness to labor" (247), or increase potential for transfer (Stuckey et al.). Overall, the most common reasons for regulations revolve around developing: (1) knowledges about rhetoric and writing processes, and/or critical knowledges; (2) a psychology defined by a sense of agency, reduced stress, confidence, self-efficacy, academic habits of mind, and writerly or professional identities; and (3) identification with an academic community, shared with peers.

Epistemic Goals of Behavioral Regulation

Some argue grading contracts themselves help focus on writing processes (Danielewicz and Elbow; Litterio, "Contract"; Stuckey et al.; Kostelich and Cowan) and help students understand expectations for the course and for course assignments (Stuckey and Wilson; Watson, "Easing,"; Litterio, "Blending"); however, at the same time, teachers also regulate specific behaviors to promote certain knowledges and types of attention.

Many hope students build knowledge about rhetoric and writing processes. Danielewicz and Elbow argue regulating writing process behaviors may support learning about rhetoric by encouraging rhetorical thinking (Danielewicz and Elbow 254–255), while Nancy Reichert suggests students may better understand rhetorical situations by writing in different genres (Reichert 65). Lisa Litterio argues students may better identify genre expectations of professional rhetorical situations when they deliberate assignment expectations ("Blending"). Increasingly, teachers regulate behaviors to encourage students to understand linguistic diversity as a rhetorical asset (Tinoco et al.; Fernandes et al.). Regulating writing processes may also help students learn about what those processes look like (Blackstock and Exton 282) and what writers do. Through such regulation, many suggest, students can improve their writing aptitude or proficiency (Reichert; Potts; Hendrickson) and their ability to analyze writing (Litterio, "Blending"). Thus, behavioral regulations tend to sustain and generate knowledge about rhetoric, language, and writing.

Teachers may also regulate behaviors hoping students develop critical thinking and critical knowledges. For example, several regulate discussion behaviors, hoping students develop critical knowledges (Shor, "Critical Pedagogy," *When Students*; Thelin; Spidell and Thelin). Other behaviors may also contribute to critical knowledges; for example, Marc Santos argues the extra "labor opportunities" he provides students (which includes things like utilizing the writing center, attending office hours, or contributing more to discussions) help students understand the "hidden curriculum" of college (169–170), while Inoue argues his course ecology can help students demonstrate awareness of the politics of language through behaviors like reflecting on peer response, journaling, and posing questions (*Labor-based* 276–280).

Like Inoue, other teachers may regulate behavior to produce awareness of certain issues. Beyond an awareness of rhetoric, Jennifer Consilio and Sheila Kennedy argue some metacognitive behaviors can increase their present-moment awareness and self-awareness (38), while Cruz Medina and Kenneth Walker argue grading contracts and their regulations can help draw attention to explicit pedagogical values (53). Thus, teachers may regulate behaviors to promote certain kinds of knowledge and attention.

Psychological Goals of Behavioral Regulation

Behavioral regulations may also impact student psychology. Some attribute psychological outcomes to contract use alone, arguing that grading schemes are motivational devices (Elbow, "Time Out" 12–13) and contracts help students access their intrinsic motivations (Danielewicz and Elbow 257; Inoue, *Labor-based*; Reichert; Blackstock and Exton; Mateo-Girona and Dean; Watson, "Integrated"). Still, some suggest correspondences between particular behaviors and affective outcomes. One striking example is when Inoue suggests practicing "compassionate behaviors" might lead to more empathetic feelings and compassionate actions over time (181–182). While empathy is not a common affective goal, many similarly regulate behaviors to promote students' sense of agency, confidence, habits of mind, and self-efficacy.

Perceptions of Agency

Behavioral regulations may affect a sense of agency. For example, Petra Baruca writes students may feel increased autonomy and agency when they select or design learning opportunities for higher grades (Tinoco et al. 4). Some also argue greater agency results from deciding what work to complete or not to complete (Danielewicz and Elbow; Litterio, "Contract"; Klotz and Whithaus). Deliberating and negotiating the design of assignments and assessment criteria, and evaluating writing may also contribute to student agency (Litterio, "Blending"; Consilio and Kennedy). Thus, teachers often try to promote agency by encouraging students to select and pursue particular learning opportunities and to help create evaluative criteria and practicing assessment.

Anxiety, Stress, and Confidence

Many connect grading to stress and anxiety. Some find students resist and feel "dissonance" about contract grading (Inman and Powell; Thelin)—especially among high-performing students (Spidell and Thelin) and White students (Inoue, "Racial Formations" 90–91). However, most suggest contract grading reduces stress and anxiety (Potts; DasBender et al.). This appeals to many teachers, believing students will experiment or take more risks in their writing when they are under less stress (Inman and Powell; Fernandes et al.; Blackstock and Exton) and develop confidence as writers (Stuckey et al.; Potts; Klotz and Reardon). Emily Watson, whose scholarship offers extensive consideration of the psycho-emotional outcomes of contract grading, finds that under conditions of less stress, students may also build or exhibit better academic behaviors related to coping and self-worth protection, such as avoidance/procrastination and social comparison ("Achieving"). Thus, teachers may use grading contracts to indirectly promote other behavior they see as valuable, especially taking risks and exhibiting coping behaviors they believe contribute to academic success.

Self-Efficacy

Teachers may also regulate student behaviors to develop their self-efficacy. Elbow and Danielewicz argue grading contracts can help self-efficacy, enabled particularly by the behaviors of using feedback and exerting control over learning outcomes ("Appendix" 1–2). More recently, Gita DasBender, Nate Mickelson, and Leah Souffrant argue their style of contract grading contributes to a "self-efficacious writerly habitus," and that self-efficacy in particular is a result of taking intellectual and writerly risks (14). Similarly, Watson found that under an assignment graded by contract, some secondary students experienced increased challenge appraisal that increased self-efficacy (Ward [Watson], "Easing" 7).

Habits of Mind

Most do not explicitly invoke the habits of mind or *Framework for Success* statements, and Inoue even questions these habits, yet many still privilege dispositions that overlap with the habits and regulate behaviors to promote these dispositions. Most often, teachers aim to cultivate engagement and responsibility, in addition to metacognition. While metacognitive regulation is previously discussed, engagement and responsibility are worth dwelling on. The *Framework for Success* document defines engagement as "a sense of investment and involvement in learning" (1), and teachers often promote engagement though sharing and responding behaviors (Stuckey et al.; Klotz and Reardon), participation behaviors (Shor and Freire 103; Gomes et al.), and metacognitive writing behaviors (Katen 18). Responsibility, defined as "the ability to take ownership of one's actions and understand the consequences of those actions for oneself and others" (*Framework* 1), is often promoted by regulating:

- planning and monitoring individual progress;
- radically revising writing;
- participating in peer evaluations and teacher conferences;
- leading class sessions;
- signing grading contracts.

The other habits of mind appear less frequently but all appear in some fashion, including persistence (Inoue, *Labor-based*; Mateo-Girona and Dean; Stuckey et al.); openness to self-critique and revision (Stuckey and Wilson); open-mindedness (Blackstock and Exton); and creativity (Luckert and McCormick).

Developing and Changing Identities

Behavioral regulations also impact student identities. Marino Ivo Lopes Fernandes, Alicia Clark-Barnes, and Christina Ortmeier-Hooper highlight the "identity work" (75) of schooling, arguing teachers should promote plurilingual identities (80–89). Their interest in plurilingual identity is unique; most often, teachers regulate behaviors to promote writerly and professional identities. DasBender, Mickelson, and Souffrant describe courses that promoted "writerly identities more than judgments about the quality of their writing" (2) and encouraged students to "develop positive affective ties to writerly identities" by making active choices about their writing (3). Asking students to imagine themselves as professional, creative writers and to develop "a writing identity" (111), Bishop encouraged students to practice "writerly disclosure" and to go "public with exploratory thinking" (112). Amy Cicchino's class asked students to develop their professional identities through tasks like creating professional portfolios or composing blog or vlog posts (8). All suggested regulations help teachers encourage writerly and professional identities.

Social Goals of Behavioral Regulation

Teachers also regulate behavior to create particular classroom dynamics and social environments. Some common aims are to:

- reduce grade conflict and antagonism between teachers and students;
- de-mystify institutional and cultural power;
- privilege democracy and collective deliberation;
- de-center and refigure hierarchical relations
- contribute to others' learning; or
- contribute to cultures of compassion.

However, the most common goal is simply for students to be part of a community with shared values. Treating a classroom as a "community" may be problematic (Inoue, *Antiracist* 162–165), but many instructors ultimately find community a desirable outcome and make students work and learn together. For Inoue, emphasizing collective interests also resists the White supremacist habit of "hyperindividualism," which "tends to ignore the larger social community and its well-being" (*Cripping* 5). However, many instructors simply frame their classrooms as a common, shared social space, to which students must continually return and contribute. Teachers hope to create such a community by prompting students to attend and speak in class (Gomes et al.), practice class behaviors (Shor, *When Students*; Inoue, *Labor-based*; Cicchino), work with peers (Spidell and Thelin; Thelin), or contribute to peer learning in some way (Inoue, *Labor-based*; "Sara," in Sims; Katopodis and Davidson).

Grading Contracts and the Behavioral Commonplaces of Composition

Contract scholarship indexes a tendency to regulate and require behaviors based on generalizations, and especially in the writing of those critical of contracts, it helps reveal behavioral regulation as a major and growing equity concern. If we have rejected "behaviorism," this scholarship illustrates a persistent strain of hopefulness that we still might just make students "do the things that we think will lead to learning" (Elbow, "Grading" 133). Contract scholarship suggests norms form most often around writing, participation, and metacognition behaviors. It suggests we should continually interrogate *how* we regulate behaviors, and what we assume about the normative outcomes of behaviors.

We often standardize writing, participation, and reflective behaviors. While scholars increasingly argue that required forms of participation may disadvantage some students (Birdwell and Bayley; Price), we should also scrutinize compulsory writing and metacognitive behaviors. For example, we should continue questioning the role of peer response in our classrooms. The emphasis on peer response in contract literature echoes broader disciplinary advocacy (Melzer; *Framework*). However, peer response is also part of the "figured world" of composition discourse, with a "naturalized-yet-constructed meaning," that privileges how students may learn about writing (Martorana 63–64). Peer response can also value learning or writing development over student emotions (Heard), conveniently redistribute pedagogical labor (Ching 312), and circulate White language ideologies (Inoue, *Labor-based* 274–281). Thus, peer response runs the risk of reconstructing emotional, social, and racial harms. Still, we tend to minimize or suppress these risks in favor of the normative benefits associated with peer response. As we increasingly denaturalize compulsory attendance and on-time submission requirements, we should also need to denaturalize peer response, reframing it as a behavior common to academic discourse while also questioning whether it should be compulsory in all writing processes.

If generic behavioral regulations are motivated by more durable exigences, we should also be critical of those exigences. Though reasons for regulating behavior may differ, they tend to privilege disciplinary control, grounded in Western/European knowledges, the assertion of writerly and disciplinary identities, and logics of consensus and assimilation to community. We are less consistently interested in sustaining culturally relevant knowledges, privileging intersectional approaches to psychology, or highlighting opportunities for dissensus and disidentification with a class community. However, composition classrooms should better accommodate a broader range of knowledges, psychologies, and social relationships.

Epistemically, contract pedagogies often center rhetorical, process, critical, and metacognitive knowledges. Often treating writing as a way of thinking, they center writing's capacity for representing ideas. However, these epistemic priorities reflect Western/European knowledges of rhetoric and writing. When we center these knowledges, Iris Ruiz and Raúl Sánchez argue, we commit forms of epistemic violence (xiv). Yet, the rhetorical priority is implicit in the habitual framing of writing as necessarily related to "rhetorical theory, the rhetorical tradition, the history of rhetoric" (Sánchez 87) and in our fixation on writing's capacity for representation (Sánchez 80). Instead, we might understand writing as "consequential mark-making" to further delink it from its ideological, epistemological, and rhetorical baggage" (Sánchez 88). Standards for writing behavior falsely limit the nature of writing, reproducing common disciplinary beliefs, while marginalizing or ignoring writing behaviors and uses of writing that exceed rhetorical and process traditions. We should ask what knowledges about writing we cultivate when we regulate writing behaviors and create further opportunities for students to practice culturally sustaining literacies.

Our psychological goals also demand scrutiny. We tend to privilege and regulate behaviors to produce writerly identities, habits, and practices. Beyond just a few critiques (Inoue, *Labor-based*; Kryger and Zimmerman), there is less consideration of intersectional approaches to the psychological effects of composition courses. However, we should better consider such effects. Useful as they may be in some academic contexts, critiques of the "habits of mind" highlight how they may:

- produce a "normative mandate" (Jack 33);
- valorize traits that, under austere economic conditions, are efforts "simply to survive" (Kalish et al. 272);
- promote a positive psychology, by promising increasingly inaccessible "fantasies of successful personhood" (Gross and Alexander 288);
- reflect habits of Whiteness (Inoue, *Labor-based* 24).

In short, the habits of mind seem most accessible and valuable to White, able-bodied, economically privileged subjects. Therefore, regulating behaviors to sustain these habits of mind risks reproducing a classroom space that defines success in White, able-bodied, and classed terms.

We should also be careful with the identity work we ask students to do and resist the imperative to compel students to identify as writers. Valerie Kinloch argues some students reject such identifications as "performances of resistance" that help "protect and safeguard themselves from the harmful, potentially painful, damaging forms of interaction" (27). Such performances can present as opposition to "official school sanctioned practices, expectations, and behaviors" that often seek to surveil and other them. In one study, Kinloch identifies two Black students who reject writerly identities in school. One, Christina, rejects the identity as an "attempt to protect herself from [Kinloch's] gaze" (26) while the other, Derek, rejects it partly because of a fear of disappointing those in his life (36–37). Both resist writerly identifications to protect themselves from a school system that tends to devalue them. Instead of making students identify as writers, Kinloch urges teachers to "work with students to co-construct classroom spaces that support multiple literacy engagements and perspectives," which better validates "who students are and their ways of knowing" (38). Composition may tend to see the extension of writerly identity as empowering; however, imposing such an identity can dehumanize students when we position them to either assimilate to writerly identities or fail.

We might also reconsider compelling students to behave as part of a shared community. Regulations often support, or even demand, relationships of identification, agreement, consensus, and trust. These can be positive social goals, but such relationships also entail risks which are magnified for marginalized student populations. For example, Carillo argues negotiating common course expectations can compel disabled students to make uncomfortable disclosures, creating forced intimacy. Pertaining to race, Sherri Craig highlights the extraordinary demands for trust contract grading can place upon students of color whose experiences and futures likely involve "traditional writing assessment practices" (145–46). Laila McCloud further explicates the types of trust in an instructor, in their expertise, and in the efficacy of new ways of learning (103). Both speak to a condition of "exposure," which Ruha Benjamin explains, are racialized circumstances of visibility, potential financial loss, or a lack of protection (67). They often entail heightened scrutiny, being misread (69), exoticization, surveillance (75), and a loss of privacy (84). While I generally also hope students form identifications with peers, the course, and its content, it is important to recognize the risks of visibility in school for some students, refigure the social space of the classroom as heterogeneous, and design classrooms and assessments to acknowledge and reduce the possible harms of exposure.

Conclusion

To perpetuate and foster plural, meaningful writing and learning behaviors without centering White discourses and values, we should look to culturally sustaining pedagogies (CSPs) and the emerging literature on culturally sustaining assessments or CSAs (Randall et al.). CSPs and CSAs aim to "perpetuate and foster—to sustain—linguistic, literate, and cultural pluralism" (Paris 93; Randall et al. 596), responding directly to "largely assimilationist and often violent White imperial project" of U.S. schooling (Alim and Paris 1). They emphasize "explicitly pluralist outcomes that are not centered on White, middle-class, monolingual, and monocultural norms of educational achievement" (Paris and Alim, 95), dynamic conceptions of culture, and willingness to critique hegemonic aspects of culture (Alim and Paris, 10–11). CSAs therefore decenter Whiteness, attempting to integrate "the sociocultural identities of BIPOC students…in every planning/development phase of the assessment" (Randall et al. 85), by drawing upon their "funds of knowledge," connecting to their lives, providing multiple ways to demonstrate expertise, and "embedded within a culturally sustaining curriculum" (Randall et al. 596).

Culturally sustaining pedagogies overlap considerably with the antiracist and decolonial commitments present in more recent contract pedagogies (Inoue; Tinoco et al.) and particularly share an interest in sustaining student languages and literacies. We should approach classroom assessments and designs with a culturally sustaining ethic that is especially considerate of how the behavioral expectations of school can displace and overwrite non-academic discourses. CSPs supply a useful perspective on behavior, encouraging teachers to "view resistances as invitations into learning" and helping us understand "how students of color sustain their heritage and community practices, how they access power and opportunity in schools, and how they see themselves" (Kinloch 38). Without limiting learning opportunities to students whose bodies meet White, able-bodied, class-privileged ideals, we must also actively cultivate classroom environments that enable students to "perpetuate and foster" meaningful writing and learning practices, especially those adjacent or in opposition to White supremacist discourses.

In writing and learning, a "culturally sustaining" ethic might invite instructors to elicit (without requiring or merely extracting) meaningful modes of invention, transcription, sharing, response, evaluation, and iteration, and the other behaviors writing and learning may entail. Hannah Rule argues we should treat writing as an "emplaced physical activity" and ask students to research and represent their writing processes (109–125) that are focused on spatial immediacies and affective dimensions of writing (110) to counter "disembodied and placeless" ways of teaching writing processes. This may be one option that illuminates students' culturally-meaningful literacy and languaging practices, alongside the behaviors and tasks we encourage. We might be particularly attentive to the ways students share and elicit response to their writing, especially if peer response is a risky and potentially exploitative behavior. Yet, these practices should not be compulsory, and instructors should respectfully acknowledge that students may reasonably choose not to share these behaviors. Nevertheless, learning more about meaningful literacy and learning behaviors, when students are willing to share, can help instructors support more capacious and meaningful literacy and language practices.

Finally, we should remember that all grading models ultimately rationalize an unjust and unproductive pedagogical behavior. Many who advocate for contracts recognize grading as a problem. Hence, my recommendations are intended to reduce the harms of assessment in school environments intrinsically hostile toward students of color, disabled students, and those whose bodies chafe against the codes of academic spaces. However, grading tools will always have limited value for producing just educational outcomes. Additional scholarship and advocacy should intervene in academic institutional requirements for grades, considering universities like Antioch, Sarah Lawrence, Evergreen State, Reed, Bennington, Oregon State, and Brown University, where grades may not be required (Potts). Finally, as Sherri Craig, Barclay Barrios, and Jeffrey Galin remind us, we must also look beyond individual classrooms to identify points of leverage "across scales within the entire complex system that is the target of change" (52). Programmatic and pedagogical actions are necessary to help schools be more culturally sustaining spaces.

Notes

1. Inoue has recently addressed some of these criticisms, offering insights for "cripping labor in grading ecologies," and classes with labor-based contract grading. Several recommendations implicate student behavior, such as requiring fewer on-time assignment submissions (117-118), eliminating compulsory sequences of process activities (118-119), suggesting ranges of time on labor instructions (119–120), increasing planning activities (121-122), and negotiating word counts (122).

2. Like Lockett et al., I capitalize the term White to "draw attention to the fact of race as a social construct mediated by language, technologies, and communication" and to "appropriately recognize a deliberate expression of identity that is . . . inextricably connected to architectures of White supremacy, capitalism, and patriarchy, which are residual designs of colonialism, feudalism, and autocracy" (4).

3. Several major models make this premise explicit; for example, Danielewicz and Elbow argue both learning and attitudes may be outcomes of "going through the motions" (261); Inoue similarly argues "doing" leads to both "learning" (Labor-based 112) and "feeling" (Labor-based 181). Outside of these models, others also assert that practice can "make perfect" (Reichert 60) or "build proficiency" (Hendrickson 131).

4. The 1990s marks the period when scholarship about grading contracts in composition began to be published more regularly. While there are some descriptions and examples published before this time, many are not for composition courses, and thus are less relevant to developing modern, disciplinary understandings of behavior.

Online Appendix: Commonly Regulated Behaviors and Motivations Among Reviewed Examples

Access the online appendix through the QR code below or at compstudies-journal.com/wp-content/uploads/2025/04/gomes-online-appendix.docx

Works Cited

Aryal, Bhushan, Brody Bluemel, and A. Myrna Nurse. "Negotiating Traditions and Charting a Different Future at an HBCU: The Composition and Speech Program at Delaware State University." *Composition Forum*, vol. 49, 2022, compositionforum.org/issue/49/delaware-state.php.

Bawarshi, Anis S. and Mary Jo Reiff. *Genre: An Introduction to History, Theory, Research, and Pedagogy.* Parlor P; WAC Clearinghouse, 2010, wac.colostate.edu/books/referenceguides/bawarshi-reiff/

Benjamin, Ruha. *Race after Technology: Abolitionist Tools for the New Jim Code*, Polity P, 2019.

Bishop, Wendy. "Contracts, Radical Revision, Portfolios, and the Risks of Writing," *Power and Identity in the Creative Writing Classroom: The Authority Project*, edited by Anna Leahy, Multilingual Matters, 2005, pp. 109–20.

Blackstock, Alan, and Virginia Norris Exton. "'Space to Grow': Grading Contracts for Basic Writers." *Teaching English in the Two-Year College*, vol. 41, no. 3, 2014, pp. 278–93.

Carillo, Ellen C. *The Hidden Inequalities in Labor-Based Contract Grading.* Utah State UP, 2021.

—. "What I Learned about Teaching while Teaching *Mrs. Dalloway* during the Pandemic." *Pedagogy: Critical Approaches to Teaching Literature, Language, Composition, and Culture*, vol. 23, no. 1, 2023, pp. 1–9.

Cicchino, Amy. "Preparing Students to Compose across Media for Various Audiences: Syllabus for an Upper-Level Professional Writing Course." *Syllabus*, vol. 10, no. 1, 2021.

Consilio, Jennifer and Sheila M. Kennedy. "Using Mindfulness as a Heuristic for Writing Evaluation: Transforming Pedagogy and Quality of Experience." *Across the Disciplines*, vol. 16, no. 1, 2019, pp. 28–49, DOI: doi.org/10.37514/ATD-J.2019.16.1.04.

Cowan, Michelle. "A Legacy of Grading Contracts for Composition." *Journal of Writing Assessment*, vol. 13, no. 2, 2020, escholarship.org/uc/item/0j28w67h#author

Craig, Sherri. "Your Grading Contract Ain't It." *WPA: Writing Program Administration*, vol. 44, no. 3, 2021, pp. 145–46.

Craig, Sherri, Barclay Barrios, and Jeffrey Galin. "Toward More Sustainable Antiracist Practices." *WAC Journal*, vol. 34, 2023, pp. 40–63, doi.org/10.37514/WAC-J.2023.34.1.04.

Czarnecki, Seth. "Labor-Based Grading: A New Ethic for Writing Feedback." *English Journal*, vol. 112, no. 6, 2023, pp. 56–62, doi.org/10.58680/ej202332488.

Danielewicz, Jane, and Peter Elbow. A Unilateral Grading Contract to Improve Learning and Teaching. *College Composition and Communication*, vol. 61, no. 2, pp. 244–68.

—. "Appendix to 'A Unilateral Grading Contract to Improve Learning and Teaching.'" scholarworks.umass.edu/cgi/viewcontent.cgi?article=1035&context=emeritus_sw

DasBender, Gita, Nate Mickelson, and Leah Souffrant. "Contract Grading and the Development of an Efficacious Writerly Habitus." *Journal of Writing Assessment*, vol. 16, no. 1, 2023, pp. 1–18, doi.org/10.5070/W4jwa.231.

Elbow, Peter. "Grading Student Writing: Making it Simpler, Fairer, Clearer." *New Directions for Teaching and Learning*, 1997, pp. 127–40, https://doi.org/10.1002/tl.6911.

—. "Taking Time Out from Grading and Evaluating While Working in a Conventional System." *Assessing Writing*, vol. 4, no. 1, 1997, pp. 5–27 doi.org/10.1016/S1075-2935(97)80003-7.

Fernandes, Marino Ivo Lopes, Alicia Clark-Barnes, and Christina Ortmeier-Hooper. "Units of Exchange: How Teachers Develop Assignments with Academic Currency for Plurilingual Identities." *Plurilingual Pedagogies for Multilingual Writing Classrooms,* edited by Kay M. Losey and Gail Shuck, Routledge, 2022, pp. 75–91.

Framework for Success in Postsecondary Writing. Council of Writing Program Administrators, the National Council of Teachers of English, and the National Writing Project. wpacouncil.org/aws/CWPA/asset_manager/get_file/350201?ver=7548

Gallagher, Chris W. "What Writers Do: Behaviors, Behaviorism, and Writing Studies." *College Composition and Communication*, vol. 68, no. 2, pp. 238–65.

Gomes, Mathew, Bree Bellati, Mia Hope, and Alissa LaFerriere. "Enabling Meaningful Labor: Narratives of Participation in a Grading Contract." *Journal of Writing Assessment*, vol. 13, no. 2, 2020.

Gorzelsky, Gwen, Dana Lynn Driscoll, Joe Paszek, Ed Jones, and Carol Hayes. "Cultivating Constructive Metacognition: A New Taxonomy for Writing Studies." *Critical Transitions: Writing and the Question of Transfer*, 2016, pp. 215–28.

Gross, Daniel M., and Jonathan Alexander. "Frameworks for Failure." *Pedagogy: Critical Approaches to Teaching Literature, Language, Composition, and Culture*, vol. 16, no. 2, 2016, pp. 273–95.

Hendrickson, Jason. "Life, Learning, and the Liberal Arts: A Hybrid Contract Grading Model." *Zeal: A Journal for the Liberal Arts*, vol. 1, no. 2, 2023, pp. 127–33.

Inman, Joyce Olewski, and Rebecca A. Powell. "In the Absence of Grades: Dissonance and Desire in Course-Contract Classrooms." *College Composition and Communication*, vol. 70, no. 1, 2018, pp. 30–56.

Inoue, Asao B. *Antiracist Writing Assessment Ecologies: Teaching and Assessing Writing for a Socially Just Future*. WAC Clearinghouse, 2015.

—. *Cripping Labor-Based Grading for More Equity in Literacy Courses*. The WAC Clearinghouse; UP of Colorado, 2023. doi.org/10.37514/PRA-B.2023.2203.

—. "A Grade-less Writing Course That Focuses on Labor and Assessing." *First-Year Composition: From Theory to Practice*, edited by Deborah Coxwell-Teague and Ronald F. Lunsford, Parlor P, 2014, pp. 71–110.

—. "Grading Contracts: Assessing Their Effectiveness on Different Racial Formations." *Race and Writing Assessment*, edited by Asao Inoue and Mya Poe, Peter Lang, 2012, pp. 79–94.

—. *Labor-Based Grading Contracts: Building Equity and Inclusion in the Compassionate Writing Classroom*. 2nd ed., WAC Clearinghouse, 2022.

Katen, Jesse. "Performance Across the Disciplines: Envisioning Transdisciplinary Performance Pedagogies in Postsecondary Education." *Futures of Performance*, edited by Karen Schupp, Routledge, 2024, pp. 13–27.

Katopodis, Christina and Cathy Davidson. "Contract Grading and Peer Review." *Ungrading: Why Rating Students Undermines Learning (and What to Do Instead)*, edited by Susan Blum, West Virginia UP, 2020, pp. 105–22.

Kalish, Katie, Holly Hassel, Cassandra Phillips, Jennifer Heinert, and Joanne Baird Giordano. "Inequitable Austerity: Pedagogies of Resilience and Resistance in Composition." *Pedagogy: Critical Approaches to Teaching Literature, Language, Composition, and Culture*, vol. 19, no. 2, 2019, pp. 261–81, doi. org/10.1215/15314200-7295934.

Kinloch, Valerie. "'You Ain't Making Me Write': Culturally Sustaining Pedagogies and Black Youths' Performances of Resistance." *Culturally Sustaining Pedagogies: Teaching and Learning for Justice in a Changing World*, edited by Django Paris and H. Samy Alim, Teachers College P, 2017, pp. 25–41.

Klotz, Sarah, and Kristina Reardon. "Crafting a Writing Response Community through Contract Grading." *Journal of Response to Writing*, vol. 8, no. 2, 2022, pp. 106–26.

Klotz, Sarah and Carl Whithaus. "Contract Grading as Anti-Racist Praxis in a Community College Context." *Empowering the Community College First-Year Composition Teacher: Pedagogies and Policies*, edited by Meryl Siegal and Elizabeth Gilliland, U of Michigan P, 2021, pp. 62–80.

Kostelich, Callie F., and Michelle Cowan. "Subverting from the Inside: Inclusive Assessment Practices in First-Year Writing." *Peitho*, vol. 26, no. 1, 2023.

Kryger, Kathleen and Griffin X. Zimmerman. "Neurodivergence and Intersectionality in Labor-Based Grading Contracts." *Journal of Writing Assessment*, vol. 13, no. 2, 2020. journalofwritingassessment.org/article.php?article=156

Litterio, Lisa. "Contract Grading in a Technical Writing Classroom: A Case Study." *Journal of Writing Assessment*, vol. 9, no. 2, 2016, journalofwritingassessment.org/article.php?article=101

—. "Contract Grading in the Technical Writing Classroom: Blending Community-Based Assessment and Self-Assessment." *Assessing Writing*, vol. 38, 2018, doi.org/10.1016/j.asw.2018.06.002.

Lockett, Alexandria L., Iris D. Ruiz, James Chase Sanchez, and Christopher Carter. *Race, Rhetoric and Research Methods.* WAC Clearinghouse and UP of Colorado, 2021. wac.colostate.edu/docs/books/race/rhetoric.pdf

Luckert, Erika, and Jason McCormick. "Grading What We Value: A Conversation for Creative Writing." *Journal of Creative Writing Studies*, vol. 6, no. 2, 2021.

Mallette, Jennifer C., and Amanda Hawks. "Building Student Agency Through Contract Grading in Technical Communication." *Journal of Writing Assessment*, vol. 13, no. 2, 2020, journalofwritingassessment.org/article.php?article=158

Martorana, Christine. "Through the Lens of Figured Worlds: A Heuristic for Productive Collaboration." *Composition Studies*, vol. 45, no. 1, 2017, pp. 59–73.

Mateo-Girona, M. Teresa, and Christopher Dean. "Digital Writing and Labor-based Grading: An Equitable and Inclusive Approach to Undergraduate Writing Instruction." *Perspectiva Educacional*, vol. 62, no. 2, 2023, pp. 87–113, doi.org/10.4151/07189729-vol.62-iss.2-art.1404.

McCloud, Laila I. "Keeping Receipts: Thoughts on Ungrading from a Black Woman Professor." *Zeal: A Journal for the Liberal Arts*, vol. 1, no. 2, 2023.

Medina, Cruz, and Kenneth Walker. "Validating the Consequences of a Social Justice Pedagogy: Explicit Values in Course-based Grading Contracts." *Key Theoretical Frameworks: Teaching Technical Communication in the Twenty-First Century*, edited by Angela M. Haas and Michelle F. Eble, Utah State UP, 2018, pp. 46–67, doi.org/10.7330/9781607327585.c002.

Melzer, Dan. "Placing Peer Response at the Center of the Response Construct." *Journal of Response to Writing*, vol. 6, no. 2, 2020, pp. 7–41, scholarsarchive.byu.edu/journalrw/vol6/iss2/2

O'Meara, Kat. "Building Response into Labor-Based Grading Contracts." *Journal of Response to Writing*, vol. 8, no. 1, 2022, pp. 81–91, scholarsarchive.byu.edu/journalrw/vol8/iss1/4

Paris, Django, and H. Samy Alim. *Culturally Sustaining Pedagogies: Teaching and Learning for Justice in a Changing World.* Teachers College P, 2017.

—. "What Are We Seeking to Sustain through Culturally Sustaining Pedagogy? A Loving Critique Forward." *Harvard Educational Review*, vol. 84, no. 1, 2014, pp. 85–100, 10.17763/haer.84.1.982l873k2ht16m77

Potts, Glenda. "A Simple Alternative to Grading." *Inquiry*, vol. 15, no. 1, 2010, pp. 29–42.

Randall, J., M. Poe , and D. Slomp. "Ain't Oughta Be in the Dictionary: Getting to Justice by Dismantling Anti-Black Literacy Assessment Practices." *Journal of Adolescent & Adult Literacy*, vol. 64, no. 5, pp. 594–99.

Reichert, Nancy. "Practice Makes Perfect: Contracting Quantity and Quality." *Teaching English in the Two-Year College*, vol. 31, no. 1, 2003, pp. 60–68.

Rule, Hannah J. *Situating Writing Processes.* WAC Clearinghouse, 2019.

Ruiz, Iris D., and Raúl Sánchez. *Decolonizing Rhetoric and Composition Studies: New Latinx Keywords for Theory and Pedagogy.* Springer, 2016.

Sánchez, Raúl. "Writing." *Decolonizing rhetoric and Composition Studies: New Latinx Keywords for Theory and Pedagogy*, edited by Iris D. Ruiz and Raúl Sánchez. Springer, 2016, pp. 77–90.

Santos, Marc. "How I Implemented Asao B. Inoue's Labor-Based Grading and Other Antiracist Assessment Strategies." *CEA Critic*, vol. 84, no. 2, 2022, pp. 160–79, doi.org/10.1353/cea.2022.0019.

Schwarz, Virginia. *(De)Norming Classroom Merit: Grading Contracts as an Assessment Genre.* 2020. University of Wisconsin-Madison, PhD Dissertation.

—. "Patterns, Negotiations, and Ideologies: Contract Grading as Genre." *Writing the Classroom: Pedagogical Documents as Rhetorical Genres*, edited by Stephen E. Neaderhiser, Utah State UP, 2022, pp. 60–76.

Shor, Ira. "Critical Pedagogy is Too Big to Fail," *Journal of Basic Writing*, vol, 28, no. 2, 2009, pp. 6–27.

—. *When Students Have Power: Negotiating Authority in a Critical Pedagogy.* U of Chicago P, 1996.

Shor, Ira, and Paulo Freire. *A Pedagogy for Liberation: Dialogues on Transforming Education.* Bergin and Garvey, 1987.

Sims, Mikenna Leigh. "Shifting Perceptions of Socially Just Writing Assessment: Labor-Based Contract Grading and Multilingual Writing Instruction." *Assessing Writing*, vol. 57, 2023, pp. 1-14.

Smith, John A. "Contracting English Composition: It Only Sounds Like an Illness." *Teaching English in the Two-Year College*, vol. 26, no. 4, 1999, pp. 427–30.

Spidell, Cathy, and William H. Thelin. "Not Ready to Let Go: A Study of Resistance to Grading Contracts." *Composition Studies*, vol. 34, no. 1, 2006, pp. 35–68.

Stanback, Emily B. "The Borderlands of Articulation." *Pedagogy: Critical Approaches to Teaching Literature, Language, Composition, and Culture*, vol. 15, no. 3, 2015, pp. 421–40, doi.org/10.1215/15314200-2917009.

Stuckey, Michelle A., Ebru Erdem, and Zachary Waggoner. "Rebuilding Habits: Assessing the Impact of a Hybrid Learning Contract in Online First-Year Composition Courses." *Journal of Writing Assessment*, vol 13, no. 2, 2020, escholarship.org/uc/item/9sp0g53j

Stuckey, Michelle and Gabriella Wilson. "Learning to Unlearn: Grading Contracts in the Online Classroom." *Better Practices: Exploring the Teaching of Writing in Online and Hybrid Spaces*, edited by Amy Cicchino and Troy Hicks, UP of Colorado, 2024, pp. 419–46, doi.org/10.37514/PER-B.2024.2241.

Thelin, William. "Understanding Problems in Critical Classrooms." *College Composition and Communication*, vol. 57, no. 1, 2005, pp. 114–41.

Tinoco, Lizbett, Scott Gage, Ann Bliss, Petra Baruca, Christen Barron, and Curt Meyer. "Openings, Risks, and Antiracist Futures at a Hispanic-Serving Institution." *Journal of Writing Assessment*, vol. 13, no. 2, 2020, journalofwritingassessment.org/article.php?article=151

Trimble, Thomas, and Adrienne Jankens. "Using Taxonomies of Metacognitive Behaviors to Analyze Student Reflection and Improve Teaching Practice." *Pedagogy: Critical Approaches to Teaching Literature, Language, Composition, and Culture*, vol. 19, no. 3, 2019, pp. 433–54, doi.org/10.1215/15314200-7615400.

Ward [Watson], Emily. "An Integrated Mixed-methods Study of Contract Grading's Impact on Adolescents' Perceptions of Stress in High School English: A Pilot Study." *Assessing Writing*, vol. 48, 2021, pp. 1–14, doi.org/10.1016/j.asw.2020.100508.

—. "Easing Stress: Contract Grading's Impact on Adolescents' Perceptions of Workload Demands, Time Constraints, and Challenge Appraisal in High School English." *Assessing Writing*, vol. 48, 2021, pp.1–11, doi.org/10.1016/j.asw.2021.100526.

Watson, Emily. "Setting and Achieving High Goals: The Impact of Contract Grading on High School Students' Academic Performance, Avoidance Orientation, and Social Comparison." *Journal of Writing Assessment*, vol. 16, no. 1, 2023, pp. 1–26, doi.org/10.5070/W4jwa.249.

Wood, Shane A. "Engaging in Resistant Genres as Antiracist Teacher Response." *Journal of Writing Assessment*, vol. 13, no. 2, 2020, escholarship.org/uc/item/2c45c0gf

Mathew Gomes is assistant professor in the English department at Santa Clara University. His work has been published in journals including *Assessing Writing*, *WPA: Writing Program Administration*, *Communication Design Quarterly*, and in edited collections. He is associate editor at the *Journal of Writing Assessment*.

Aligning with and through Difference: Tracing the Thingifications of a Multi-Campus Outcomes Statement

Jessica Ouellette and Ryan J. Dippre

In an article chronicling the revised WPA Outcomes Statement (WPA-OS), WPA scholars note that "WPA Outcomes Statement 3.0 continues to function as a boundary object: a statement speaking to common outcomes that can be adapted to local conditions" (Dryer et al. 140). This article traces the ways in which we, as co-authors of our own system-wide outcomes statement (and co-authors of this article), were placed in a position that caused the term "boundary object" to break down as we both wrote and enacted the document on our individual campuses. As WPAs trained in programs with different emphases and members of different writing programs on different campuses, we found ourselves constructing the language of the Outcomes Statement (OS), the document itself, and the implications of that document in different ways. Therefore, this piece looks at the impact of our collective and individual "thingification" (another concept we build on in this article) of the University of Maine System Outcomes Statement (UMS-OS).

Introduction

In his essay, "What is First-Year Composition?," Doug Downs writes that first-year composition "can and should be *a space, a moment, and an experience*—in which students might reconsider writing apart from previous schooling and work, within the context of inquiry-based higher education" (50). Higher education, however, has made the process of defining first-year composition a complicated one due to the various stakeholders interested and invested in how it gets defined. The role of a writing program administrator (WPA) involves not only acknowledging and balancing the different and, oftentimes, competing definitions but also challenging them at times.

As of this writing, two powerful challenges to our ongoing understanding of first-year writing—and, more broadly, writing across campus—are the increasing consolidation of colleges and universities (Kurzweil et al.) and the privileging of STEM over the humanities in contemporary discourse (Taylor et al.). Both of these pressures are felt across higher education, but they are felt acutely in writing courses. The push for deliverables, for ease of skill transfer from one course to another, and for writing (and other gen ed) courses as requirements to be "gotten out of the way" are difficult to navigate for WPAs, and, in many ways, the pressures have only just begun.

In this article, we propose a course of action for handling these pressures by drawing on the opportunities presented by the consolidation of public higher education. Drawing on our experiences working with WPAs at other campuses of the University of Maine System (UMS) (a statewide system of universities undergoing unified accreditation), we—the Director of Writing Programs at the University of Southern Maine and the Director of College Composition at the University of Maine—trace our work to implement a system-wide outcomes statement in our respective campuses and the resulting opportunities that emerged from that work. Our campuses, situated in a comparatively tightly-knit university system, offer a strategic research site (Bazerman) for understanding how the pressures of higher education consolidation might be mobilized to combat the pressures the humanities are facing.

We begin the article by contextualizing our work as WPAs within the system-wide initiative to align writing outcomes across campuses, detailing the collaborative process and challenges involved. Using theoretical frameworks such as boundary objects, thingification, and splicing from actor-network theory (ANT), as explained by Clay Spinuzzi, we examine how the OS became an adaptable and transformative "living document" within each of our campuses, reshaping pedagogical practices and institutional support for writing. By tracing the OS's integration at the University of Southern Maine and the University of Maine, we show how cross-campus collaboration and a shared document fostered both local innovation and systemic change. We conclude with insights for WPAs engaged in multi-institutional work, suggesting that the thingification of shared documents can cultivate a valued writing culture and sustain cross-campus collaboration.

Seizing an Opportunity: Program Innovation in the University of Maine System

During the 2016–2017 academic year, the Vice Chancellor for Academic Affairs in the UMS announced a round of funding to support program innovation throughout the system. This proposal was part of a broader movement to increase cross-campus collaboration throughout the UMS,[1] and it was aligned with (although separate from) the later development of unified accreditation that the UMS Board of Trustees would pursue.

University consolidation has been on the rise for some time now. In 2013, Clayton Christensen claimed in Forbes magazine that twenty-five percent of colleges and universities would merge or close within ten to fifteen years. While the specific number is questionable, a trend of closures and consolidations is clearly underway. Besides Maine, state school systems in Pennsylvania, Georgia, and Wisconsin have all engaged recently in some form of consolidation (Horn); in Vermont, schools have merged into new entities, which, it is hoped, will have a more sound financial footing (Knox). While some circumstances in Maine are specific to the state and the particular makeup of the UMS, the movement we have experienced as faculty is generally in line with a nationwide trend.

To be sure, the increase in multi-campus collaborations, and even the later recommendation for unified accreditation, was not a new trend in the system. Efforts to align what is happening across UMS campuses have been an ongoing concern. For instance, the General Education Transfer Block agreement with the Maine Community College System (MCCS) shapes transfer at all UMS campuses. First-year writing is often caught up in all of these consolidation and alignment maneuvers, which tend to treat it similarly across campuses. But, is it? WPAs across UMS campuses were not actually sure; we did not have the opportunity to sit down and talk about what we do, how we do it, why we do it, and how what we do shapes the writing trajectories of our students. The program innovation funds offered us the opportunity to do just that: engage in collegial discussions about what we do and why and attempt to put meaningful, site-specific insight into the claims of alignment that these larger institutional moves were making. In other words, we could use these funds as an opportunity to develop community while also productively and meaningfully aligning our work together in ways that would benefit not only us as teachers and administrators but also our students. Toward that end, seven WPAs from throughout the UMS proposed developing a set of unified outcomes for first-year writing courses. The team received notice that this project was funded in May 2017, and we began our work in the fall semester.

The working group of WPAs met twice in fall 2017 and spring 2018 to develop an outcomes statement. We shared what we called "program snap-shots" of what was happening on each campus: the courses offered for first-year writing, the number of sections offered, the number of students served, and so on. Through these snapshots, we got a sense of how our various offerings overlapped and diverged. With this as a starting point, we identified what we later termed the "proto-goals" of our courses: general topics we all agreed with but still needed considerable articulation.

This articulation occurred both synchronously and asynchronously throughout the fall 2017 semester. By late November, we had a working draft that we were willing to share with stakeholders on our various campuses. During a three-week open comment period, WPAs on each campus held meetings, encouraged written feedback, and shared what they were hearing with the rest of the team. On December 9, 2017, we closed the discussion window and went to work on the final round of edits.

Our work to identify these outcomes, however, was just the starting point. Over the next year and a half, we worked to use this document—what we called the University of Maine System Outcomes Statement (UMS-OS)—at our various campuses to assess our programs, bring about change, and continue to build a common language both within and across campuses about the kinds of work we do when teaching our first-year writing courses. We met further in spring 2018, and in the 2018–2019 academic year, we invited one another to our campuses to share knowledge and discuss insights. From these interactions, we built some joint projects that ended up in reading groups, conference presentations, and—as of now—published manuscripts.

However, it would be wrong to see the OS document as an inert object or something that emerged as part of a broader initiative to encourage cross-campus collaboration. In many ways, the collaborations that emerged during and after the program innovation project drew, were shaped by, and, in turn, transformed our understandings of the OS. The OS is a living document in several senses of the word: it has played and continues to play an active role in the ways we and our campuses understand what first-year writing does, as well as what the role of writing instruction and expertise in teaching writing is on campus. In the following section, we draw on concepts from the social sciences to help define and concretize the impacts and interactions that emerged from the OS as a living document on our own campuses. Drawing on language in ethnomethodology and ANT, we explore how our two campuses worked—individually and together—to "thingify" the OS and, as a result, shift our notions about the teaching of writing and the administration of writing programs on our campuses. Paying attention to thingification can help WPAs make sense of how particular documents are taken up in particular times and places—and, by extension, suggest how we might influence that take-up.

Encountering a Document: Ethnomethodological Insights

Discussing the revised WPA-OS, Dylan B. Dryer, Darsie Bowden, Beth Brunk-Chavez, Susanmarie Harrington, Bump Halbritter, and Kathleen Blake Yancey note that "WPA Outcomes Statement 3.0 continues to function as a boundary object: a statement speaking to common outcomes that can be adapted to local conditions" (140). The concept of "boundary objects" emerged in the late 1980s in the field of sociology—more specifically, in the sociology of science. Susan Leigh Star and James R. Griesemer, writing in *Social Studies of Science*, examined the interactions between amateurs and professionals in the field of zoology to suggest that there are objects used by all members of the interaction that are "both plastic enough to adapt to local needs and the constraints of the several parties employing them, yet robust enough to maintain a common identity across sites" (393). For them, boundary objects served as an analytic unit that helped them understand how people collaborated despite differing interests and social groupings; in other words, they allowed "heterogeneity and cooperation" to operate successfully side by side (414).

Boundary objects, as a concept, proved to be useful and durable to social scientists, and the term was picked up by writing studies scholars, particularly through the work of Etienne Wenger. In *Communities of Practice: Learning, Meaning, and Identity,* Wenger frames one of the connections between communities of practice as boundary objects, which he defines as "artifacts, documents, terms, concepts, and other forms of reification around which communities of practice can organize their interconnections" (105). Boundary objects, to Wenger, are the phenomena "that connect us in various ways to communities of practice to which we do not belong" (107).

These characterizations of boundary objects give those objects a sense of durability to researchers. That is, while certain communities of practice may privilege certain parts of an object over others, the object itself remains unchanged and, through that unchangingness, flexible and adaptable to the needs of the participants in multiple communities. This approach is extended by Wenger into "boundary practices," or "idiosyncratic ways of engaging with one another, which outsiders cannot easily enter" (113). The move from object to practice has proven a useful one in writing studies, helping scholars to understand the complexities of performing literate action in different kinds of social configurations.

The OS, however, put us as co-authors in a position that caused the term "boundary object" to break down: we were both writing *and* enacting the document on our individual campuses. In order to make further sense of how we negotiated the creation and enactment of this OS, we turned to the proto-ethnomethodological work of Harold Garfinkel—particularly his 1950s work *Toward a Sociological Theory of Information*, published in 2008.

The focus of this work is, as the title indicates, an attempted sociological theory of information. At the heart of this theory is the idea that information is always incomplete. The work that individuals do to make sense of the world around them, to make themselves sensible to others, is always done with and through incomplete understandings. This is true not only for individuals but for organizations as well.

By framing information sharing as happening amidst incomplete knowledge, the researcher is able to focus attention on what kind(s) of work actors do together to make and define information via interaction. Garfinkel treats information exchange as something that is constituted, something that is the result of ongoing work. More importantly, information can only count as information through the act of being constituted as information. Leaning in particular on Garfinkel's other work (*Seeing Sociologically*; *Ethnomethodology's Program*; *Studies*), we can make sense of the "constitution" of information as happening in the ongoing social construction of order. In our interactions with one another, we draw upon our joint attention and interactions to turn the inert world around us into "things"—objects that count socially for us. We "thingify" the world around us with and through others, determining what "counts" in a particular social situation, what needs to be attended to, what matters, etc.

Garfinkel also emphasizes the newness of information. Something that is information is, at its heart, anomalous in some way. If it wasn't new and if it wasn't something that actors on a scene needed to contend with, it would not be information: it would just be another object talked and acted into being through the constitutive nature of social order. When we encounter information, though, we're encountering something that we have not encountered before in some way. We have to work together to figure out what it is, why it's there, and what we might do with it.

The examination of our joint OS fit well with Garfinkel's notion of information as an anomaly. Rather than seeing the OS as both durable and malleable, we saw it as co-constructed into being with greater or lesser levels of certainty among different groups of people: the team of WPAs working on it, the teachers in the program who would work with and give feedback on it, and the higher-level administrators who might be interested in it. In doing so, the two of us came to notice new aspects of the statement, new revisions we might make, and new ways of bringing it to life on our campuses. The work that our campuses had to do to make sense of this object—and, for that matter, the work we had to do to write it—was well explained, retroactively, as an ongoing, multi-site process of rendering the anomalous into a thing.

As WPAs trained in programs with different emphases and as members of different writing programs on different campuses, we found ourselves constructing the language of the OS, the document itself, and the implications of that document in different ways. In other words, we thingified the OS in ways that aligned without overlapping. In the next section, we draw on some understandings from ANT to help us position the concept of thingification as a useful lens for understanding the complexity of how the OS was taken up at our campuses.

Splicing in the OS

One of the valuable aspects of ANT is its tendency to treat the world as flat—that is, as having chains of associations that historically sediment instead of a complex web of difficult-to-trace social forces. Trying to consider how actants come together to practice the production of social activity through concepts like splicing and betrayal can be useful for highlighting the ongoing, material work of thingifying the OS.

A particularly useful term for our purposes is "splicing." Spinuzzi contrasts splicing in ANT with weaving in cultural-historical activity theory (CHAT). According to Spinuzzi, CHAT calls attention to woven networks, which are "exemplified by the artisan who weaves nets for fishermen" (33). Interrelated activities carried out by different individuals work together toward a particular outcome. But, these interrelated activities do not provide us with a helpful mechanism for seeing what happened when the OS showed up at our institutions. For that, we turned to ANT and the concept of splicing.

For Spinuzzi, the splice is the first move of ANT—namely, it is how objects work their way into a setting. "[S]pliced networks," Spinuzzi argues, "are exemplified by the technician who splices together disparate electrical devices and existing networks to respond to unforeseen alliances and uses" (34). When an object (such as the OS) arrives at a site, it is immediately situated in relation to other objects, and it is through this interaction that all objects come to define each other.

That in-the-moment act of ongoing mutual interactional definition is particularly useful for our study of the OS. The OS does not simply arrive on the scene of an ongoing Burkean parlor of sorts, looking for a way to jump into the conversation the way Ryan did at his first writing studies conference. Instead, the ongoing conversation shifts in relation to the OS: talk, tools, and texts shift in how they interact with one another and the OS so that new alliances (in ANT parlance) are formed, old ones are broken, and a new configuration of actants can emerge. This new configuration can sediment and become stable for a period of time as other configurations are built atop it. But—and this is crucial, not just for our current project but for our ongoing work as WPAs—new actants can always be spliced into the network and transform that network in unpredictable ways.

Through ANT, we can imagine that the OS is spliced into the ongoing work of our programs—that is, it moves into some kind of ongoing relationship with the other talk, tools, and texts of our programs in some way. These ways might not be what we intend, expect, or hope for, of course, but the splicing is nonetheless evident and traceable. We can document the introduction of the OS at a staff meeting, trace the ways in which its language seeps into syllabi, rubrics, and assignments, and hear the echoes of its use in hearing students and teachers talk about writing.

Our use of the term "thingification" helps us to understand the complexity of this splicing a bit more finely. When the OS arrives at a campus, it does not remain unchanged. It is not a catalyst, in the sense that chemists use the term. Rather, it is talked and acted into being and brought to life by the ongoing work of the program, becoming a thing that people think, talk, and act with and through again and again. In short, the act of rendering the OS as a thing transforms it in that context for the purposes of those engaging with it.

This mutual construction—between the ongoing practices of a program and the OS—is important if we are to understand the multifaceted ways in which a program might deal with a new set of outcomes. The OS can be spliced into the heart of what a program does; it can transform assessments, assignment design, feedback, and classroom activities. It might also be a translational device for making sense of transfer agreements. If we can imagine these choices not as historical accidents or the result of conscious, individual choice and instead as the ways in which people, tools, and talk come together to co-construct some possibilities with this document, then we can better trace the patterns of interaction that led to these outcomes being taken up in the way that they were.

But situating splicing in relation to thingification lets us move one step further, as well: it also calls attention to the ongoing negotiation that happens among actants beyond the moments of thingification that we are able to home in on. Since spliced networks of actants "grow through opportunistic alliances, through unpredictable jumps and sideways connections" (Spinuzzi 35), we can use splicing to track the trajectories of meaning and action that shape and are shaped by the acts of thingification we engage in. These acts give rise to the sedimentation of particular alliances of actants. In other words, "[c]ommitments multiply and are built on previous commitments" rendering the configuration of actants stable (if only for now).

In the next two sections, we put thingification, splicing, and sedimentation to work, tracing the splicing of the OS at our respective institutions (the University of Southern Maine and the University of Maine) and the acts of thingification that both constitute and are impacted by the splicing of the OS. These acts of splicing and thingification then, as we will come to see, sediment into stable-for-now alliances of actants that constitute our sense of the programs that we currently direct.

Rhetoric, University of Southern Maine, and Institutional Change

One of the two sites this study focuses on is the University of Southern Maine (USM). USM has two campuses—one located in Gorham, where the majority of students reside on campus, and one located in the city of Portland, where many students commute to and from campus. Prior to fall 2021, USM offered one first-year writing course—ENG 100: College Writing—to all students as part of the general education core curriculum. The combined campuses delivered close to forty sections of ENG 100 each year, taught mostly by adjunct faculty.

When Jessica began her career as the Director of Writing Programs at USM in 2016, the University of Maine System (UMS) had just charged its campuses with developing state-wide learning outcomes for first-year composition. Indeed, the OS grant project came at an opportune time for Jessica, as it afforded her a collaborative experience that would later contribute to shaping her role as a WPA and facilitating some major changes at her university.

As we began our work on the OS, we quickly learned the differences between our campuses. There were differences, for example, in curriculum design as well as differences in financial support, faculty and staff numbers, and student demographics on each campus. USM, for instance, has an extremely diverse student population—diverse in the sense of educational experience, socio-economic background, and geographic location. This kind of diversity, of course, brings with it a spectrum of literacies that arguably cannot be met with a "one-size-fits-all" writing course. For Jessica, the work on the OS aided her in reenvisioning the writing curriculum at USM.

As a new WPA, Jessica saw many potential areas for improvement and expansion. While the writing curriculum at USM was strong in the areas of reading and expository writing, some elements were missing—rhetoric being one of them. As a "rhetoric person" (within the context of the composition-rhetoric divide), Jessica's approach to the teaching of writing involves seeing writing situations as rhetorical situations—a pedagogical approach that helps students view writing as situational and strategic and as a means to discover and reconsider ideas by understanding and practicing how to negotiate things like context, purpose, audience, and conventions. Part of her vision, too, is responding to the changing nature of writing in the age of digital culture and information technologies. Given the rapidly changing landscape of communication—one that directly impacts higher education—Jessica saw the OS as a potential invocation for stakeholders invested in college composition to address new conceptions of what it means to be a writer in the twenty-first century.

When the OS made its way to USM, its movement—its thingification—helped actualize an attention to writing that was previously nonexistent, at least in scope and scale. The English department revived its college writing committee, and this committee took up the OS as a visionary document: they studied it, shared it with other colleagues, and discussed what it meant for students at USM. This localized interaction led to a revision of the ENG 100 learning outcomes. Indeed, while the course's outcomes were revised to reflect the OS, the acts of reflection and revision allowed for new pedagogical insights, including a greater emphasis on rhetoric.

The thingifying that occurred—the interaction between the OS and USM's pre-existing outcomes—served as cause for further action. When other stakeholders, including department chairs across campus and USM administrators (e.g., the Deans, Provost, and President), encountered the OS statement alongside the new outcomes for ENG 100, conversations about practice and assessment began to percolate. How, for example, do we deliver the new ENG 100 outcomes—the vision described in the OS—in just one semester? The answer became clear: you can't.

Working with the Core Curriculum Committee, Jessica utilized the OS and the new ENG 100 learning outcomes as grounds for proposing a new, more robust core writing sequence. The uptake of these documents resulted in a decision to move beyond a modification of core writing outcomes to a broader reenvisioning of what first-year students need most, both in the first year and beyond, to succeed in subsequent courses. The decision was made to eliminate USM's "Entry Year Experience" (EYE) course and propose a new three-course writing sequence requirement that would retain the most important elements of EYE (e.g., collaboration with others and engagement with diverse viewpoints) while refocusing the curriculum on writing, reading, and inquiry as central and essential skills.

The proposal for the new writing sequence quickly moved from the Core Curriculum Committee to the Faculty Senate for a vote. More thingifying occurred as faculty considered the new sequence in relation to their own disciplines. Some expressed concerns over the credit footprint, while others inquired about assessment and alignment with national standards. The reemergence and recirculation of the OS served as a response to those concerns, as it reflected both state-wide efforts to improve writing curricula across the UMS and state-wide efforts to align those curricula with national models of writing standards in general education. In this sense, the statement functioned as a "translational device," one that, on the margins, helped realize the possibility of implementing not two but three new writing requirements. The proposal was met with success, and USM implemented its three-course writing sequence, "Writing, Reading, and Inquiry" (WRI), in fall 2021.

Alongside this significant university-wide curricular reform, the thingification of the OS resulted in yet another instance of change—the development of a writing center. As response to institutional priorities with which the OS aligns, this parallel activity represents another moment where interactions between people, tools, and talk about the "thing" culminated in a reassessment of USM's support for student writing, resulting in the creation of a resource intended to help sustain and strengthen USM's newly energized focus on writing.

If we think of the institutional changes that took place at USM as a sedimentation of a living document, we can trace the chain of interactions that led to such changes. The thingification of the OS helped bring into existence several things: an English department reassessing and reenvisioning of the role of writing on their campus; connections between disparate groups of faculty, staff, and administration; a new, robust core writing sequence that encourages students to be active agents in their education and communities; the development of a writing center; ongoing faculty development that ensures best practices in the teaching of writing; and, most importantly, institutional change in the form of a visibly reinvigorated attention to writing across the USM campus. Indeed, the thingification of the OS changed the nature of writing at USM; it bolstered the creation of new opportunities and goals for students and faculty, and we imagine that it will continue to do so. But it also did something else: it spoke into existence a language—a rhetoric, if you will—that values writing. And that is perhaps one of the best outcomes we could have imagined.

Composition, University of Maine, and Literate Action

The other site that this study focuses on is the Orono campus of the University of Maine (UM). This campus runs roughly forty sections of English 101, Translingual English 101, and a "stretch" alternative each semester, staffed by about twenty graduate teaching assistants in a two-year MA program, nine or so adjuncts, and a handful of full-time lecturers and tenured or tenure-track instructors. The program has historically served nearly seventy percent of each graduating class.

This program, operated by a Director of College Composition (Ryan), an Associate Director of Assessment and Program Research, and an Assistant Director of College Composition, was decidedly on the "composition" side of the rhet-comp divide. College Composition courses take up a writing about writing (WAW) curricula, shaped further by a discussion-based class format and an assignment sequence-based approach to curricula in the tradition of Theodore Baird and David Bartholomae. At the end of each semester, students submit a portfolio (two academic essays and a critical reflection) to be assessed by at least two teachers other than their own. These teachers must agree (independently) that the portfolio holistically meets the criteria listed in the Portfolio Assessment Rubric (PAR) in order for students to pass the class. Composition teachers meet three times a semester to calibrate to the rubric before the portfolio review begins.

As the above description indicates, the Orono campus has a fairly well-sedimented set of pedagogical and curricular approaches in place. There is a fair amount of homogeneity of experiences created across sections because of the similarities in subject matter, approaches to class activities, and understandings of the course outcomes as listed on the PAR. The OS was certainly built with the experiences of the Orono campus in mind, of course, but the integrating of Orono's pre-existing outcomes with the goals, values, and language of other campuses served to create a document that might, perhaps, be spliced into the ongoing sedimentation of Orono's campus.

Toward that end, Ryan received a small grant from the university's Office of Assessment to convene a small team of first- and second-year TAs, as well as adjunct instructors, to revise the PAR in light of the new OS document. This group of instructors met regularly throughout the summer of 2018 to discuss the connections and disconnections between the documents, recent experiences using the current PAR, and general ideas for reshaping the document. The final document, what we came to call "PAR 5.0," was drafted, piloted against past portfolios, revised accordingly, and approved by August 2018.

The work of this portfolio revision was only the start of the splicing of the OS into the ongoing practice of the College Composition program. Once we were able to make sense of the demands that the OS made for the assessment of end-of-term portfolios, we quickly found that our work was just beginning. The OS proved to be a valuable document to share with other stakeholders (department chairs across campus, academic support staff, etc.) and served to unsettle, revise, and re-sediment new relationships among those stakeholders while also changing their understandings of what was happening in College Composition.

But this also caused some challenges. Previously, the PAR did double duty as both an assessment tool and a place for course outcomes. With the splicing in of the OS, the relationship between course outcomes and the rubric changed. The rubric was now the place where some of the course outcomes were actualized and assessed. Other aspects of the OS that were less easily observed via our current portfolio assessment—such as "flexible composing practices"—were now more visibly accounted for by final course grades issued after the "Pass/Fail" decision had been made.

The OS also productively complicated the relationship between College Composition and rhetoric, generally speaking. As Director, Ryan's past training in education and composition heavily tilted the program toward composition and composition research—though, to be fair, the program was already tilted in that direction prior to his arrival in 2015. A substantial discussion took place across several meetings about the role that rhetoric was to play in a program shaped by the OS. In the end, rhetoric was thingified through a composition lens—as Latour might say, the concatenation of actants betrayed the gestures toward rhetoric in the OS. The phrase "rhetorical concepts" would indeed be included in the new PAR, but it would be understood capaciously, as any concept that could encourage students to use language strategically would "count" as such a concept.

What we can see happening, both at this site and at Jessica's campus, is a slower sedimentation than we might have originally expected. The new document was cause for some specific actions (such as the PAR revision), but the overall practices of the program remained rather stable, even several years in. Below, we consider what such a thingification of the document means at both of these sites and what might happen further now that the OS is firmly in place at both campuses.

Thingifying Together, Thingifying Apart: Takeaways for WPAs in Multi-Institutional Work

Looking across these two instances of thingifying the OS, we can identify a few takeaways—some implications of what we have seen that might be of assistance to other state university systems engaged in (or hoping to engage in) similar multi-campus initiatives. The foremost insight that we took from looking across these campuses is that the work we do to thingify a document doesn't just make the document real—it also shapes who we see ourselves as and the work we see ourselves capable of doing as WPAs. The recurring work of thingifying the OS among different groups of people gave us a sense of how we might act with and through the language of that document and how we might use it to triangulate ourselves in the complex bureaucracy of our respective universities.

We made sense of these options, in part, by talking to one another, which was another important take-away of the thingification of the OS. It was a document that we brought to our campuses, certainly, but it was also a common text that gave us (1) an exigence for discussion and (2) a shared text during that discussion. While we have both established professional relationships and friendships with others on our own campuses, there are times when it helps to have a sympathetic ear from someone in a similar situation. The OS gave us an exigence and a referent to begin those conversations, and those conversations, in many ways, led to the writing of this article.

The thingification of the OS also created a context in which writing was valued, and expertise in teaching writing was valued along with it. The OS was evidence that there was expertise across the UMS and that the work going on in local writing programs was both drawing on and contributing to that expertise. It is difficult to overstate how important this work was on both of our campuses. By showing that we knew what we were talking about—and that we had access to others who also knew what they were talking about—we were able to thingify the OS as the tip of the iceberg and as a particular instantiation of a wealth of coordinated knowledge. Given the current circumstances of higher education in general, with funding (and values) shifting from the humanities to STEM, this move to emphasize, value, and act on expertise in the teaching of writing is one that we hope we can build upon on our campuses in the coming years.

The thingification of the OS might be most tangible, though, in the cross-institutional work we've engaged in since its publication: the sharing of not just war stories from our work but also initiatives, funding ideas, and curricular reforms. For instance, USM, using the Orono campus's model, decided to pilot a "stretch" course—a year-long course dedicated to students who may need more time and exposure to writing. The benefit of a course like this—a course where students remain with the same instructor and peers for the entire academic year—involved not only aspects of high-impact student learning but also the time and space for students to build a repertoire of writing practices that they could then apply in other courses as well as in professional contexts beyond the university. Not to mention, such a course would be extremely effective in terms of retention: if students at USM feel strongly invested in by their instructor and their peers, especially over a long period of time, they are more likely to stay at that institution.

There was a slight hiccup in this pilot: it didn't work. Why it didn't work has a lot to do with the student dynamic on the USM campuses. Many students at USM are non-traditional students. They have full-time jobs, families, and other commitments that tend to dictate their schedules. Therefore, a year-long course—and the advanced planning over two semesters it required—was daunting to USM students. However, the failure of the initial idea of the stretch eventually gave way to a revamped writing sequence, which drew on some of what the USM team knew about the struggles in implementing curricular reform.

The Orono campus, likewise, drew inspiration from some of the changes implemented by the USM Writing Program. USM proposed a WID Faculty Fellows program to support the faculty who wish to develop writing-intensive courses for upper-level undergraduates in their majors. The program involves an application for interested teachers, a stipend, and a week-long series of workshops focused on pedagogical practices for teaching writing in their disciplines. In addition to the workshops, faculty fellows work with the Director of Writing Programs to discuss, design, develop, and/or revise syllabi and assignments. The goal of this program is to encourage collaboration and mentorship among faculty with the intention of fostering a community of educators committed to best practices in teaching and supporting student writing in the disciplines.

Ryan and other members of the College Composition program have been watching the rollout of the WID Faculty Fellows program in hopes of designing something similar for interested teachers on the Orono campus in the future. The actual structure, funding, and activities of Orono's approach will likely need to adapt to the specifics of the Orono campus; after all, the faculty fellows will have to be thingified, just as the OS was. But with the work at USM as a starting point, and the OS as a shared document guiding work on both campuses, the Orono campus will be able to hit the ground running—or, at least, with minimal stumbling.

We also hope that our work with thingifying an outcomes statement can help WPAs, in the future, attend carefully to the local ways outcomes and outcomes statements are talked and acted into being. University systems—and even collaborations with colleagues across multiple systems—may prove a useful middle ground between the local actors of individual programs and campuses as imagined by Chris W. Gallagher and broader initiatives that have been thoughtfully complicated by Charlotte Asmuth. It can also speed the valuing of difference that Carrie S. Leverenz calls for, highlight the problems that may arise if outcomes fail to capture learning as intended (Weisse; Zito), and allow for easier identification of accessibility issues (Benander and Rafaei). Exploring this middle ground may help WPAs to see the ways in which our seemingly stable understandings of texts and language are competently and consequentially negotiated time and again in the ongoing work of working our writing programs.

Tracing the thingification of the OS has highlighted, for us, the multi-faceted impact that such a document has had. Thingifying it has shaped our sense of identity as WPAs, created the conditions for a community of WPAs across campuses, underscored the value of writing and writing expertise, and served as a pipeline for sharing ideas on pedagogy and curricula. Continuing to trace its ongoing thingification—to other campuses, perhaps, or to colleges and universities outside of the UMS but within the state of Maine—might reveal even more insights. We offer these takeaways as starting points to help other WPAs working across institutions imagine the kinds of documents they might create that would enable these and similar actions in their thingification across campuses.

Note

1. The University of Maine System, established in 1968, stands as Maine's largest educational organization. Enrolling nearly 30,000 students each year, it significantly enhances the lives of hundreds of thousands of Mainers through its academic programs, cultural contributions, and outreach efforts that serve individuals, businesses, organizations, and policymakers. The System ensures accessibility with seven universities—many featuring multiple campuses—along with a law school, thirty-one additional learning locations, and Cooperative Extension services spread throughout the state ("About the University of Maine System").

Works Cited

"About the University of Maine System." University of Maine System, www.maine.edu/.

Asmuth, Charlotte. *Re-localizing Writing Assessment: Sites of Knowledge Mobilization.* 2022. U of Louisville, PhD dissertation. https://doi.org/10.18297/etd/3809.

Bazerman, Charles. "Theories of the Middle Range in Historical Studies of Writing Practice." *Written Communication*, vol. 25, no. 3, 2008, pp. 298–318.

Benander, Ruth, and Brenda Refaei. "Access, Outcomes, and Diversity: Opportunities and Challenges in Basic Writing." *Improving Outcomes: Disciplinary Writing, Local Assessment, and the Aim of Fairness*, edited by Diane Kelly-Riley and Norbert Elliot, Modern Language Association, 2020, pp. 67–78.

Downs, Doug. "What is First-Year Composition?" *A Rhetoric for Writing Program Administrators*, edited by Rita Malenczyk, 1st ed., Parlor P, 2013, pp. 50–63.

Dryer, Dylan B., Darsie Bowden, Beth Brunk-Chavez, Susanmarie Harrington, Bump Halbritter, and Kathleen Blake Yancey. "Revising FYC Outcomes for a Multimodal, Digitally Composed World: The WPA Outcomes Statement for First-Year Composition (Version 3.0)." *WPA: Writing Program Administration*, vol. 38, no. 1, 2014, pp. 129–43.

Gallagher, Chris W. "The Trouble with Outcomes: Pragmatic Inquiry and Educational Aims." *College English*, vol. 75, no. 1, 2012, pp. 42–60.

Garfinkel, Harold. *Ethnomethodology's Program: Working Out Durkheim's Aphorism*, edited by Anne Warfield Rawls, Rowman & Littlefield Publishers, 2002.

—. *Seeing Sociologically: The Routine Grounds of Social Action*, edited by Anne Warfield Rawls, Routledge, 2005.

—. *Studies in Ethnomethodology*. 1st edition, Polity, 1991.

—. *Toward a Sociological Theory of Information*, edited by Anne Warfield Rawls, Routledge, 2008.

Horn, Michael B. "Will 25 Percent of Colleges Consolidate? An Update on a Prediction." *Forbes*, 20 Aug. 2024, www.forbes.com/sites/michaelhorn/2024/08/13/will25percent-of-colleges-consolidate-an-update-on-a-prediction/.

Knox, Liam. "Praying for a Merger Miracle." *Inside Higher Ed*, 1 Sept. 2023, www.insidehighered.com/news/business/mergers-collaboration/2023/09/01/can-consolidation-save-vermonts-public-four-year.

Kurzweil, Martin, Melody Andrews, Melody, Catharine Bond Hill, Sosanya Jones, Jane Radecki, and Roger C. Schonfield. "Public College and University Consolidations and the Implications for Equity." *Ithaka S+R*, 30 Aug. 2021, doi.org/10.18665/sr.315846.

Latour, Bruno. *Reassembling the Social: An Introduction to Actor-Network Theory*. Oxford UP, 2007.

Leverenz, Carrie S. "Redesigning Writing Outcomes." *WPA: Writing Program Administration*, vol. 40, no. 1, 2016, pp. 33–49.

Spinuzzi, Clay. *Network: Theorizing Knowledge Work in Telecommunications*. Cambridge UP, 2008.

Star, Susan Leigh, and James R. Griesemer. "Institutional Ecology, 'Translations' and Boundary Objects: Amateurs and Professionals in Berkeley's Museum of Vertebrate Zoology, 1907–39." *Social Studies of Science*, vol. 19, no. 3, 1989, pp. 387–420.

Taylor, Barrett J., Brendan Cantwell, and Sheila Slaughter. "Quasi-Markets in U.S. Higher Education: The Humanities and Institutional Revenues." *Journal of Higher Education*, vol. 84, no. 5, 2013, pp. 675–707.

Weisse, Kathleen Daly. "When Learning Outcomes Mask Learning, Part 1: The Promises and Pitfalls of Learning Analytics." *Adapting the Past to Reimagine Possible Futures: Celebrating and Critiquing WAC at 50*, edited by Megan J. Kelly, Heather M. Falconer, Caleb L. González, and Jill Dahlman, WAC Clearinghouse, 2023, pp. 143–54. doi.org/10.37514/PER-B.2023.1947.2.10.

Wenger, Etienne. *Communities of Practice: Learning, Meaning, and Identity*. Cambridge UP, 1998.

Zito, Angela J. "When Learning Outcomes Mask Learning, Part 2: Probing Assumptions about Assessment via Disciplinary Genres." *Adapting the Past to Reimagine Possible Futures: Celebrating and Critiquing WAC at 50*, edited by Megan J. Kelly, Heather M. Falconer, Caleb L. González, and Jill Dahlman, WAC Clearinghouse, 2023, pp. 155–68. doi.org/10.37514/PER-B.2023.1947.2.11.

Jessica Ouellette is associate professor of English and women and gender studies and the director of writing programs at the University of Southern Maine. She is the co-editor of the collection, *Feminist Connections: Rhetoric and Activism Across Time, Space, and Place* and has appeared in the journals *Peitho*, *Computers and Composition*, and *Harlot* as well as the edited collection, *Composing Feminist Interventions: Activism, Engagement, Praxis*.

Ryan J. Dippre is associate professor of English and the director of college composition at the University of Maine. His research interests include writing program administration, writing through the lifespan, and the teaching of writing.

Through Thick and through Thin: Domains of and Tensions Surrounding Expertise in a Subset of Writing Studies Scholarship

James P. Purdy

Writing studies teacher-scholars have worked hard to articulate what writing studies as a discipline is and does and why it is relevant. This task is made more important with the rapid adoption of generative artificial intelligence that writes and assesses writing because it challenges the expertise of writing studies professionals. The issue of expertise, therefore, needs to figure more substantively into discussions of disciplinarity. This article advocates for more thorough attention to expertise in writing studies by sharing results of a thin and thick analysis of a corpus of writing studies articles that use the word "expert*" (the wildcard "*" indicates variations in language). I enact a thin approach by compiling a corpus based on the presence and prevalence of the keyword "expert*" and identifying patterns and relationships among its uses. I enact a thick approach by performing close reading and content analysis on corpus texts. The thin approach identifies five domains of expertise discussed in the corpus. The thick approach reveals three underlying tensions that complicate the field's assertion of its expertise. Awareness of these domains and tensions prepares us to articulate, defend, and (re)focus the work of writing studies.

Introduction

With the public release and rapid adoption of generative artificial intelligence (AI) that writes and assesses writing, the expertise of writing studies teacher-scholars is being challenged. Such challenges are not new. Writing studies teacher-scholars historically have worked hard to articulate what writing studies as a discipline is and does and why it is relevant. This work has entailed defining and analyzing its keywords (Dryer; Heilker and Vandenberg; Horner *Rewriting*; Ruiz and Sánchez), examining terms used to label the field and its work (Lauer; Miller; Moxley), and explaining its threshold concepts (Adler-Kassner and Wardle, *Naming*) and subfields (Ritter and Matsuda). However, the issue of expertise has not figured substantively enough in these discussions. As Brenton Faber argues about the concept of "professional" in professional writing, discussions about the disciplinarity of writing studies "have progressed largely without developing a robust and theoretically sound framework" (307) for understanding writing studies expertise, especially to expose contradictions in claims to expertise for the field. This article advocates for more thorough attention to expertise in writing studies by sharing results of what Derek Mueller might call a "thin" and "thick" analysis of a corpus of writing studies articles that use the word "expert*." In this article, I use "expert*" with the wildcard "*" to account for variations in this language (e.g., "experts," "expertise").

This study builds on prior expertise scholarship. K. Anders Ericsson, Michael J. Prietula, and Edward T. Cokely affirm that becoming an expert takes 10,000 hours of deliberative practice, arguing that expertise is learned rather than innate. They, together with other scholars in the multidisciplinary field of expertise studies (e.g., Ericsson et al.; Feltovich et al.; Ward et al.), have explored, largely from cognitive and psychological perspectives, what constitutes expertise, how it develops, and ways in which it is performed, assessed, and (un)recognized. Some of this work touches on writing as an activity or profession (e.g., Kellogg), but none directly acknowledges writing studies as an academic discipline. With few exceptions (e.g., Trimbur), writing studies scholarship on expertise studies writing practices of experts and/or novices (e.g., Adler-Kassner and Wardle, *Writing*; Beaufort; Geisler). I do not seek to replicate that work. Rather than focusing on expertise in writing *practices*, this study addresses expertise in writing *studies*—what writing studies teacher-scholars write about when they use language of expertise.

Writing studies has a fraught relationship with expertise, because writing is an activity with a low threshold for participation but a high threshold for success. It is simultaneously easy to do (for those without disabilities) and hard to master (for everyone). Thus, the gap between expert and non-expert writer is simultaneously wide and blurry. Linda Adler-Kassner and Elizabeth Wardle identify two associated difficulties: non-writing experts claim to know what constitutes good writing, and writing experts struggle to translate their knowledge of good writing to non-experts (*Naming* 6). Ericsson adds a third difficulty: non-experts sometimes cannot identify experts, so they do not recognize expertise when they encounter it (4). In discussing the "problem of expertise," Sherry Lee Linkon explains why: "As experts, we use conceptual, content, and strategic knowledge with great facility. . .but often we're not even aware of what we're doing" (256). This situation has contributed to a lack of recognition and respect for writing studies as a discipline. Na Luo and Ken Hyland affirm, "many English teachers struggle to have their expertise recognized in their institutions and among their colleagues" (435). The stakes of understanding what expertise means in writing studies, then, are high.

Tension has long characterized the field's relationship with expertise. Cheryl Geisler, for example, contends expertise has two "problem spaces": domain content knowledge and rhetorical understanding (82–84). Expertise, in other words, is characterized by tension between what Erika Lindemann terms "what-centered" and "how-centered" knowledge (228–30). Michael Carter addresses this tension by analyzing the complementary approaches to writing expertise espoused by cognitive and social-epistemic theories of composing. He seeks to advance a "pluralistic theory of expertise in writing" that allows for a continuum of writing expertise development (267). Yet, despite this foundational scholarship's enormous contributions, this work is limited. Geisler studies expertise broadly as part of academic literacy rather than writing studies' treatment of expertise specifically. Writing studies, moreover, has largely moved beyond cognitive and social-epistemic approaches. This article seeks to redress these limitations by focusing on writing studies' treatment of expertise and accounting for newer perspectives.

To work towards a fuller concept of writing studies expertise, this article examines how the notion of expertise is defined, discursively constructed, appropriated, (mis)understood, and/or dealt with in some of the field's articles. Teacher-scholars who use the word "expert*" in these articles cast the field's expertise as simultaneously diffuse and narrow. This representation of expertise can be a problem when it muddles what it means to be a writing studies expert and makes asserting our expertise difficult. In this study, I follow Faber, who reviews a corpus of professional communication articles to determine how scholars in that field conceptualize the term "professional." In this article, I do similar work with the term "expert*."

Examining references to "expert*" in journal articles is important for several reasons. It contributes to the field's longstanding attempts at self-definition, explains the domains of expertise studied by writing studies teacher-scholars, and uncovers underlying tensions with expertise affecting work in the field. Awareness of these domains and tensions prepares us to articulate, defend, and (re)focus the work of writing studies. In this era when AI can generate human-sounding prose, we must clarify what writing studies expertise means.

Method

This study combines what Mueller calls "thin" and "thick" methodological approaches. Mueller presents "thin" inquiry as akin to Franco Moretti's concept of distant reading and Heather Love's notion of thin description. Through surface engagement with a textual corpus, thin inquiry provides "tentative and provisional" insights into "disciplinary emergence and maturation" that can make "dynamic disciplinary patterns obvious." "Thick" inquiry, on the other hand, hearkens to anthropologist Clifford Geertz's concept of thick description and his method of ethnography that involves in-depth accounts of behaviors, actions, and contexts (3). For this study, I enact a thin approach by compiling a corpus of articles based on the presence and prevalence of the keyword "expert*" and identifying patterns and relationships among its uses. I enact a thick approach by performing close reading and content analysis on corpus texts. The thin approach provides insight into domains of expertise discussed in the corpus. The thick approach reveals underlying tensions that complicate the field's assertion of its expertise. To understand these tensions, we need first to understand how the conversation on expertise occupies five distinct domains.

For the corpus, I amassed writing studies journal articles indexed in major databases; see table 1. I searched these journal runs from their beginning to the end of their moving wall for articles mentioning "expert*." Searches for "expert" included the related terms "experts," "expertise," and "inexpert." This approach resulted in a corpus of 148 articles.

Table 1.
Journals Searched

Database	Journal(s)	Time period	# Articles in corpus
JSTOR	*College Composition and Communication (CCC)*	Origin to September 2018	18
	College English (CE)		6
	Composition Studies (CS)		8
	Journal of Advanced Composition (JAC)		2
	Journal of Basic Writing (JBW)		4
	Research in the Teaching of English (RTE)		12
	Writing Center Journal (WCJ)		15
	Writing on the Edge (WoE)		3
ScienceDirect	*Computers and Composition (C&C)*	Origin to October 2021	45
Project Muse	*Pedagogy*	Origin to October 2021	10
SAGE	*Written Communication (WC)*	Origin to November 2021	25

Next, I read these articles for the domain(s) of expertise discussed. I first read the abstract, introduction, and conclusion. Then, I searched for "expert*" in the text and read the sentence before, after, and including every instance where it appeared. Instead of taking a purely grounded theory approach, I used

Jenny Rice's concepts to develop initial categories. However, I also let codes for expertise domains emerge as I read. Rice, whose article includes the most mentions of "expert*" in the corpus at 283, claims definitions of expertise as "either the acquisition of skills or the acquisition of ethos" are "common ways expertise has been discussed in rhetoric and composition" (118). My study finds that what skills and whose ethos are discussed vary. Authors discuss expertise related to writing and reading practices and to teaching writing across the first-year writing (FYW) classroom, the WAC/WID classroom, the writing center, and the workplace and civic spaces. (I use the term "WAC/WID" to represent the various institutional models for teaching writing across campus after the first year.) Authors discuss establishing ethos as a student/novice, scholar/expert, and teacher/tutor. To arrive at the three tensions I identified in the thick analysis, I first noted who or what were identified as agents in discussions of "expert*" and then with what or whom they were opposed.

This method of selecting objects of analysis is imperfect. First, this list of journals is incomplete, leaving out important publications. However, this list includes National Council of Teachers of English flagship journals and major publication venues in writing studies indexed by accessible databases. Second, this corpus excludes other forms of publication, including books, and texts that discuss expertise without using that word. Regrettably, I had to limit the corpus, and journal articles are often the first way readers become acquainted with the field. Third, relying on database searches leaves out open access journals (e.g., *Enculturation*, *Kairos*) and articles published after a database's moving wall. JSTOR searches, for example, did not include *CCC*, *CE*, *CS*, and *RTE* articles published after 2018, potentially excluding relevant articles.

Given these limitations, this article offers only a partial picture of the field, as Mueller concedes thin methods do (13, 41). Including additional journals, more recent articles, monographs and edited volumes, and texts discussing expertise with different terms could change the results. Yet despite these limitations, this study seeks to serve as a productive starting point for developing a more robust concept of expertise in writing studies.

Thin Results

Analysis of the corpus reveals five domains of expertise, as shown in table 2. This list is not exhaustive; however, it represents the five major categories generated by adapting Virginia Braun and Victoria Clarke's thematic analysis approach. Articles that address multiple domains of expertise were coded in multiple categories.

Table 2.

Expertise Domains in the Study Corpus

Domains of expertise	Student/novice	Scholar/expert	Teacher/tutor
Academic writing practices	23	16	56
Academic reading practices	5	8	2
Writing studies as a content area	7	12	8
Disciplinary content outside writing studies	21	35	8
Writing technology use	15	20	8

Table 3 provides definitions of and examples for each of the five categories.

Table 3.

Definitions and Examples of Five Domains of Expertise Discussed in the Study Corpus

Expertise domain	Definition	Example
Academic writing practices	How writers, usually students, learn and demonstrate the ability to write texts that meet conventional Western academic standards in source use and citation, information literacy, and process-based writing, primarily in FYW courses	Denise K. Comer and Edward M. White report on their assessment of "Achieving Expertise," a FYW course taught as a MOOC (massive open online course) that centered on "collective inquiry into writing expertise: What does expert writing look like? How does it vary across contexts? How does one develop writing expertise? Who defines what is or is not effective writing?" (324).

Expertise domain	Definition	Example
Academic reading practices	How people learn and demonstrate skills of academic reading—the ability to comprehend, summarize, and paraphrase accurately scholarly texts, especially peer-reviewed journal articles and serious news publications—and how teachers teach these skills, primarily in FYW and undergraduate coursework	Ellen C. Carillo, in discussing "what it means to teach reading within our current post-truth culture" (135), claims the Common Core State Standards prevent students from developing expertise in reading because they focus too heavily on "argument and objectivity" to the exclusion of personal and creative texts (136). She worries reading becomes "reverence" and students are not learning the critical, reflective stance toward texts that being an expert reader—and ultimately an effective participant in a democracy—demands (155).
Writing studies as a content area	Knowledge of the academic discipline of writing studies, its history, theories, and research	T J Geiger II, via his study of the undergraduate writing major, argues for seeing "writing as a content worthy of study in its own right" (96). He concludes "expertise *about* writing is as important as the teaching *of* writing" in the discipline (109; italics in original).
Disciplinary content other than writing studies	Discussion of knowing disciplinary content to write and/or teach writing effectively in a particular field	Nancy Sommers and Laura Saltz contend, "disciplinary expertise in content and method" is necessary for students to succeed as writers after their first year in college. They elaborate, "If students are only writing to understand their personal experiences, if their expertise comes only from their personal connection with the material, or if they see the personal and academic as opposites," they will not become expert writers (146).

Expertise domain	Definition	Example
Writing technology use	Study of use of digital technologies to create, circulate, receive, assess, and/or teach writing	Virginia Anderson laments that writing studies teacher-scholars—especially computers and composition teacher-scholars—are expected to develop "technological expertise" to be "socially responsible educators" and teachers of writing (124). Via a case study of her university's switch to a new content management system, Oncourse, she concludes, "[c]omposition's revision of its mission to make compositionists players in the fast-moving world of futuristic innovation can exacerbate class divisions" (124).

In addition to helping me identify domains of expertise discussed in corpus articles, a thin reading reveals the frequency and depth of engagement with these domains. This information can help readers better know where to find sought information, identify where they might want to publish, and understand writing studies as a field.

This thin reading reinforces the strength of the pedagogical imperative in writing studies. In the corpus, articles with more mentions of "expert*" are more likely to discuss expertise related to teaching. Nine of the 15 (60%) articles with the most mentions of "expert*" comprise this category. Outpacing all other categories with 56 articles (see Table 2), expertise in teaching academic writing is the domain of expertise addressed most in the corpus. These results suggest expertly teaching academic writing remains a central concern in the field.

The most addressed domains of expertise reflect ongoing attention to FYW and WAC/WID. Expertise in academic writing practices and in disciplinary content other than writing studies are the two domains of expertise discussed most frequently; see Table 2. The prevalence of these two categories evidences scholarly attention to both of Geisler's "problem spaces" of expertise, skill and content. However, this content is mainly outside the field.

A thin reading shows comparatively little attention paid in the corpus to expertise in the content area of writing studies. Articles referencing expertise in disciplinary content other than writing studies account for more than twice the number referencing expertise in writing studies: 67 to 30. Authors attend more to expertise in content areas other than their own. This finding illustrates writing studies' difficulty in asserting its own disciplinary identity. The exception is articles connected to the Writing about Writing (WaW) movement, which foreground focus on writing studies as a content area.

Corpus articles on writing centers show particular concern with content expertise. Nearly half (9 of 20) of articles about expertise in tutoring writing also discuss the role disciplinary content knowledge plays, especially in being an expert tutor. For instance, Sue Dinitz and Susanmarie Harrington classify writing center consultants as "experts" when they have majors or have taken coursework that matches that of the student with whom they are working. This content knowledge, claim Richard Haswell et al., can help consultants read more rhetorically and attend to a text's intended effect as compared to the audience's likely reception.

A thin reading also identifies which journals most and least discuss expertise. The corpus includes the most articles from *C&C* and *WC* at 45 and 25 articles, respectively. These journals mention "expert*" 602 and 844 times, respectively. Only two articles in *JAC*, three articles in *WoE*, and four articles in *JBW* address "expert*" for a total of 16, 42, and 30 mentions, respectively. Apart from Rice's *CE* article, most in-depth treatment of expertise is in *WC*.

A thin reading likewise provides insight into the foci of writing studies journals, including which address which expertise domains. For instance, corpus articles addressing expertise in using digital writing technologies are most likely to appear in *C&C*. While unsurprising given *C&C*'s explicit focus, surprising is that articles discussing reading expertise appear almost exclusively in *Pedagogy* (with *WoE, WCJ, and JBW* each having only one article). Of the 12 articles addressing scholar expertise in writing studies content, half are from *CCC*. The only other journal to address this topic in more than one article is *WCJ*. With eight articles, *WCJ* addresses student expertise in disciplinary content outside writing studies twice as much as any other journal. *WC* has four. *WC* and *C&C* each address scholar expertise in disciplinary content outside writing studies most at eight articles each.

Connections among domains of expertise in corpus articles suggest expertise in skill is understood relationally, while expertise in content is understood individually. For instance, seven articles (of 16, or 44%) about expert writing practices also discuss novice writing practices. This approach suggests many articles define expertise in relation to non-expertise. However, articles treating content expertise operate differently. Nearly all corpus articles discuss either student or scholar expertise in disciplinary content. Only three articles discuss both. Likewise, no article addresses both student and scholar expertise in writing studies content. They are always addressed separately.

This thin analysis is limited. My biases inevitably shape my reading of the field's scholarship. Others might identify different domains of expertise or classify articles differently. However, this attention to a subset of journals' treatment of expertise helps us recognize the range of expertise studied by writing studies teacher-scholars and where these discussions are found.

Thick Results

Thick analysis of the corpus reveals three systemic tensions that affect writing studies teacher-scholars' ability to assert their expertise. One tension is that while writing studies needs to demonstrate expertise to succeed as a discipline, writing studies teacher-scholars may not want or be able to claim expertise. Relatedly, the desire to expand who can be(come) writing experts can threaten the notion that expertise is defined by exclusivity. Finally, labor practices that allow for staffing writing programs can undermine the notion that teaching writing requires expertise. I explain these tensions more fully in the following subsections.

Discomfort and Difficulty in Claiming Expertise

Thick analysis shows the notion of expertise can oppose tenets of the field. For example, in her analysis of climate change stories, Nancy Bray aligns expertise with "rational and scientific terms," "technical information," "data," and "decontextualized knowledge" as opposed to narrative and subjective meaning-making. She professes, "the narrative paradigm of thought is one that is accessible without expertise" (96–97). In Bray's conceptualization, writing studies is already marginalized from expertise. Thus, writing studies teacher-scholars can feel uncomfortable claiming expertise. They may not want to associate with statistics, disassociate from narrative, or view themselves as "rational and scientific." Publishing scholarship and teaching students to develop expertise can be difficult when teacher-scholars themselves are hesitant to be(come) experts.

Other authors suggest expertise is more compatible with quantifiable and objective disciplinary ways of knowledge-making. For instance, Christopher Eisenhart, in his case study of a humanities scholar who struggled to be acknowledged as a public expert in the Branch Davidian standoff in Texas, notes, "research tends to define expertise in such a way as to presume technical expertise. Taking the hard and social sciences as its 'paradigm,' expertise is often defined in terms of generating facts" (151). Experts, he concludes, are to be objective and disinterested. Consequently, scholarship on expertise tends to "neglect" humanists (159). As such, expertise fits uncomfortably with writing studies, which recognizes objectivity as impossible and encourages writers to expose their positionality.

Still other corpus authors find problematic the patriarchal nature of expertise. Rachael Sullivan, for instance, affirms that teacher-scholars too often rely on "patriarchal definitions of expertise" that erase material and bodily components of expertise, present males as the prototypical experts, and suggest reliance on instructional materials is counterpoised to expertise (53–54). For her, "The language we use to discuss technical expertise and the ways that we perform responses to technical difficulty in the classroom can reinforce or counteract cultural narratives about who 'belongs' in a high-tech classroom and world" (51). This scholarship reinforces that not everyone gets the opportunity to be considered an expert.

Yet, even if they wanted to be recognized as experts, some writing studies teacher-scholars find it strategically advantageous to deny their expertise. For instance, Faye Halpern reports a case study of her difficulty recruiting faculty to teach FYW, arguing that insisting special expertise is required to teach FYW scares away faculty from other disciplines. Rather, she calls for adopting a stance of "strategic disingenuousness" where WPAs "withhold" not only their own expertise but also the notion that teaching writing requires expertise—at least expertise different than what faculty in other disciplines already have (644). From this perspective, while writing studies teacher-scholars must claim expertise to achieve disciplinary status, they must deny expertise to staff their courses. To be respected as researchers, they need to establish what they know that others do not. To staff the writing programs they supervise, they need to deny that teaching writing requires special knowledge or skills.

Expansion and Restriction of Expertise

Expertise is required for disciplinary status in the academy. In describing how medicine became a profession in the early nineteenth century, Dara Rossman Regaignon explains expertise is "a domain of specialized and restricted knowledge" (145). Writing studies requires this same specialization and restriction of knowledge to be considered a discipline. Teacher-scholars must demonstrate they are recognized as subject matter experts to be tenured and promoted.

However, writing studies simultaneously seeks to make writing expertise accessible to others. Corpus articles evidence belief that novices can and should become expert writers. Authors profess expertise extends across the student-teacher dyad. For instance, in their study of the "Writing II: Rhetorical Composing" MOOC, Michael Blancato and Chad Iwertz report, "[i]nstead of conforming to the roles of either passive learner or expert teacher," both students and teachers in the MOOC moved along a spectrum between knowledge consumption and knowledge production (47). Blancato and Iwertz share, "it increasingly became difficult to point to specific 'experts' in the MOOC, as that role was adopted by both instructors *and* participants" (49; italics in original). The teacher was not always the expert, and the student was not always the non-expert (55). For Blancato and Iwertz, this finding troubles the prevailing construction of MOOCs, where "the success or failure of the course depends not upon the measured learning of students but upon the establishment of the instructors as *experts*" (49; italics in original). They worry such a framework precludes the possibility that all participants, students and teachers, can perform expertise.

Others agree. Corpus articles on multimodal/multimedia composing argue writing technologies can flatten classroom hierarchies built around expertise because students can be the experts in how to use them. Sullivan, for instance, notes discussions of technical difficulty in computers and composition tend to "sidestep" "expert/non-expert dualisms in favor of play and experimentation" (51). Such scholarship focuses on how everyone can learn by playing rather than who is the expert. As Collin Brooke argues in describing new media pedagogy, "Teachers must abandon the notion that all expertise must flow from the front of the classroom, particularly when it comes to technology." He elaborates, "Even those who are considered experts or 'power users' cannot expect to master every single program or application" (182). Brooke recognizes that new media composing requires expertise in many technologies, platforms, and media, and one person having such diverse expertise may be infeasible. However, some teachers may have difficulty ceding this expertise, and play is generally not viewed as scholarly.

Designating students as experts is complicated, as Sandra Tsui Eu Lam's study of Chinese L2 students' use of the platform SWoRD for peer review illustrates. She uses the terms "expert-learner" and "teacher-expert" (6) to highlight that both students (the learners) and teachers can be experts—or at least treated as such. She identifies two potential expert roles in peer review, "Teacher as Expert" and "Peer as Expert" (8). In her study, expertise entails knowledge both of how to write and of teacher expectations for an assignment. In other words, the expert knows exactly what is expected in a particular writing situation, a view consistent with Dinitz and Harrington's findings. Ostensibly, the teacher would fill this role, and Lam indeed found that students afforded more expertise to teachers than peers (8). However, students were not more likely to accept suggestions from the "Teacher as Expert." She reports, "feedback from a 'nonexpert peer' had greater influence than 'expert' teacher feedback" (19). Lam's use of scare quotes highlights that designations of "expert" are not automatically accepted and can depend on the audience. That is, expertise is subjective. Students did not necessarily do what their teachers told them to do in peer review, even if students considered their teachers to be experts. Sometimes they followed their peers' advice instead, even though their peers were non-experts. Experts were not automatically heeded.

In tension with efforts to expand who can gain expertise is the notion that expertise is a scarce commodity. Eisenhart calls this "the market economy of expertise" (153) where "factual knowledge is viewed as the commodity an expert produces" (152). Jim Webber explains this view when he suggests writing studies practitioners are recognized as experts when they provide something no one else can—in his example, when they do writing assessment that cannot be replicated by machines or people outside the academy (124). In other words, they are experts when they provide a distinctive service. Such is Stanley Fish's position when he declares, "in order for a discipline to survive[,] it needs to be seen as doing something other disciplines do not" (162). Faber concurs, affirming, "Expert knowledge and self-agency only become available and accessible when nonprofessionals become more embedded in the professional system. However, this system is structured to keep nonprofessionals out" (318). Writing studies thereby faces a conundrum: broadening who can become writing experts diminishes the value of writing expertise.

Writing Program Labor Practices and Expertise

Thick analysis of the study corpus uncovered a third tension: WPA work manifests writing studies' struggles with expertise. First, WPAs are often not treated as disciplinary experts. In its position statement "Evaluating the Intellectual Work of Writing Administration," the Council of Writing Program Administrators puts this situation starkly: "administration—leadership of first-year writing courses, WAC programs, writing centers, and the many other manifestations of writing administration—has for the most part been treated as a management activity that does not produce new knowledge and that neither requires nor demonstrates scholarly expertise and disciplinary knowledge." Corpus article authors agree. They work to redress this perception by explaining the expertise needed for administrative work.

Second, labor practices of FYW, WAC/WID, and writing centers can undermine that content expertise is required to teach writing. Most FYW courses are not staffed by writing studies teacher-scholars. Rather, most instructors come from literary studies and creative writing, with many being hired as adjuncts shortly before classes start. Moreover, when such courses are staffed by writing studies teacher-scholars, they are usually beginning rather than established scholars—either graduate students or assistant professors (i.e., experts-in-training). Halpern admits, "we cannot have the assurance that the professors teaching [FYW courses] already have the knowledge of what to do inside themselves" (654). Yet sometimes they are hired anyway.

Articles on WaW address this issue by arguing for FYW to become a course about writing studies rather than a course in how to write in college. For instance, Douglas Downs and Elizabeth Wardle assert,

When we continue to pursue the goal of teaching students 'how to write in college' in one or two semesters—despite the fact that our own scholarship extensively calls this possibility into question—we silently support the misconceptions that writing is not a real subject, that writing courses do not require *expert* instructors, and that rhetoric and composition are not genuine research areas or legitimate intellectual pursuits. (553; italics added)

Following Downs and Wardle entails requiring expertise in writing studies content to teach FYW. Given the diversity of domains of expertise in the study corpus, doing so is no small task.

My point is not that folks from other disciplines or experts-in-training cannot teach FYW well. They can (see McClure). Nor is it that writing programs do not offer effective training in teaching writing. WPAs often make heroic efforts to prepare instructors under challenging circumstances. The point is that corpus articles suggest staffing models often do not privilege—or even allow for—hiring writing studies experts to teach FYW. If we as writing studies professionals claim that writing studies is a discipline in which people can be experts and that expertise is required to teach writing, we need to define that expertise and employ staffing models that enact those beliefs. What would it mean to have FYW predominately taught by writing studies experts? We have never had the chance to find out.

The realities of WAC/WID instruction also oppose the notion that teaching writing requires expertise. WAC/WID courses are usually taught not by writing studies faculty but by faculty in other disciplines. Until the 2000s, faculty at many institutions were often assigned to teach these courses with little to no discussion of how or why (Salem and Jones 63). On one hand, having disciplinary faculty teach their own WAC/WID courses is necessary. They know best about writing in their field. Writing studies faculty cannot know the writing practices and genres in every academic discipline. Even if they did, few institutions employ enough writing studies faculty to teach writing in every discipline across campus. On the other hand, this model hinges on the idea that, with minimal or no training, anyone can teach others how to write.

Writing center staffing likewise downplays that content expertise is required to teach writing. In conflict with findings that writing center consultants are seen as experts when they possess disciplinary content knowledge are claims that consultants do not need disciplinary expertise to be effective. In their analysis of writing center consulting sessions, for instance, Dinitz and Harrington claim expertise in tutoring writing entails "knowledge of writing in the discipline" (79). Isabelle Thompson et al. concur, characterizing writing center consultants as experts when they have "more knowledge and experience [. . .] in the subject matter or skill" than the student with whom they are working (81). Elsewhere Thompson presents this "expert-novice relationship" as essential for successful writing center sessions (419).

Others offer a different view. Rebecca S. Nowacek and Bradley Hughes, for instance, advocate for writing center consultants to take on the role of "expert outsider." They explain this "paradoxical" role entails "knowledge of writing processes and genres, as well as the affective, institutional, and ideological contexts for writing," while recognizing that "tutors cannot possibly hope to be content experts for every writer and draft they encounter" (181). For them, expert outsiders can teach novices how to do certain things with writing (e.g., decipher a writing prompt, conform to genre expectations), even if they do not know disciplinary content. In Geisler's terms, they profess writing center sessions can be successful when tutors have rhetorical but not content expertise.

Regardless of which belief is embraced, writing centers face infrastructural and theoretical challenges regarding expertise. Most staffing models do not permit the approach Dinitz and Harrington and Thompson et al. advocate. Though some writing centers have professional or faculty tutors, staffs usually comprise undergraduates. They are not staffed by experts but rather operate on a peer tutoring model. Nor do these peer consultants have disciplinary content knowledge of all the majors for which students bring in writing. Most peer tutors are English majors. Peer tutoring in writing has enormous benefits. Part of what makes writing centers successful is that students engage as peers without fear of evaluation. As Lam finds, students more readily accept peer feedback. However, we need to acknowledge openly the limits to content expertise with this model. Furthermore, even if writing consultants were content experts, the explicit goal of most writing centers is to teach students to write and revise themselves, without depending on the expertise of the writing center. Thus, the mission of most writing centers is at odds with a notion of expertise as a protected commodity. Writing centers strive to share their expertise.

This thick analysis of the study corpus reveals that, at best, writing programs illustrate expertise can be held across populations. However, this belief conflicts with the ideas that expertise is a restricted commodity and that teaching writing requires disciplinary content knowledge about writing. If expertise is (to be) held by only a select few, it seemingly cannot simultaneously be held by broader populations—at least not without understanding expertise differently.

Conclusion

This article advocates for greater attention to expertise in writing studies through both thin and thick studies of disciplinarity. A thin study of a corpus comprising writing studies articles that reference "expert*" reveals that writing studies practitioners discuss five domains of expertise, with expertise in disciplinary content other than writing studies and expertise in academic writing practices as the two most popular. Awareness of this diversity of expertise domains can help us articulate for both internal and external audiences the range of what writing studies practitioners study. It can also raise awareness of how we construct our expertise—in this corpus, as focused mainly on doing and teaching academic writing. These foci establish a narrow view of the field in tension with calls to extend writing studies' purview to all literate practice (e.g., Bazerman). Concomitantly, attention to this range can explain the field's challenges in achieving disciplinary recognition. Because the status of academic disciplines depends on their ability to establish themselves as experts in content knowledge, it is crucial for writing studies to establish what that content is—and to ensure it represents what the field values. If writing studies is serious about embracing a broad focus on literate practice, attention to expertise should include and extend beyond academic writing practices and teaching academic writing.

Thick analysis of the corpus reveals three tensions in the field's treatment of expertise. First, while writing studies needs to claim expertise to succeed as a discipline, writing studies teacher-scholars may not want or be able to do so. Second, writing studies teacher-scholars' desire to expand who can be experts threatens the notion of expertise as exclusive. Third, labor practices that allow for staffing writing programs can undermine the notion that teaching writing requires expertise. Recognizing these tensions can help us (re)consider how to invite more diverse populations to become experts in writing studies as well as how we want to (discuss how we) staff the writing programs we oversee. The study corpus shows our scholarship is conflicted. We want the protection and status of disciplinary expertise but are uncomfortable with the inherently exclusionary nature of expertise. Acknowledging these tensions challenges us to consider to what extent we want to embrace the neoliberal ideal that scarcity brings value. It also challenges us to consider ways to achieve expertise that do not downplay the need for expertise.

Writing programs might benefit from explicitly acknowledging these tensions surrounding their labor practices. If the basis for current staffing models is to get bodies into classrooms for the lowest cost rather than to achieve instructional goals for writing, that is a problem. This is not news to writing studies teacher-scholars (Horner "Grounding"; Kahn; Mendenhall). But the stakes are now different. In situating writing courses as capable of being taught by anyone, regardless of expertise, we lower the bar for such courses to be taught (in part or in whole) by AI. To protect our expertise, we need to argue for hiring writing studies experts (or experts-in-training) to teach, co-teach, and train others to teach FYW and WAC/WID courses (see Scott). While such approaches entail significant logistical challenges, they are necessary if we take seriously that expertise in writing studies is required to teach and research writing and that work cannot be outsourced to AI.

This study is only a beginning. Follow-up research should examine texts excluded from this study corpus, especially edited volumes where disciplinary reflection often occurs (e.g., Malenczyk et al.). More sophisticated statistical analysis of mentions of "expert*" would also enrich our understanding of expertise in writing studies. Likewise, follow-up research could ask writing studies practitioners themselves to reflect on the role of expertise in their research, pedagogy, and service. This study reinforces that expertise plays a crucial role in all three areas. While claims to expertise are fraught in writing studies, they will continue to require attention if we (want to) exist as an autonomous discipline.

Works Cited

Adler-Kassner, Linda, and Elizabeth Wardle, editors. *Naming What We Know: Threshold Concepts of Writing Studies*. Utah State UP, 2015.

——. *Writing Expertise: A Research-based Approach to Writing and Learning Across Disciplines*. UP of Colorado, 2022.

Anderson, Virginia. "Supply-Side Dreams: Composition, Technology, and the Circular Logic of Class." *Computers and Composition*, vol. 27, no. 2, 2010, pp. 124–37, doi.org/10.1016/j.compcom.2010.03.002.

Bazerman, Charles. "The Case for Writing Studies as a Major Discipline." *Rhetoric and Composition as Intellectual Work*, edited by Gary A. Olson, Southern Illinois UP, 2002, pp. 32–38.

Beaufort, Anne. "Learning the Trade: A Social Apprenticeship Model for Gaining Writing Expertise." *Written Communication*, vol. 17, 2000, pp. 185–223.

—. *Writing in the Real World: Making the Transition from School to Work*. Teachers College P, 1999.

Blancato, Michael, and Chad Iwertz. "'Are the Instructors Going to Teach Us Anything?': Conceptualizing Student and Teacher Roles in the 'Rhetorical Composing' MOOC." *Computers and Composition*, vol. 42, 2016, pp. 47–58, doi.org/10.1016/j.compcom.2016.08.002.

Braun, Virginia, and Victoria Clarke. *Successful Qualitative Research: A Practical Guide for Beginners*. Sage, 2013.

Bray, Nancy. "Epiphanies of the Ordinary: Personal Stories of Climate Change." *Writing on the Edge*, vol. 29, no. 1, 2018, pp. 91–108.

Carillo, Ellen C. "Reading and Writing Centers: A Primer for Writing Center Professionals." *Writing Center Journal*, vol. 36, no. 2, 2017, pp. 117–45.

Carter, Michael. "The Idea of Expertise: An Exploration of Cognitive and Social Dimensions of Writing." *College Composition and Communication*, vol. 41, no. 3, 1990, pp. 265–86.

Comer, Denise K., and Edward M. White. "Adventuring into MOOC Writing Assessment: Challenges, Results, and Possibilities. *College Composition and Communication*, vol. 67, no. 3, 2016, pp. 318–59.

Council of Writing Program Administrators. *Evaluating the Intellectual Work of Writing Administrators.* 17 July 2019, wpacouncil.org/aws/CWPA/pt/sd/news_article/242849/_PARENT/layout_details/false.

Dinitz, Sue, and Susanmarie Harrington. "The Role of Disciplinary Expertise in Shaping Writing Tutorials." *Writing Center Journal,* vol. 33, no. 2, 2014, pp. 73–98, www.jstor.org/stable/43443372.

Downs, Doug, and Elizabeth Wardle. "Teaching about Writing, Righting Misconceptions: (Re)Envisioning FYC as Intro to Writing Studies." *College Composition and Communication,* vol. 58, 2007, pp. 552–84.

Dryer, Dylan B. "Divided by Primes: Competing Meanings among Writing Studies' Keywords." *College English,* vol. 81, no. 3, 2019, pp. 214–55.

Eisenhart, Christopher. "The Humanist Scholar as Public Expert." *Written Communication,* vol. 23, no. 2, 2006, pp. 150–72, doi.org/10.1177/0741088306286392.

Ericsson, K. Anders. "An Introduction to *Cambridge Handbook of Expertise and Expert Performance*: Its Development, Organization, and Content." *The Cambridge Handbook of Expertise and Expert Performance,* 2nd ed., edited by K. Anders Ericsson et al., Cambridge, 2006, 3–19.

Ericsson, K. Anders, Neil Charness, Paul J. Feltovich, and Robert R. Hoffman, editors. *The Cambridge Handbook of Expertise and Expert Performance,* 2nd ed., Cambridge, 2006.

Ericsson, K. Anders, Michael J. Prietula, and Edward T. Cokely. "The Making of an Expert." *Harvard Business Review,* 2007, hbr.org/2007/07/the-making-of-an-expert.

Faber, Brenton. "Professional Identities: What Is Professional About Professional Communication?" *Journal of Business and Technical Communication,* vol. 16, no. 3, 2002, pp. 306–37.

Feltovich, Paul J., Kenneth M. Ford, and Robert R. Hoffman, editors. *Expertise in Context: Human and Machine.* MIT P, 1997.

Fish, Stanley. "Them We Burn: Violence and Conviction in the English Department." *English as a Discipline: Or, Is There a Plot in This Play?,* edited by James C. Raymond, U of Alabama P, 1996, 160–73.

Geiger, T J. "An Intimate Discipline? Writing Studies, Undergraduate Majors, and Relational Labor." *Composition Studies,* vol. 43, no. 2, 2015, pp. 92–112, www.jstor.org/stable/45157101.

Geisler, Cheryl. *Academic Literacy and the Nature of Expertise.* Lawrence Erlbaum, 1994.

Halpern, Faye. "Strategic Disingenuousness: The WPA, the 'Scribbling Women,' and the Problem of Expertise." *College Composition and Communication,* vol. 66, no. 4, 2015, pp. 643–67, www.jstor.org/stable/43491904.

Haswell, Richard, Terri L. Briggs, Jennifer A. Fay, Norman K. Gillen, Rob Harrill, Andrew M. Shupala, and Sylvia S. Trevino. "Context and Rhetorical Reading Strategies: Haas and Flower (1988) Revisited." *Written Communication,* vol. 16, no. 1, 1999, pp. 3–27.

Heilker, Paul, and Peter Vandenberg, editors. *Keywords in Writing Studies.* Utah State UP, 2015.

Horner, Bruce. "Grounding Responsivity." *JAC*, vol. 34, no. 1/2, 2014, pp. 49–61.

——. *Rewriting Composition: Terms of Exchange*. Southern Illinois UP, 2016.

Kahn, Seth. "Anyone Can Teach Writing." *Bad Ideas about Writing*, edited by Cheryl E. Ball and Drew M. Loewe, West Virginia University Libraries, pp. 363–68.

Kellogg, Ronald T. "Professional Writing Expertise." *The Cambridge Handbook of Expertise and Expert Performance*, edited by K. Anders Ericsson, et al., 2nd ed., Cambridge UP, 2006, pp. 413–40.

Lam, Sandra Tsui Eu. "A Web-Based Feedback Platform for Peer and Teacher Feedback on Writing: An Activity Theory Perspective." *Computers and Composition*, vol. 62, 2021, pp. 1–27, doi.org/10.1016/j.compcom.2021.102666.

Lauer, Claire. "Contending with Terms: 'Multimodal' and 'Multimedia' in the Academic and Public Spheres." *Computers and Composition*, vol. 26, no. 4, 2009, pp. 225–39, doi.org/10.1016/j.compcom.2009.09.001.

Lindemann, Erika. *A Rhetoric for Writing Teachers*, 2nd ed. Oxford UP, 1987.

Linkon, Sherry Lee. "The Reader's Apprentice: Making Critical Cultural Reading Visible." *Pedagogy*, vol. 5, no. 2, 2005, pp. 247–73, muse.jhu.edu/article/182336.

Luo, Na, and Ken Hyland. "Intervention and Revision: Expertise and Interaction in Text Mediation." *Written Communication*, vol. 34, no. 4, 2017, pp. 414–40, doi.org/10.1177/0741088317722944.

Malenczyk, Rita, Susan Miller-Cochran, Elizabeth Wardle, and Kathleen Blake Yancey. *Composition, Rhetoric, and Disciplinarity*. Utah State UP, 2018.

McClure, Randall. "Being COMPetitive." *Inside Higher Ed*, 6 April 2011, www.insidehighered.com/advice/2011/04/06/being-competitive.

Mendenhall, Annie S. "The Composition Specialist as Flexible Expert: Identity and Labor in the History of Composition." *College English*, vol. 77, no. 1, 2014, pp. 11–31, www.jstor.org/stable/24238502.

Miller, Susan. "Writing Studies as a Mode of Inquiry." *Composition as Intellectual Work*, edited by Gary A. Olson, Southern Illinois UP, 2002, pp. 41–54.

Moxley, Joseph M. "Writing Studies." *Writing Commons*, writingcommons.org/section/writing-studies-definition/.

Mueller, Derek N. *Network Sense: Methods for Visualizing a Discipline*. WAC Clearinghouse, 2017, wac.colostate.edu/books/writing/network/.

Nowacek, Rebecca S., and Bradley Hughes. "Threshold Concepts in the Writing Center: Scaffolding the Development of Tutor Expertise." *Naming What We Know: Threshold Concepts of Writing Studies*, edited by Linda Adler-Kassner and Elizabeth Wardle, Utah State UP, 2015, pp. 171–85.

Regaignon, Dara Rossman. "Anxious Uptakes: Nineteenth-Century Advice Literature as a Rhetorical Genre." *College English*, vol. 78, no. 2, 2015, pp. 139–61, www.jstor.org/stable/44075104.

Rice, Jenny. "Para-Expertise, Tacit Knowledge, and Writing Problems." *College English*, vol. 78, no. 2, 2015, pp. 117–38.

Ritter, Kelly, and Paul Kei Matsuda, editors. *Exploring Composition Studies: Sites, Issues, Perspectives*. Logan: Utah State UP, 2012.

Ruiz, Iris, and Raúl Sánchez, editors. *Decolonizing Rhetoric and Composition Studies: New Latinx Keywords for Theory and Pedagogy*. Palgrave, 2016.

Salem, Lori, and Peter Jones. "Undaunted, Self-Critical, and Resentful: Investigating Faculty Attitudes Toward Teaching Writing in a Large University Writing-Intensive Course Program." *WPA: Writing Program Administration*, vol. 34, no. 1, 2010, associationdatabase.co/archives/34n1/34n1salem-jones.pdf.

Scott, Tony. "Subverting Crisis in the Political Economy of Composition." *College Composition and Communication*, vol. 68, no. 1, 2016, pp. 10–37, www.jstor.org/stable/44783525.

Sommers, Nancy, and Laura Saltz. "The Novice as Expert: Writing the Freshman Year." *College Composition and Communication*, vol. 56, no. 1, 2004, pp. 124–49, dx.doi.org/10 .2307/4140684.

Sullivan, Rachael. "Troubling Structures: A Material-Embodied Pedagogy of Technical Difficulty." *Computers and Composition*, vol. 53, 2019, pp. 47–59, doi.org/10.1016/j.compcom.2019.05.004.

Thompson, Isabelle. "Scaffolding in the Writing Center." *Written Communication*, vol. 26, no. 4, 2009, pp. 417–53, doi.org/10.1177/0741088309342364.

Thompson, Isabelle, Alyson Whyte, David Shannon, Amanda Muse, Kristen Miller, Milla Chappell, and Abby Whigham. "Examining Our Lore: A Survey of Students' and Tutors' Satisfaction with Writing Center Conferences." *Writing Center Journal*, vol. 29, no. 1, 2009, pp. 78–105, www.jstor.org/stable/43442315.

Trimbur, John. *Solidarity or Service: Composition and the Problem of Expertise*. Boynton/Cook, 2011.

Ward, Paul, Jan Maarten Schraagen, Julie Gore, and Emilie Roth, editors. *The Oxford Handbook of Expertise*. Oxford UP, 2020.

Webber, Jim. "Toward an Artful Critique of Reform: Responding to Standards, Assessment, and Machine Scoring." *College Composition and Communication*, vol. 69, no. 1, 2017, pp. 118–45, www.jstor.org/stable/44784334.

James P. Purdy is professor of English and University and Community Writing Center director at Duquesne University. In his two co-authored books, four edited volumes, and numerous peer-reviewed articles and chapters, Purdy studies research-writing activities, particularly as mediated by digital technologies and intersecting with issues of intellectual property and expertise.

The Eco-Cosmopolitan Campus: Expanding Place-Based Writing Instruction through Ecocomposition

Luke Rodewald

This article demonstrates how the theoretical configuration of ecocomposition—the study of the dynamics between environments and discourse, and between ecology and composition—complicates conventional approaches to place-based writing pedagogy. Here, I seek to reimagine the parameters of recurring place-based writing assignments that often focus explicitly on local spaces to, instead, broaden their considerations toward an "eco-cosmopolitan" awareness, using Ursula K. Heise's ecocritical framework to orient student writing toward a more holistic consideration of place. Such expansion of scope resonates in a planetary era where spatial boundaries are increasingly porous. First, I examine how ecocomposition aligns with and ultimately extends existing conceptions of place-based pedagogy, arguing for more explicit intersections between these two fields of composition instruction. I, then, detail a specific place-based writing assignment that initially fixates student focus on a particular, local place—our university's campus—before extending outward to consider regional and global entanglements. Through a discursive analysis of students' projects and reflective writing, I show how an ecocomposition approach to place-based writing not only facilitates meaningful composition about the ecological dynamics of local places but also enables more complex spatial considerations altogether.

Introduction

On each pane of the revolving glass door through which I almost-daily enter my university's library, there are small white signs bearing the phrase, "revolve to save energy." The text suggests that my decision to push open this particular door is—somehow—an explicitly "sustainable" action, or, at the very least, a more environmentally-friendly choice than using one of the automatic-opening doors that sit on either side of it. With somewhat regularity, the signs give me pause. Although vague, they insinuate that my miniscule choice to (or not to) manually revolve the door is—again, somehow—linked to larger efforts elsewhere to reduce energy usage. I spotlight this particular encounter to illustrate one of the (admittedly lackluster) ways in which my university campus uses writing to situate its individual "greening" initiatives within a larger context of environmental consciousness (Emanuel and Adams). The signs imply that what might appear to be a standalone action or location is entangled with something much more complex altogether. When noticed, such public writing facilitates my understanding of this particular site—my campus—not as an isolated entity but rather, a "complex system" that is "composed of many elements that interact across space and time" within both local and bioregional contexts (Posner and Stuart 265–66). Yet, this acknowledgment of the site's larger, subliminal ecological networks often fails to materialize within a landscape as carefully constructed and presumably contained as today's university campus.

As curriculum theorist Gillian Judson suggests, the difficulty in gauging how a nuanced, interrelated sense of place exists on the university campus correlates with a larger lack of pedagogical attention to campus place in higher education. This absence endures, in part, because of the campus's perceived "invisibility," due to the fact that, in general, "'the everyday,' by its very nature, is difficult to grasp" (234). An increasing number of composition scholars have drawn attention to the invisible, often-unacknowledged characteristics of place, including its agency and influence on discourse. Katrina M. Powell identifies Nedra Reynolds, Robert E. Brooke, and Jenny (Edbauer) Rice, for instance, as figures who have "shown the continuing relevance and importance of understanding material contexts and physical locations for insight into the ways writers write and audience read" (Powell 179). Gregory L. Ulmer, Jeff Rice, and Felicita Arzu Carmichael further extend the conception of "place" as it impacts writing to encompass digital environments and online learning locations. Yet, as Isabel Galleymore has argued, in contemporary writing pedagogy—and in particular, *place*-based writing pedagogy—the role of place is often relegated to an overwhelmingly "local" construction, omitting the concealed, networked connections underlying the reality of today's globalized world. Such limited scope emerges as problematic for place-based writing instruction, which often seeks to engage students in ecocritical or environmentally-conscious composition assignments centered on ideas of sustainability or community conservation—concepts that inherently transcend the imagined boundaries between the local and the global.

This article demonstrates how the theoretical configuration of ecocomposition—the study of the dynamics between environments and discourse—complicates and ultimately enriches conventional approaches to place-based writing pedagogy. In particular, I illustrate how integrating ecocomposition—with its overt focus on recognizing place not as a stable entity but as an interconnected network or system—might generate a more nuanced understanding of place as it relates to student writing. As such, I seek to reimagine the parameters of place-based writing assignments that often focus explicitly on local spaces to, instead, broaden their concerns toward an "eco-cosmopolitan" understanding, using ecocritic Ursula K. Heise's framework to orient student writing about place onto a more holistic consideration. Heise's eco-cosmopolitan configuration avers that our age of globalization "entails the emergence of new forms of culture that are no longer anchored in place" (10). As I argue here, through a similar "deterritorialized" emphasis on spatial networks and fluidity, eco-composition's complex understanding of what "place" means as it relates to composition offers an approach for student writing about place that more accurately accounts for the networked world outside instructors' classrooms (10).

In what follows, I examine how ecocomposition aligns with and ultimately extends existing conceptions of place-based pedagogy and argue for more explicit intersections between these two fields of composition instruction. To illustrate how "enmeshed the world of words, of text, and the natural world" are even within a landscape as seemingly insular as the university campus, I then detail a specific place-based writing assignment that initially fixates student focus on a particular, local place before extending their attention outward toward regional and even global entanglements (Dobrin and Weisser 1). As the signs on my library's doors allude, even the most presumably-simple actions in a particular place are implicated in existential scales. Through a discursive analysis of students' projects and reflective writing, I show how integrating ecocomposition into place-based writing not only facilitates meaningful composition about the ecological dynamics of local places, but also enables students to embark on more complex, eco-cosmopolitan spatial considerations. As a result, place becomes repositioned in such pedagogy as not just an immediate location to write "about," but also as a multilayered construct of planetary scope and significance that influences writing itself.

Broadening the Parameters of Placed-Based Writing via Ecocomposition

Championed by educators such as David Sobel and David Greenwood, place-based pedagogies posit that fostering an individual's "sense of place" correlates to their heightened attachment and engagement in learning. Moreover, such pedagogies seek to offer organic opportunities for facilitating environmentalist thinking that transcends the classroom, often harnessing student interest through centering local landscapes, texts, and cultural artifacts which center accountability toward their neighboring communities (Ball and Lai). Consequently, this instruction—particularly when it is informed by critical race theory and Indigenous land-based epistemologies—also provides opportunities for students to unearth suppressed histories of both people and the environment by "re-embedding them in the land-connected social relationships" that settler-colonial worldviews often ignore (Wildcat et al. iv).

Place-based composition instruction, consequently, most often facilitates this critical inquiry through student writing about place. Jennifer Case, reflecting on place-centric approaches to creative writing pedagogy, notes that embracing local place in the composition classroom can "demystify the university" and "facilitate a greater sense of agency for student writers" (6). Lauren Esposito likewise asserts that "place influences our interactions by shaping the genres, texts, and languages we use as writers and readers," and advocates for integrating student writing about community concerns (70). Such testimonies aver that writing instruction rooted in considering place not only offers students a resonant curriculum but also steers them toward a heightened sense of their own participatory roles in their surrounding communities (Brooke).

Unabashedly endorsed in these espousals is the value of local place, a sentiment which recurs in most approaches to place-based writing instruction. Galleymore underscores this trope, arguing that "place" is almost always "synonymous" with locality in such pedagogy (26). While Galleymore's assessment focuses primarily on creative writing instruction, a quick survey of argumentative and analytical place-based composition ventures reveals a similar pattern. For example, in *Composition and Sustainability*, Derek Owens argues that writing instruction requires not "higher," abstract levels of critical thinking but "lower learning," orienting students toward a deeper understanding of their local communities through assignments like a "place portrait" wherein students describe "where you're living right now" so that an unfamiliar reader can acquire an accurate picture of the place (75; 185). Likewise, Allison B. Wallace describes a "place journal" assignment where students repeatedly visit a location, record observations via both writing and sketching, and reflect on the changes witnessed during the semester and, as such, become more "placed" in this landscape (103). In a similar field journal assignment, Summer Harrison's students regularly observe and visually-depict various sites on campus: an attempt to "defamiliarize" the everyday by becoming more attune to subtle changes over time, which helps "engender a sense of empowerment for students as they become more capable of understanding the places in which they find themselves" (41). Aligned with many of place-based pedagogy's objectives, these tasks engage students in a critical exploration of where they are, claiming that such inquiry will also facilitate a recognition of the complex biological relationships coexisting within this space.

I spotlight these examples to illustrate the repeating motif of how spatial attunement in place-based writing instruction is often explicitly local in its orientation. While local place may, indeed, exist as a phenomenon rich for examination in the composition classroom—both as a topic for writing and as an agent influencing such writing, as Christopher Keller, Christian Weisser, Ryan David Leack, and Hannah Rule have convincingly shown—I concur with Galleymore that contemporary place-based writing instruction also remains hindered by a preoccupation with this limited realm of spatial consideration.

As Deborah Brandt has suggested via the notion of literacy sponsors, it is imperative to recognize the fluid range of "literacy's materiel" and the "things that accompany writing and reading and the ways they are manufactured and distributed" (168). In an increasingly globalized world, where the presumed boundaries between local, regional, and planetary spaces frequently blur, place-oriented writing pedagogy must also account for such viscosity.

Instructive for Galleymore is Ursula K. Heise's configuration of eco-cosmopolitanism: "an attempt to envision individuals and groups as part of planetary 'imagined communities' of both human and nonhuman kinds" (61). Arguing that the traditional, localist construction of a "sense of place" fails to adequately yield meaningful environmental interventions, Heise posits that an eco-cosmopolitan understanding of place generates a more dynamic, provocative "sense of planet": an attunement to the political, economic, technological, social, cultural, and ecological networks that govern everyday locations and behaviors, like writing (55). Such holistic consideration echoes the notion that writing shapes and is shaped by "ongoing context-construction" and a myriad of influences across a writer's lifespan (Dippre and Smith 33). While theories of cosmopolitanism have been contested by scholars like Rosi Braidotti due to risks of over-simplifying "the complexity of the global condition" (10), Heise's use of the construct is intended to "provide a shorthand for a cultural and political understanding that allows individuals to think beyond the boundaries of their own cultures, ethnicities, or nations to a range of other sociocultural frameworks" (60). Drawing from Ramachandra Guha and Juan Martínez-Alier, Heise's notion offers, in part, a method for "envisioning contemporary modes of consciousness that might be commensurate with intensified global connectedness" (57). Consequently, if place-based pedagogies are, as Robert E. Brooke has long emphasized, designed to facilitate ideas of ecological citizenship for students beyond just instilling a "migratory" set of disciplinary skills, then a broader, more nuanced, and ultimately eco-cosmopolitan understanding of place in student writing must also emerge (Lipscomb).

I turn to the construction of ecocomposition to complicate and enrich conventional ideas about location for place-based writing pedagogy in ways that resonate with Heise's eco-cosmopolitan framework. Ecocomposition's regard of both place and writing as complex, intersecting systems broadens place's potential for student composition in ways that reflect spatial entanglements inherent by modern globalization. As defined by Sidney I. Dobrin and Christian Weisser, ecocomposition "is the study of relationships between environments (and by that we mean natural, constructed, and even imagined places) and discourse (speaking, writing, and thinking)" (6). While a complete chronology of ecocomposition is beyond the scope of this article—and is crystallized elsewhere by Madison Jones—the conception springs from acknowledging the physical and metaphorical dynamics between composition and environments, such as Richard M. Coe's espousal of a systems theory-based approach to composition and Marilyn Cooper's formation of an ecological model for writing. Overarching such scholarship is the notion that an ecological understanding of composition highlights the enmeshed reality of what "place" and "environment" mean, as well as the active influence they exert on writing.[1] For example, in her foreword to Weisser and Dobrin's *Ecocomposition*, Cooper remarks, "the systems that constitute writing and writers are not just *like* ecological systems, but are precisely ecological systems," and claims, "there are no boundaries between writing and the other interlocked, cycling systems of our world" ("Foreword" xiv, emphasis original). Put shortly, an ecocomposition approach casts place as an engaged actor in the complex network of relationships and interactions that constitute writing.

It is this reiterative emphasis on systems and networks by Cooper and other ecocomposition scholars that intrigues me for place-based writing and how their instructional approaches might more explicitly intersect. Dobrin underscores the imperative to better integrate systems and fluctuation theories into ecological considerations of writing because of their attention to instability, complexity, and "their focus on wholes rather than parts" (142). Jones likewise argues that by perceiving place in ecocomposition as "premises" we might better recognize how place correlates to composition "not as a fixed entity but as fluid, complex, and emergent" ("Writing Conditions"). Both Jones and Dobrin gesture here toward a multifaceted, eco-cosmopolitan understanding of place. In this era of globalization—where, returning to Heise, "both local cultural and ecological systems are imbricated in global ones"—it is critical for place-centric writing instruction to similarly avoid an over-romanticization of local place as an impetus for environmental thinking, and to, instead, open its concerns up to a "less territorial and more systemic sense" of global entanglements (59; 56).

If, as Dobrin suggests, ecocomposition offers "a more complex notion of ecological methodologies" that "account for the complexity of writing as a system," then its integration into place-oriented writing instruction might also help instructors re-conceive "place" as a more intricate, systemic iteration which better grasps the network reality of geospatial globalization (142). In turn, place-based composition pedagogy offers—indeed, grounds—ecocomposition with an immediate origin point from which students can begin to identify, recover, and create material spaces and places that "teach us how to live well in our total environments . . . and identify and change ways of thinking that injure and exploit other people and places" (Greenwood, "The Best of Both Worlds" 9). Such emphases, in particular, speak to the type of nuanced awareness that eco-cosmopolitan thinking offers—an "understanding of larger salient connections . . . of biospheric connectedness"—and which might also be better accounted for in place-based composition pedagogy today (Heise 62).

Applying Ecocomposition to Place-Based Writing Pedagogy: A Case Study

The previously-mentioned instructional assignments from Owens, Wallace, and Harrison exemplify how place-based composition approaches often solicit local environments as their foci for student writing. Common variations on those assignments—for example, nature journals, observational logbooks, and other descriptive writing exercises about a particular place—reiterate objectives that extend beyond developing compositional proficiencies: students sharpen perception and observation skills, think critically about their intersections with a place's multispecies inhabitants, evaluate a site's status as it relates to conservation or accessibility, and detail its physical intricacies through purposeful imagery. My intent here is not to dismiss the merits of these projects nor their objectives. Indeed, I have incorporated similar assignments and found them to yield engaging, creative pieces that largely achieve the learning outcomes suggested by these instructors. I agree with Greenwood that, through such instruction, students come to see how "place" becomes more than some "thing" inert or merely a marker on a geographic map; rather, all places become recognized as social constructions and cultural products, which provides a "locally relevant pathway for multidisciplinary inquiry and democratic participation" ("Place-Based Education" 148). The popularity of these projects—as evidenced by their recurring appearance in archived syllabi on the Association for the Study of Literature and the Environment's teaching database—speaks to their pragmatism ("Sample Syllabi"). However, I am interested in how an *extension* of these project's current spatial considerations might better account for an ecocosmopolitan sense of place that acknowledges the networked ties underlying all locations. How might the "placed" sensation Wallace advocates for or the "defamiliarized," deepened understanding of location Harrison envisions *also* enable students to grasp the globalized connections with which they are entangled?

While preparing to teach a lower-division writing course, I was intrigued by the potential to integrate this broadened spatial inquiry into a place-based curriculum. In an assignment that echoes eco-cosmopolitan thinking, Peter Goggin and Zach Waggoner's first-year writing students generated shopping lists and then deconstructed them via a rhetorical analysis while pondering the concept of environmental footprints implicit in such items. Such an exercise, they note, helps students "recognize that the choices we overtly or tacitly make as consumers have important consequences" (59). I also drew inspiration from James J. Farrell's *The Nature of College* and his reflections on teaching sustainability issues based in the university setting. One experience Farrell records featured students writing publicly about local environmental concerns through a "campus annotation" assignment. Occasioned during Earth Week, Farrell's students would "annotate" his campus of St. Olaf College by creating and posting signs that would "reveal the invisible complexity of the campus environment" through concise "blurbs" of information (159). Student considerations oscillated from critique to admiration and ranged from the campus's artificial environment—carpeting, roofing materials, elevators, window sizes, on-site dining options—to the natural, such as its surrounding prairie landscape.

Although Farrell's assignment was taught in an environmental studies seminar, I saw value in retooling aspects of his project as a way for composition students to both think critically about their local campus environment, highlight ecological links connecting it to a larger "sense" of place beyond its parameters, and contemplate how to convey such observations to a general audience. Farrell's annotations also made me think back to the vague message about energy conservation suggested by the signs on my library's revolving doors. How could my students take the idea *behind* the signs' purpose—to inform, raise awareness, or even influence a reader's behavior—and create more compelling, informative pieces of ecocomposition that might better articulate the ecological dynamics at work within their campus?

I explored this question with "sensing place/s" as a thematic focus for a lower-division composition course. In initial units, students considered how everyday locations are defined and represented through composition via signs, the names of apartment and subdivision communities, and even maps. From these discussions, we moved into an examination of how our university used modes of writing to convey environmental information about its campus to the public, such as through its Office of Sustainability's website and promotional materials for upcoming initiatives, and the Office of Planning, Design, and Construction's published "scorecards," which assess development projects for their environmental efficiency. One objective of this inquiry was to articulate what understandings of the campus might emerge through such communication. We discussed, for example, what impression is given by a building's designation as a "platinum" or "gold" structure by LEED (Leadership in Environmental Energy and Design), and how the university's Greenhouse Gas Emissions Inventory, an annual documentation of estimated facility emissions, employs visual rhetoric via graphs to communicate its progress—or lack thereof —toward meeting carbon neutrality goals.

While these inquiries fashioned an understanding of the dynamics between writing and individuals' perceptions of the campus, I wanted students to move beyond looking at this location as an isolated entity and scan for its regional or global ties. To introduce this aspect of Heise's eco-cosmopolitanism, students examined an excerpt from Michael Pollan's *The Omnivore's Dilemma*, where the author traces a fast-food meal back to its "source": a steer in Kansas and a cornfield in Iowa. Pollan observes the steer's disturbing existence in an industrial feedlot and notes, "He's a link in a food chain, a thread in a far-reaching web of ecological relationships. Looked at from this perspective, everything going on in this cattle pen appears quite different, and not nearly as far removed from our world as this manure-encrusted patch of ground here in Nowhere, Kansas, might suggest" (81). Reflecting on how the health of this individual animal and its unnatural corn diet are inextricably linked to those of distant eaters, Pollan articulates an awareness of his geospatial bonds: "I thought of the other places connected to this place by the river of commodity corn" (83). From a field in Iowa, to nitrogen fertilizer runoff in the Gulf of Mexico, to the extractive petroleum sourced from the Persian Gulf, Pollan identifies the connected segments of this international food chain that are often obscured into "boneless abstractions" (114). Heise also gestures toward this sort of awareness with a hypothetical exercise involving an imported commodity—in her case, a banana—and tracing where it came from, under what conditions it grew, and how it was eventually transported to its current location. This probing, Heise suggests, "open[s] the local out into a network of ecological links that span a region, a continent, or the world" (56).

After considering Pollan's experience, students then turned to selections from Farrell's *The Nature of College* in which he explores the ecological ties underpinning everyday aspects of university life: energy consumption, clothes, electronics devices, and the material culture of parties, where even a swig of beer is, to quote Farrell, "an extensive environmental activity" (167). Students were placed into groups, assigned different chapters, and then coalesced to create a list of cultural artifacts and routinized actions that illustrate the "system of invisible complexity" at work on the college campus, and which connect this particular locality to global environmental concerns (Farrell 46). Through such analysis, students began to think more comprehensively and critically about their presence on campus.

From here, I introduced a modified version of Farrell's annotation assignment. Working in groups, students would select some aspect of the campus landscape, research its ties to larger ecological considerations, and create short annotations which would eventually be posted on campus near an annotation's subject. Their goal was to provide readers insight into the often-overlooked, networked connections and ecological implications that underlie everyday locations, behaviors, and decisions. To begin, students generated topics that represented a holistic consideration of the campus environment. Like the open parameters of Farrell's prompt, students could choose aspects of the campus they found either commendable or problematic: landscaping, water, power, waste, food and dining options, architecture, and other physical structures, as well as aspects of material culture and everyday "stuff" like clothes, decorations, and cosmetics were listed. The subsequent annotations' content was derived from students' firsthand observations, their exploration of public writing by the university, and—most significantly—contextualizing this writing with research into this aspect of campus "place" that situated it on a more eco-cosmopolitan scale. This final prewriting step was critical for students to reorient the presumed locality of their subject into a broader understanding of spatial connectivity. An in-class workshop involved peer reviewing groups' preliminary work to assess the geospatial scope of each inquiry. For example, the workshop facilitated one group's expansion of their topic—comparing the environmental footprint of the coffee sold in the university's national chain establishments to the brand offered in the residential dining halls—to move beyond domestic distribution sites and trace the commodity's origin to even more specific, and geographically further, destinations.

The assignment culminated in groups creating annotations: short blurbs—about a paragraph in length—that condensed this information via the use of succinct, clear, prose. A final workshop focused on sharpening language and tone, with students offering suggestions to enhance the rhetorical impact of an annotation, as well as discussing what sort of impression—intended or not—it might give a reader about the place examined. In-line with Dobrin and Weisser's vision for ecocomposition pedagogy, the workshop's emphasis on language offered students a way to "be cognizant not only of the words they write . . . but also of the environments from which those words grow and in turn influence" (150). Upon submission, annotations were typed in fonts visible to readers from a vantage point of several feet away, printed on bright green cardstock, and posted near the site of the subject of inquiry.

The annotations directed readers toward an eco-cosmopolitan awareness of their place on campus. For example, two of my students, Kaitlyn and Micah,[2] addressed the energy consumption caused by taking the elevator in our classroom's building instead of climbing the stairs:

> Going up? A single ride to the third floor in this 16-years-old elevator uses 0.3 kilowatt-hours of electrical power—roughly the same as burning a lightbulb for 7 hours straight. Each and every floor the elevator climbs past expends almost as much energy as it would take to charge half of your iPhone's battery. By contrast, walking all the way up the stairs just down the hall burns energy of a very different type: anywhere from 5 to 8 calories per trip.

The annotation reflects the research involved in Kaitlyn and Micah's pre-writing process. The pair first discovered the brand, model, and year of the elevator, researched the machine's estimated energy costs, and then contextualized the power expended from the singular act of using the elevator with that "consumed" by other everyday actions. Their annotation was posted next to each floor's elevator call button, providing readers with an opportunity to pause and consider the environmental implications entangled in what might have otherwise been an unquestioned action.

Other projects spoke more explicitly to the links between the campus and physically remote locations. Dawson and Aaliyah's annotations looked at water usage and the environmental impact of waste in residence hall bathrooms. Two of their submissions, in particular, traced the origins and destinations of the water used in this location:

> The water pouring out of this faucet has traveled further than you might think. It originates in the lower Floridan Aquifer, which lies up to 2,000 feet beneath the surface of much of the state's northwestern half. Over 2 billion gallons of water are extracted from this location everyday and are sent as far north as the middle of Georgia. Our particular university's water is pulled from a wellfield almost 5 miles north of this building, tested at the region's treatment center on the outskirts of town, and then distributed through sixteen different locations on campus.

> Ever think about what happens *after* the flush? The water from this toilet is pumped through the university's sewer system until it arrives at the reclamation facility on the southern edge of campus, which takes in over 3 million gallons of water each day. Here, the majority of this water is filtered, treated, and disinfected to be used for irrigation and fertilization—and can be found in structures like cooling towers as far away as Sarasota.

In these annotations, Dawson and Aaliyah underscore how a seemingly "small" element encountered everyday—water flowing through a residence hall's facilities—is enmeshed in a complex system that traverses beyond the "local" and is entangled with more distant places and bodies. As such, their work illuminates to readers just one aspect of their "connectedness with both animate and inanimate networks of influence and exchange" that often lie outside the frame of daily recognition (Heise 61).

Students' annotations allowed them to, as Farrell ascribes, "wake up to systems thinking—to see the systems that operate beneath the surfaces of everyday life" and thereby acknowledge their enmeshed ties to more distant places and beings (32). Recognizing the campus as, to use Steven Marx's articulation, "a physical, economic, and political entity within history, situated on the land in the community," my students' projects articulated a more holistic understanding of the networked connections with which *all* locations are involved (Marx). To these ends, the university campus—deemed a material and functional "settler space" by postcolonial scholars—emerges as a landscape rife with pedagogical possibilities for unburying its past and complicating its present and future through direct study within the writing classroom (Smith et al. 143; Seawright). Several annotations delved into this tension by addressing the various campus landmarks devoted to the Timucua people, the region's first documented Indigenous inhabitants, and the extent to which such memorials adequately—or inadequately—account for ongoing legacies of settler colonialism on this site. Others examined the history of the campus's physical development and how notions of "progress" and facility expansion are intertwined with environmental justice questions regarding housing, resource access, and futurity for the community's non-university residents. In both cases, annotations linked campus-specific histories of erasure and displacement with broader legacies of oppression in this bioregion.

Perhaps unsurprisingly, projects that consistently exhibited the most expansive sense of spatial connectivity were those concerning food and campus vegetation. Student work that examined university dining options attempted to ground what Kevin Morgan, Terry Marsden, and Jonathan Murdoch have called the "placeless foodscape" generated by international corporations that obscure the origins and growing conditions of food (14). The presence of transnational corporations on campus—both dining enterprises and also commodities sold in the university's bookstore and vending machines—inspired several student projects, which identified the global roots wrapped up in such purchases. For example, one of Justin's annotations spotlighted the difference in originating distance between similar menu items in two student union offerings: first, from a recognizable chain—whose French fries were concocted from potatoes grown in the Pacific Northwest—and then, from an adjacent, locally-derived establishment which sourced its produce from within the state. In another one of his submissions, Justin highlighted the oily ties underpinning the coffee served in the university's most popular coffee stops:

> Wake up and smell the...gasoline? Using the <u>closest</u> possible starting point, the beans brewed into your medium-roast coffee at this franchise traveled at least 1,500 miles to reach your cup, almost entirely by truck.

Other students found analogous considerations emerging from campus landscape design. Maya's annotations, for instance, identified non-native plants routinely cropping up in university green spaces:

> While palm trees may seem synonymous with our state's imagery, most of the palms on campus aren't Floridian at all. The tree next to this table is actually native to northern Africa and was introduced to this region by Spanish colonizers in the mid 17th century. Today, our state has more than 117 identified non-native species now growing freely in natural areas, a high number of which are invasive and continue to threaten the health of native plant communities.

Maya's additional annotations explored the complex relationships embodied by campus flora, drawing attention, for instance, to invasive species of vines jeopardizing native plants' livelihood in some of the campus's designated wooded areas. Another student traced the probable origins of the mulch needles found at the base of a plaza's flower bed, suggesting that the decomposing bark likely originated from trees several states away. Beyond plants, other projects spotlighted the vast spatial connections embedded in the materiality of electronic devices—such as a residence hall's TV and a library floor's common printer—as well as the plastic items populating the shelves and desks of dorm rooms. Another pair considered the university's transit system, posting annotations at campus stops to inform riders about, for example, the environmental implications of the biodiesel fuel powering most buses and the trade-offs between these models and those designed as hybrid vehicles. Throughout these different foci, students' work steered readers toward an awareness of their implicit spatial connectivity to more remote locations and concerns.

As a means of gauging students' own cultivation of an eco-cosmopolitan sense of the campus, the final segment of the assignment concerned reflective writing. In these responses, students discussed the rhetorical strategies of their annotation's composition, justified their decisions, and articulated their takeaways from this project's experience. In the latter regard, reflections consistently gestured to a heightened understanding of the global connectivity underlying their daily existence in this location. For example, Lauren observed:

> I have never really thought about where the food I eat comes from. Now I can't stop thinking about it. I opened my mini-fridge this morning and saw a carton of blueberries from California and an orange that (I think?) was from Mexico. And here they were, sitting in my fridge, after thousands of miles of transit and encountering people that I'll never meet at each destination along the way.

Lauren's reflection both mimic Heise's hypothetical exercise with a banana and Pollan's own awakening to the "web" of relationships inherent in his fast food meal by articulating her increased awareness of how an array of ecological networks are tied to something as small and mundane as a piece of fruit. Likewise, Miguel offered a retrospect on how, by taking the bus to his chemistry lab three times a week, he routinely stepped into the globally-oriented "embodied energy" (Costanza) of the vehicle, bound up in a planetary-spanning system of energy, labor, and production, noting that:

> . . . the bus itself is a conglomerate of materials derived from somewhere far from here, which I've never really thought about until now. The plastic seat I'm on—where did <u>that</u> come from? I'm also the last stop on the bus before it refuels. When it fills up with biodiesel fuel in a few minutes, where did the plants that laid the basis for that liquid originally grow? And which traveled further: the seat or the biofuel?

Miguel's questions concerning the past and future spatial connections of his transit echo Lauren's increased awareness of the transnational links existing in her dorm room. Returning to the philosophies of place-based education advocates, such observations embody the ecocritical thinking about place that enable students to become more informed, engaged "environmental citizens" (Schild). In line with eco-cosmopolitan thinking, their reflections also indicate a more complex understanding of place and environmentalism—one "detached" from the imagined boundaries of any particular site (Heise 13).

Beyond noting an expanded awareness, student reflections also repeatedly identified that the assignment's public-facing element infused their writing with a deep level of purpose and precision. Aaliyah highlighted:

> The fact that we knew the signs were going to be up in the restroom—<u>my</u> restroom, specifically—made us more careful in how we worded our annotations. We didn't want to come across as preachy or condescending, but we did want someone who read it to really think about where all the water in here came from…and where it was going next. I think the language reflects this frankness and curiosity. I would hope someone who looked at the sign while running the tap water would reflect on its use and relative precarity.

Inherent here is Aaliyah's recognition that the rhetoric she and her partner used to construct their annotations would impact how a reader might view the space. Others emphasized the assignment's presumed relevancy. For example, one student's annotations augmented the numerical messages about plastic "saved" in his residence hall's water bottle-filling stations to contextualize this information. His reflection noted:

> I liked knowing that people could see it [the annotation], even if they just were stumbling on it, randomly. For the 15 seconds or so that it takes them to fill up their Hydroflask, they're learning something more than just "x" number of plastic bottles have been saved. The information I selected for each annotation was meant to show how plastic reduction seems so simple but is a part of so many other crises we're facing today.

Such testimonies indicate that the assignment's public output facilitated a close consideration of rhetoric in students' projects and infused the task with an organic sense of pragmatism. By creating works of ecocomposition situated in the places they inhabit, students became participatory agents within this environment, emerging as writers who could better see that their words can have genuine impact in local debates (Dobrin and Weisser 142). Furthermore, by allowing students to recognize that their published words could influence how readers came to view these places, the assignment concretized the seemingly abstract, yet networked dynamic existing between "the biosphere and the semiosphere" and between discourse and all environments (157).

Conclusion

In a lament on the state of higher education published over thirty years ago, David Orr declared that "now, more than ever, we need people who think broadly and who understand systems, connections, patterns, and root causes" (23). To Orr, the planet's ecological crises were exacerbated by their lack of engagement in higher education, thereby warranting a complete overhaul of its pedagogical objectives. Decades later, his call for students to better perceive the systems, connections, and patterns entangled with their lives and dwellings continues to resound. Eileen Schell, Charlotte Hogg, and Kim Donehower's introduction to *enculturation's* special issue on rhetoric and climate change, for instance, underscores the need for a more explicit embrace of eco-oriented writing pedagogy that addresses environmental crises. As the distinctions between local and global spaces continue to fade through nascent technology and globalization, however, it also becomes critical to assess the parameters of place-based education.

For writing instructors seeking to engage students in ecocritical or sustainability themes, an embrace of ecocomposition pedagogy opens up the "sense of place" that more accurately captures the networked connectivity implicit in all sites today. Furthermore, by expanding the foci of conventional place-based writing explorations, instructors might continue to cultivate sustainability literacies grounded in local context for students, while also prompting their consideration of far-reaching spatial impacts and systems-level ecological connections. The assignment outlined here articulates one method through which instructors might merge the ambitions of place-based writing and ecocomposition. Other assignments predicated on exploring the features of specific environments might similarly be modified to reflect this more holistic conception of place and account for the fluid dynamics between local, regional, and transnational communities, and to offer students public-facing opportunities to enter such communities as participatory members in discourse exchange.

Like Farrell, I focused here on a place-based ecocomposition assignment rooted in the urban college campus to "offset pedagogical approaches that endorse overly privileged, polarized, or escapist conceptions of the environment" and to, instead, "conceive of the environment more comprehensively" (Hothem 36; 38). Variations on this assignment might direct student attention more explicitly to the intersections of place, race, settler colonialism, and environmental justice and how these phenomena coalesce on the university campus. Such a focus would be further enriched by foregrounding Indigenous and non-Global North land-based education philosophies regarding literacy and rhetoric (Styres et al.; Ríos) as well as considering topics which allow students to draw from personal memory and cultural knowledge. Additional explorations might situate place-based investigations into what anthropologist Marc Augé has termed "non-places": spaces and sites of transience where people merely "pass-through" and, due to increasing cultural homogenization, often forego establishing lasting connections, such as airports, shopping malls, highways, hotels, and online forums (109). Whatever the approach, by broadening the definition of place as it relates to writing, instructors can also instill an eco-cosmopolitan awareness in their students that expands notions of community engagement to become an altogether more encompassing planetary vision.

Note

1. See, too, Dobrin and Jones's co-edited *Rhetorical Ecologies* (2024) and, in particular, the chapter by Chris Ingraham and Matthew Halm.

2. Throughout, student names and identifying information have been modified for anonymity. Excerpts from student writing are used with the authors' permissions.

Works Cited

Augé, Marc. *Non-Places: Introduction to an Anthropology of Supermodernity.* 1995. Translated by John Howe. Verso, 1997.

Ball, Eric L., and Alice Lai. "Place-Based Pedagogy for the Arts and Humanities." *Pedagogy: Critical Approaches to Teaching Literature, Language, Composition, and Culture*, vol. 6, no. 2, 2006, pp. 261–87, doi.org/10.1215/15314200-2005-004.

Braidotti, Rosi. "'Becoming World.'" *After Cosmopolitanism*, edited by Rosi Braidotti, Patrick Hanafin, and Bolette Blaagaard, Routledge, 2013, pp. 8–27.

Brandt, Deborah. "Sponsors of Literacy." *College Composition and Communication*, vol. 49, no. 2, 1998, pp. 165–85.

Brooke, Robert E., editor. *Rural Voices: Place-Conscious Education and the Teaching of Writing*. Teachers College P, 2003.

Carmichael, Felicita Arzu. "'Sometimes I Forget I'm in an Online Class!' Why Place Matters for Meaningful Student Online Writing Experience." *Composition Studies*, vol. 49, no. 3, 2021, pp. 38–55.

Case, Jennifer. "Place-Based Pedagogy and the Creative Writing Classroom." *Journal of Creative Writing Studies*, vol. 2, no. 2, 2017, pp. 1–15, scholarworks.rit.edu/jcws/vol2/iss2/5/.

Coe, Richard M. "Eco-Logic for the Composition Classroom." *College Composition and Communication*, vol. 26, no. 3, 1975, pp. 232–37, doi.org/10.2307/356121.

Cooper, Marilyn M. "The Ecology of Writing." *College English*, vol. 48, no. 4, 1986, pp. 364–75.

—. "Foreword." *Ecocomposition: Theoretical and Pedagogical Approaches*, edited by Christian R. Weisser and Sidney I. Dobrin. State U of New York P, 2001, pp. xi–xviii.

Costanza, Robert. "Embodied Energy and Economic Valuation." *Science*, vol. 210, no. 4475, 1980, pp. 1219–24, doi.org/10.1126/science.210.4475.1219.

Dippre, Ryan J., and Anna Smith. "Always Already Relocalized: The Protean Nature of Context in Lifespan Writing Research." *Approaches to Lifespan Writing Research: Generating an Actionable Coherence*, edited by Ryan J. Dippre and Talinn Phillips, UP of Colorado, 2020, pp. 27–38.

Dobrin, Sidney I. *Postcomposition*. Southern Illinois UP, 2011.

Dobrin, Sidney I., and Madison P. Jones. *Rhetorical Ecologies*. National Council of Teachers of English, 2024.

Dobrin, Sidney I., and Christian R. Weisser. *Natural Discourse: Toward Ecocomposition*, State U of New York P, 2002.

Edbauer, Jenny. "Unframing Models of Public Distribution: From Rhetorical Situation to Rhetorical Ecologies." *Rhetoric Society Quarterly*, vol. 35, no. 4, 2005, pp. 5–24, doi.org/10.1080/02773940509391320.

Emanuel, Richard, and J. N. Adams. "College Students' Perceptions of Campus Sustainability." *International Journal of Sustainability in Higher Education*, vol. 12, no. 1, 2011, pp. 79–92.

Esposito, Lauren. "Where to Begin? Using Place-Based Writing to Connect Students with Their Local Communities." *English Journal*, vol. 101, no. 4, 2012, pp. 70–76, library.ncte.org/journals/ej/issues/v101-4/18751.

Farrell, James J. *The Nature of College: How a New Understanding of Campus Life Can Change the World*. Milkweed Editions, 2010.

Galleymore, Isabel. *Teaching Environmental Writing: Ecocritical Pedagogy and Poetics.* Bloomsbury, 2020.

Goggin, Peter, and Zach Waggoner. "Sustainable Development: Thinking Globally and Acting Locally in the Writing Classroom." *Composition Studies,* vol. 33, no. 2, 2005, pp. 45–67.

Greenwood, David A. "Place-Based Education: Grounding Culturally Responsive Teaching in Geographical Diversity." *Place-Based Education in the Global Age: Local Diversity,* edited by David A. Greenwood and Gregory A. Smith, Routledge, 2010, pp. 137–153.

—. "The Best of Both Worlds: A Critical Pedagogy of Place." *Educational Researcher,* vol. 32, no. 4, 2003, pp. 3–12.

Harrison, Summer. "Field Journaling in the Wild: Defamiliarizing Everyday Environments in Environmental Humanities Courses." *Ecopedagogies: Practical Approaches to Experiential Learning,* edited by Ellen Bayer and Judson B. Finley, Routledge, 2022, pp. 32–43.

Heise, Ursula K. *Sense of Place and Sense of Planet: The Environmental Imagination of the Global.* Oxford UP, 2008.

Hothem, Thomas. "Suburban Studies and College Writing: Applying Ecocomposition." *Pedagogy: Critical Approaches to Teaching Literature, Language, Composition, and Culture,* vol. 9, no.1, 2009, pp. 35–59, doi.org/10.1215/15314200-2008-016.

Jones, Madison P. "A Counterhistory of Rhetorical Ecologies." *Rhetoric Society Quarterly,* vol. 51, no. 4, 2021, pp. 336–52, doi.org/10.1080/02773945.2021.1947517.

—. "Writing Conditions: The Premises of Ecocomposition." *Enculturation: A Journal of Rhetoric, Writing, and Culture,* 2018, www.enculturation.net/writing-conditions.

Judson, Gillian. "Curriculum Spaces: Situating Educational Research, Theory, and Practice." *Journal of Educational Thought,* vol. 40, no. 3, 2006, pp. 229–45, doi.org/10.11575/jet.v40i3.52542.

Keller, Christopher J., and Christian R. Weisser, editors. *The Locations of Composition.* State U of New York P, 2007.

Leack, Ryan D. "From Chaos to Cosmos, and Back: Place-Based Autoethnography in First-Year Composition." *Composition Forum,* vol. 41, 2019, compositionforum.com/issue/41/chaos-cosmos.php.

Lipscomb, Robert. "Episode 16: Basics of Place-Conscious Education: The Nebraska Experience." *Plainstate: The Podcast,* 12 Oct. 2020, www.unl.edu/english/plainstate-podcast/episode-16.

Marx, Steven. "Think Global, Write Local: Sustainability and English Composition." UC/CSU/CCC Sustainability Conference, 3 Aug. 2008, California Polytechnic State University, San Luis Obispo, CA, www.stevenmarx.net/2008/07/think-global-write-local-sustainability-and-english-composition/.

Morgan, Kevin, Terry Marsden, and Jonathan Murdoch. *Worlds of Food: Place, Power, and Provenance in the Food Chain.* Oxford UP, 2008.

Orr, David. *Ecological Literacy: Education and Transition to a Post-Modern World.* State U of New York P, 1992.

Owens, Derek. *Composition and Sustainability: Teaching for a Threatened Generation.* National Council of Teachers of English, 2001.

Pollan, Michael. *The Omnivore's Dilemma: A Natural History of Four Meals.* Penguin, 2006.

Posner, Stephen M., and Ralph Stuart. "Understanding and Advancing Campus Sustainability Using a Systems Framework." *International Journal of Sustainability in Higher Education*, vol. 14, no. 3, 2013, pp. 264–77.

Powell, Katrina M. "Review: Location and Writing: Place-Based Learning, Geographies of Writing, and How Place (Still) Matters in Writing Studies." *College Composition and Communication*, vol. 66, no. 1, 2014, pp. 177–91.

Reynolds, Nedra. *Geographies of Writing.* Southern Illinois UP, 2004.

Rice, Jeff. *Digital Rhetoric: Rhetoric and Space in the Age of the Network.* Southern Illinois UP, 2012.

Ríos, Gabriela Raquel. "Cultivating Land-Based Literacies and Rhetorics." *Literacy in Composition Studies*, vol. 3, no. 1, 2015, pp. 60–70.

Rule, Hannah J. *Situating Writing Processes.* UP of Colorado, 2019.

"Sample Syllabi." *Association for the Study of Literature and the Environment*, ASLE, www.asle.org/teach/sample-syllabi/.

Schell, Eileen E., Charlotte Hogg, and Kim Donehower. "Introduction: Rhetorics and Literacies of Climate Change." *Enculturation: A Journal of Rhetoric, Writing, and Culture.* vol. 32, 2020, www.enculturation.net/rhetorics-and-literacies-of-climate-change.

Schild, Rebecca. "Environmental Citizenship: What Can Political Theory Contribute to Environmental Education Practice? *Journal of Environmental Education*, vol. 47, no. 1, 2016, pp. 19–34, doi.org/10.1080/00958964.2015.1092417.

Seawright, Gardner. "Settler Traditions of Place: Making Explicit the Epistemological Legacy of White Supremacy and Settler Colonialism for Place-Based Education." *Educational Studies*, vol. 50, no. 6, 2014, pp. 554–72, doi.org/10.1080/001319 46.2014.965938.

Smith, Avery, Hine Funaki, and Liana Macdonald. "Living, Breathing Settler-Colonialism: The Reification of Settler Norms in a Common University Space." *Higher Education Research and Development*, vol. 40, no. 1, 2021, pp. 132–45, doi.org/10.1080/07294360.2020.1852190.

Sobel, David. *Place-Based Education: Connecting Classrooms and Communities.* Orion, 2004.

Styres, Sandra, Celia Haig-Brown, and Melissa Blimkie. "Toward a Pedagogy of Land: The Urban Context." *Canadian Journal of Education*, vol. 36, no. 2, 2013, pp. 34–67.

Ulmer, Gregory L. *Internet Invention: From Literacy to Electracy.* Pearson, 2002.

Wallace, Allison B. "The Place of Drawing in Place Journaling." *Honors in Practice— Online Archive.* National Collegiate Honors Council, 2012, pp. 101–08.

Weisser, Christian R., and Sidney I. Dobrin, editors. *Ecocomposition: Theoretical and Pedagogical Approaches.* State U of New York P, 2001.

Wildcat, Matthew, Mandee McDonald, Stephanie Irlbacher-Fox, and Glen Coulthard. "Learning from The Land: Indigenous Land Based Pedagogy and Decolonization." *Decolonization: Indigeneity, Education and Society*, vol. 3, no. 3, 2014, pp. i–xv.

Luke Rodewald is a Marion L. Brittain Postdoctoral Fellow at the Georgia Institute of Technology. His writing appears or is forthcoming in venues such as *ISLE: Interdisciplinary Studies in Literature and Environment, Resistance: A Journal of Radical Environmental Humanities*, and the *Journal for the Study of Religion, Nature and Culture*.

Course Designs

The ACT Model in First-Year Writing: Neuroplasticity and Student Well-Being Post–COVID

Casie Fedukovich and Brooke Mulhollem

English 101: Academic Writing and Research is a 4-credit, 16-week Writing-in-the-Disciplines (WID) course that fulfills North Carolina State University's (NC State) Introduction to Writing requirement. As the sole first-year General Education writing requirement at the STEM-focused institution, the course objectives center on disciplinary writing and research practices. Most incoming students at NC State enroll in English 101, and as is the case in many first-year writing programs, the class often becomes an important site for interventions and innovations. It also becomes a site where the effects of major historical events—devastating hurricanes, national elections, pandemics—are magnified.

From July 2017 to January 2024, Casie served as Director of the First-Year Writing Program. Brooke has been teaching first-year writing full time at NC State since 2001. This course design discusses metacognitive innovations Brooke developed in response to pedagogical and student mental health challenges post–COVID.

Institutional Context

North Carolina State University is a large, public, research-intensive institution with a total enrollment of just over 38,000 and a typical incoming class of about 5,500 ("Fast Facts"). The First-Year Writing (FYW) Program is housed in the English Department, within the College of Humanities and Social Sciences, and is administered by a director and supervised by the English department head.

About 4,000 students enroll in Academic Writing and Research every academic year (AY), most of them first-year students. The approximately 220 sections per AY are largely staffed by professional track (i.e., non-tenure track, PT) faculty, with graduate teaching assistants (GTAs) teaching about 50 sections. Sections are capped at 20 seats, and approximately 70% of sections meet in seated environments. The remaining sections meet in hybrid environments (half-seated, half-remote), and only about five sections per academic year meet remotely. Remote offerings are limited by request of upper administrators.

In 2023, 30% of incoming NC State students enrolled in the college of engineering, 10% in agricultural and life sciences, and 10% in sciences ("Fast Facts"). Most first-year writing students have declared a major in engineering or the sciences. The WID focus is intended to respond to this demographic need, though many students predictably bristle at having to take a writing course, even one where they may explore writing in their STEM field.

The WID curricula also signals a deep entanglement with STEM colleges on campus. For example, a $50 million engineering enrollment initiative launched in 2023 seeks to increase enrollment in engineering and computer science by 4,000 students ("Engineering North Carolina's Future"). These students will presumably require FYW to graduate. Further, these relationships and the FYW program's position within the institutional structure introduces complicated communicative factors. Most decisions must be made through rank-and-file discussions, from program to department to college and above. Stakeholders at each tier hold different priorities, often rendering the decision-making process cumbersome and delicate.

COVID closures and reentry stressed these discussions. Like many universities, we moved fully online in March 2020. In fall 2020, upper administration brought students back to campus and required programs to offer a percentage of seated sections, with FYW staffing about 30 in-person sections, all taught by full-time PT faculty. After ten days, the "unrelenting spread" of COVID forced everyone back off campus ("NC State Students Pack Up"). Students in special circumstances, such as international students and students who aged out of foster care, could file exemptions to continue to live on campus, but communication about that process was sparse and confusing. FYW faculty stepped into the breach to guide students through complex housing situations. Though our classes met on Zoom, they were still small and discussion-based. FYW faculty remained the switchboard for information and support.

After spending spring 2021 fully remote, the university's upper administration required all courses to return fully to campus that fall, "rolling back" our course formats and pedagogical expectations to fall 2019, the last pre-COVID semester. However, we could not roll back the deeply disruptive and in many cases traumatizing experiences of living, teaching, and learning through a pandemic.

While returning to campus signaled a positive turn in events, faculty quickly reported significant teaching challenges. These challenges include what has been variously described as "student learning loss," low stress tolerance, and unfamiliarity with (or resistance to) expectations such as physical presence in class, participation in class activities, and adherence to assignment deadlines. Many students also seem to be entering first-year writing without practice in fundamental writing skills. It is impossible to know how many of our students struggled during closures, but scholarship confirms that COVID learning loss "deepen[ed] educational inequalities" (Moscoviz and Evans 1).

Brooke first created ACT (Abide/Assess, Choose/Concrete, and Take/Transition) in fall 2021, when we returned to the classroom. ACT attempted to help students develop or relearn critical and creative thinking skills that may have been left behind during COVID closures. Further, its focus on slow, metacognitive work was intended to respond to student anxiety on re-entry and bridge the gap between pandemic isolation and our new social norm.

Angela Muir and Paula Mathieu recognize the chaotic world our newest students have entered: The aftermath of a pandemic, but also heavy with global wars and genocides, the racial reckoning following the murder of George Floyd, and an all-out attack on reproductive and civil rights in the US. Muir and Mathieu follow, "This is all so traumatic to live through, let alone stand in front of a classroom and be OK, or look to our students and expect them to be OK. It's exhausting. We are exhausted" (154). The administrative imperative to "roll back to 2019" ignored these critical details and placed already-stressed faculty in difficult situations where student preparation and mental health concerns became urgent.

No one at NC State was prepared for the tragedies of 2022–23, when we experienced a great deal of loss of student life on campus. Fourteen students died: seven by suicide, two by drug overdose, four by natural causes, and one in an accident (Charalambous). Five of the seven suicides were first-year students enrolled in first-year writing, with three of the five students connected to the school of engineering. Student interviews suggest that "the stresses of being a student—including demanding STEM classes—and stress stemming from grades and social pressures" may be factors (Charalambous). The campus atmosphere was heavy. First-year writing faculty felt a deep commitment to support struggling students, without any of us quite understanding how to do it.

The student losses in 2022–23 brought our individual classroom experiences into a new light. At the same time, our institution seemed to have quickly moved on. This fraught situation led Brooke to revise her course to better meet students' metacognitive needs, particularly the gap between their expectations for first-year writing and its reality. Students' preparation for success also appeared to be deeply intertwined with their mental health. Weekly, they expressed a great deal of anguish about their writing assignments and other coursework. The institution made it clear that faculty were responsible for supporting students' mental health but gave no concrete, practical ways to do so.

This situation gave rise to ACT as a course philosophy. What began as a reflection-based intervention developed into a course re-design intended to support student learning and well-being. Brooke describes the ACT method as "helping students fight procrastination and decision fatigue and improve the writing process." Grounding the process in neuroplasticity and self-efficacy scholarship, Brooke set out to support students through new learning situations, even as they learned what it meant to learn.

She breaks down the ACT method for students as:

A: Abide in your thoughts and what your brain is working through right now, on this task, project, reading, or class discussion.

Assess what you have accomplished so far.

C: Choose action steps. What steps do you need to take to progress with this task, process, or project the next time you take it up?

Concrete: Record these steps in as much detail as possible, so you will know exactly what to do the next time you work on this task, process, or project. Write down questions you may need to investigate.

T: Takeaway: What is the most useful thing you have learned in class today?

Transition: Take a DEEP breath. You have made smart choices and good notes for your future self, so now you don't have to keep track of it mentally!

Transition to the next focus or task and direct all your mental energy on making progress there.

The goals of the ACT method are to:

- Create a decision point.
- Use self-narration to lower stress and calm the central nervous system.
- Cultivate relaxed alertness.
- Eliminate lost time remembering where you were, what you were doing, and what you need to do next.
- Eliminate decision fatigue by providing yourself with an action plan.
- Use momentum to fight procrastination.
- Help you retain more information from your work by slowing down to process information.

Brooke's development of ACT emerged out of two major pedagogical challenges: fragmentation and checkbox thinking. Compared to prior semesters, students in post–COVID classrooms—those who were in middle school to early high school during closures—seem to be even more likely to have worked with short textual excerpts, rather than whole texts. Students reported submitting major writing assignments that were fragments of an argument; for many, these major assignments constituted paragraphs at the most. Assignments were one-and-done, and graded writing was typically assessed for completeness, rather than correctness. Students further reported that certain aspects of the writing process mattered only when that aspect was the focus of a specific assessment. Once they checked the appropriate box, they could mentally move on to the next task.

These challenges emerged across sections, regardless of individual student background or demeanor. As Brooke described it, students did not read but scanned both course readings and assignment directions, filling in the blanks with their limited prior experience. The same process happened when they turned to responding to these assignments. Writing happened quickly, incompletely, and often without regard to the expectations of the assignment. Students were rushing through, short-circuiting the long writing process where they are asked to approach, explore, examine, and abide with their ideas recursively. This mismatch between expectation and production resulted in anxious students who procrastinated and ended up in a stress spiral.

Theoretical Rationale: Slowing down for ACT

Long before COVID, students procrastinated on their writing assignments, only skimmed our very-detailed assignment sheets, and submitted misaligned assignments. Alice Horning has been sounding the alarm for 15 years, alerting us to the "Demise of Reading" (2009) and "Critical Reading: Attention Needed" (2017). Victoria Appatova and Alice Horning's 2023's "Developing Critical Literacy: An Urgent Goal" defines critical literacy as "four sets of skills—critical thinking, reading, writing, and research skills—taught in the integrated manner" (100). Anecdotally, this constellation of skills created pain points for most of our students in first-year writing.

Citing Larkin's 2021 research into online learning, Appatova and Horning acknowledge that students often fail to meet expectations with regards to reading, and "the students' resistance is generally explained by the notorious TL;DR ('too long; didn't read') concept as well as the lack of time, persistence, or ability to use effective reading strategies" (101). Based on students' reports of their pandemic schooling, the move to fully remote learning in 2020 thus may have contributed to further disengagement with consuming and producing extended texts.

However, even Brooke's pared down assignment sheets and attention to active reading in class did not remedy the fragmented and checkbox thinking she observed in her students. She sought to better understand the deep neurobiological consequences of pandemic learning and support students who may feel overwhelmed in their first year. Between 2021 and 2023, the ACT course redesign gradually emerged from Brooke's intention to encourage students to slow down their reading and writing. The method expanded to guide students through critical reading and writing processes as a recursive series of assessments, decisions, and action steps, rather than a problem/solution model.

The student mental health crisis in 2022–2023 made the situation more urgent. In Brooke's words, her students appeared "shot out of a cannon" as they narrated the other exams, tests, and projects they worked on outside of English 101. Stress levels were high. Brooke saw an opportunity to expand ACT from an intervention to a course philosophy, re-framing existing assignments to signpost frequent metacognitive practice. Students were struggling, and her first-year writing course could offer a replicable method for managing the workload. This most current version of ACT references three theoretical concepts: self-efficacy, metacognition, and neuroplasticity.

Self-Efficacy

First-year students may be experiencing a fundamental challenge to their self-efficacy, as prior learning practices fail to address new challenges. Self-efficacy, or "individuals' beliefs as to whether they can perform tasks that will influence their own lives," is a practice of engagement and reinforcement (Stewart et al. 4). Graeme Stewart, Tricia Seifert, and Carol Rolheiser argue, "self-efficacy centers on whether or not students believe they can accomplish a given writing task, and whether or not they are confident that their chosen strategies will be effective" (4). Failure at these tasks "often taxes the body budget" and can be a deeply "wounding" experience for students (Comstock 717). Brooke recognized that students who perceived their work as failure were far more likely to procrastinate with future work. Stewart et al. confirm this phenomenon. They connect emotional state to self-efficacy, recognizing that "[a]nxiety . . . can be considered a consequence of low self-efficacy" (5). That is, a student who does not believe they can do the work may find themselves in a cycle of stress, anxiety, and failure. In contrast, educational researchers Renate Nummela Caine, Geoffrey Caine, Carol Lynn McClintic, and Karl J. Klimek find that learners with strong self-efficacy "believe that they can learn from mistakes" and "work harder to overcome potential obstacles" (23). The ACT method is intended to help students create flexible and replicable learning practices and habits of mind to help manage the overwhelming workload in their first year and beyond, boosting their feelings of self-efficacy.

Metacognition

ACT encourages students to reflect on their positive accomplishments, from recognizing their progress on a "task, process, or project" to acknowledging to their "future self" that they can do hard work. If self-efficacy is necessary for students to persist, metacognition may be its most potent pedagogical vehicle.

Research in metacognitive practices in writing is well traced. Given our program's WID focus, we are especially interested in the relationship between metacognition and transfer (Wardle; Portanova, Rifenburg, and Roen; Johnson). Post–COVID students are entering our classrooms with a host of challenges to their learning, including habits of mind that negatively affect their performance and persistence. In Brooke's experience, many students come to us relying on fragmentation and checkbox thinking, with little experience in slower methods of thinking and writing.

ACT is reminiscent of Kristine Johnson's course design to more explicitly integrate the habits of mind outlined in *The Framework for Success in Postsecondary Writing*. These assignments "offer students the opportunity to cultivate openness and responsibility as they develop their writing processes" while also "offer[ing] teachers a method for assessing how well individual students have cultivated particular habits of mind" (530). Brooke's focus on metacognition slows down the institution's insistence on acceleration, encouraging students to abide in reflection and habit formation in their first year.

Brooke's first iteration of ACT framed it as a method to move students from "Pandemic to Peaceful." The metacognitive focus insists that students dwell in the present moment, diverting the energy they may give to future worries and instead encourages them to scaffold their thoughts and processes. Stewart et al. extend this idea to argue, "By creating positive learning environments and interventions, anxiety can be reduced, self-efficacy can be enhanced, and the use of metacognitive strategies encouraged" (13). Brooke's holistic focus on student well-being captures this intention.

Caine et al. identify the ability to overcome challenges and build resilience as a function of neurobiology, specifically connecting higher order thinking skills and executive function to neurological processes. Brooke has adopted their concept of "relaxed alertness," defined by Caine et al. as "an optimal emotional state for learning" that "exist[s] in a learner who feels competent and confident and is interested or intrinsically motivated" (7). Students practicing "relaxed alertness" are better equipped to "be clear about their goals," "persist and overcome the confusion that naturally occurs when learning new material," and "acquire new strategies and cope with difficulties as they learn" (25). ACT offers a method for students to develop emotional competence as it prompts them to pause and think about their thinking and set goals.

Neuroplasticity

Emerging research on neuroplasticity in learning gives hope that so-described COVID learning losses can be reversed. Like self-efficacy, neuroplasticity(defined as the "brain's ability to change as a result of experience") is a process of engagement and reinforcement (Caine et al. 23). During COVID closures, students and faculty were engaged in new ways of schooling. Even those who were already teaching and learning online had to do so in the context of a global pandemic that may have affected living situations, learning environments, and health and well-being. As with any repeated practice, "new patterns of synaptic connections [were] made in the brain" (Caine et al. 23). Neuroplasticity underpins the entire ACT method as it assumes that students have control over their learning processes. Bad habits can be reversed, and the neural pathways for good habits can be formed.

Edward Comstock vividly describes neuroplasticity as "explosive potential" through "the brain's ability to reshape bad or inadequate habits" (706). Comstock's 2023 "Toward a New Neurobiology of Writing" supplements our theoretical understanding of ACT by emphasizing his "pedagogy of emotional intelligence" (724). Drawing from Chris Anson's work on failure, Comstock asserts that "there's plenty of evidence that our students are less emotionally equipped than ever to remain resilient in the face of failure" (704). The dire situation with student mental health at NC State is too complex to clearly connect to this idea of resilience; however, Comstock's point is taken, particularly as we encounter class after class of first-year students who struggle through coursework and describe feeling overwhelmed.

Critical Reflection

Many of our students operate on high alert, and it has become clear at North Carolina State that our first-year students are contending with formidable obstacles. At its core, ACT is a work-flow heuristic; however, the process offers a much broader application. ACT provides a learning method that is flexible enough to be used across disciplines but specific enough to directly apply to any course where extended reading and writing is expected. It also addresses students as whole human beings with complex lives, living through continued global upheaval and uncertainty. ACT thus becomes a heuristic for slow agency. Laura Micciche argues that "fast agency inculcates pride in getting things done swiftly, obscuring conditions that make speediness necessary and normative in the first place" (79). By slowing down students' learning, we also introduce a method of contemplation that counters the accelerated nature of higher education and intends to instill pride—or at least a sense of accomplishment and satisfaction—through deep, careful thinking.

Predictably, student responses to the ACT method are mixed. Some students report that it exacerbates their stress level by creating a subjective assignment that adds to workload. As noted, most of the students in our classrooms have declared majors in STEM fields, and some of them considered their first-year writing class (and instructor) an inappropriate space for discussions of scientific and metacognitive practice. Most of them identify "English class" as solely the domain of literature. While they accepted the scientific truth of the practice, they questioned Brooke's credibility—as an instructor of English—to present the data on neuroplasticity in service to the ACT method.

This resistance offered valuable opportunities to discuss WID in action. First, ACT's grounding in scientific data emphasized that all disciplines rely on writing to preserve, test, clarify, and convey knowledge. Second, it gave Brooke the opportunity to demonstrate that humanities scholars are not only focused on the analysis of literature. Rhetoric as a hermeneutic allows humanities scholars to read, translate, understand, and synthesize knowledge, which underscores the critical role a WID-focused course plays on a STEM-focused campus.

Implications: Cultivating Peace in Turbulent Times

The ACT method itself is constantly evolving to meet students where they are and where the world is. In the next iteration, Brooke plans to incorporate the model into an ongoing process journal, helping students concretely engage in the moment and reflect toward future tasks. This focus may help address the issues Emily J. Isaacs raises in her March 2024 *Chronicle of Higher Education* essay, "It's Time to Start Teaching Students How to Student." Issacs calls for methods to "hold students responsible for developing and practicing skills and habits that will enable them to learn." Specifically, the ACT method may provide one tool among many to help students navigate the many compounding stressors they face in their first year.

More broadly and consequentially, ACT provides classroom support during times of upheaval and crisis. Fall 2024 offered Casie and Brooke the opportunity to employ ACT in the wake of two specific crisis-level events: Hurricane Helene, which deeply affected Western North Carolina, and the reelection of Donald Trump as president. As a course philosophy, ACT reinforces the importance of slow agency, purposeful attention, and self-reflection. Students and faculty alike are struggling to operate in an ever-more "traumatic climate that can overwhelm us all and breed disengagement" (Muir and Mathieu 154). We are all still processing the trauma inflicted by living and working through a global pandemic. Current events—catastrophic natural disasters, national unrest, global genocides—can make our classroom work feel trivial. Student sentiments reflect this disengagement, with many of our students expressing resignation to a bleak future.

Muir and Mathieu advocate introducing contemplative pedagogies to help students become "more resilient and ready to learn" (156). ACT provides a model to guide students away from hyper-multi-tasking in favor of introspection and slower mono-task thinking. More importantly, we found slowing down gives students a defined space and time every week to relax and focus their thinking a bit. This relaxation may be a short respite from other pressing concerns, however it has become a reliable, almost ritualistic and sacred pause during otherwise chaotic times.

The model's focus on reflection and planning also accommodates Muir and Mathieu's holistic description of contemplative practice, which seeks to guide students to "inner and outer world connecting," in order to "integrate what they are learning in the classroom with how they operate in the world at large" (156). As global crises accrue, local communities will emerge as safe houses. Guiding students through this self-to-community thinking in a purposeful and cumulative way may encourage them toward focused coalition building or developing communities of care.

Institutionally, the struggle remains against accelerationist models that encourage students to think about higher education as a race to finish quickly. Efficiency and flexibility are the watchwords of higher administrators. ACT-style initiatives, we argue, will come from the middle: program-level directors and the like, and most critically, a deep and wide base of committed classroom instructors. Writing Program Administrators, Writing Center Directors, and faculty may become the ACT[ing] agents on their campuses, as they have access to large cohorts of students and may be able to influence programmatic structures and practices. We cannot stop the neoliberal university's press to faster degree completion, nor the tides of global politics. However, we may be able to work under the radar to influence pedagogical, programmatic, and departmental practices to support students' learning and well-being.

Edward Comstock's work reminds us of the psychic damage classrooms may inflict, where failure may be "physically and psychically taxing, at best, and, at worst, wounding or catastrophic" (717). We maintain that the converse may also be true. Our classrooms can become reflective and supportive spaces while maintaining their primary pedagogical goals. The work we do in first-year writing, as a high-impact course, has always been critical to the retention and persistence missions of the institution. Now, that work is critical to supporting students through historical shifts whose effects will be felt for decades.

Over the last three years, ACT has thus transformed from a pedagogical intervention to a course philosophy to a value statement. Slowing down counters the institutional demand for acceleration while it also provides a space for students to query their hyper-local support systems and build strong allegiances for safety. We are not suggesting that faculty achieve even greater course objectives or institute additional assessments. Instead, we propose the ACT method as a counter to—or perhaps in benevolent disobedience of—business as usual. While things continue apace in our everyday lives, it can feel like the world is burning down and yet the emails continue. The papers are written and submitted. The grades are entered. And we are all feeling the heavy fracture between world events and routine tasks. We are exhausted and disengaged, feeling "shot out of a cannon" (to recall Brooke's words).

At the end of each semester, what do we hope students take with them? The ACT method has moved beyond its original intention to complicate students' checkbox thinking. Grounded in self-efficacy, metacognition, and neuroplasticity, ACT helps us rethink the overall goals of our classroom to instead focus on students establishing confidence in their thinking, building trust in themselves, and developing their ability to work through wicked problems.

Angela Muir and Paula Mathieu summarize the urgency of the problem in front of us, "Waiting for things to let up is not an option. Teachers and students can't wait to crash or burn out. Teachers, if they hope to continue showing up and teaching with a clear-eyed sense of the world, must forge a healthier way forward for ourselves and our students" (167). Our classrooms have long moved beyond the primary focus of writing essays and correcting grammar. The ACT method offers another opportunity to teach immediately relevant habits of mind: slow thinking, discernment, care, and purposeful connection. These habits become especially critical in the context of students' mental health concerns. In the accelerated institution, slowing down is a radical act, a quiet way to counter the overwhelming speed of life.

Works Cited

Appatova, Victoria, and Alice Horning. "Developing Critical Literacy: An Urgent Goal." *To Improve the Academy: A Journal of Educational Development*, vol. 42, no. 2, 2023, pp. 99–126.

Caine, Renate Nummela, Geoffrey Caine, Carol Lynn McClintic, and Karl J. Klimek. *12 Brain/Mind Learning Principles in Action*. Corwin, 2016.

Charalambous, Peter. "After 14 Student Deaths, North Carolina State Confronts a National Crisis." ABC News, abcnews.go.com/US/challenging-year-north-carolina-state-confronts-spate-student/story?id=99008743. Accessed 3 Apr. 2024.

Comstock, Edward. "Toward a New Neurobiology of Writing: Plasticity and the Feeling of Failure." *College Composition and Communication*, vol. 74, no. 4, 2023, pp. 695–730.

"Engineering North Carolina's Future." North Carolina State University. https://think-anddo.ncsu.edu/engineering-north-carolinas-future/. Accessed 10 Apr. 2024.

"Fast Facts" Institutional Strategy and Analysis, North Carolina State University.

https://isa.ncsu.edu/facts-comparisons/fast-facts/. Accessed 3 Apr. 2024.

Horning, Alice. "Critical Reading: Attention Needed." *WPA: Writing Program Administration*, vol. 41, no. 1, 2017, pp. 125–36.

—. "The Demise of Reading?: A Meta-Analysis of Reading Studies." *International Journal of the Book*, vol. 6, no. 4, 2009, pp. 17.

Isaacs, Emily J. "It's Time to Start Teaching Your Students How to be a Student." *The Chronicle of Higher Education*, 19 Mar. 2024. www.chronicle.com/article/its-time-to-start-teaching-your-students-how-to-be-a-student.

Johnson, Kristine. "Beyond Standards: Disciplinary and National Perspectives on Habits of Mind." *College Composition and Communication*, vol. 64, no. 3, 2013, pp. 517–41.

Micciche, Laura R. "For Slow Agency." *WPA: Writing Program Administration*, vol. 35, no. 1, 2011, pp. 73–90.

Moscoviz, Laura, and David K. Evans. "Learning Loss and Student Dropouts during the COVID-19 Pandemic: A Review of the Evidence Two Years after Schools Shut Down." *CGD Working Paper 609*. Center for Global Development, 2022.

Muir, Angela, and Paula Mathieu. "Contemplative Pedagogy for Health and Well-Being in a Trauma-Filled World." *Composition Studies*, vol. 50, no. 2, 2022, pp. 154–169.

"NC State Students Pack Up, Start Moving Out After Less than a Month on Campus." abc11.com/nc-state-ncsu-raleigh-covid/6392281/. Accessed 3 Apr. 2024.

Portanova, Patricia, Michael Rifenburg, and Duane Roen, editors. *Contemporary Perspectives on Cognition and Writing*. WAC Clearinghouse, 2017.

Stewart, Graeme, Tricia Anne Seifert, and Carol Rolheiser. "Anxiety and Self-efficacy's Relationship with Undergraduate Students' Perceptions of the Use of Metacognitive Writing Strategies." *Canadian Journal for the Scholarship of Teaching and Learning*, vol. 6, no. 4, 2014, pp. 1–17.

Wardle, Elizabeth. "'Mutt Genres' and the Goals of FYC: Can We Help Students Write the Genres of the University?" *College Composition and Communication*, vol. 60, no. 4, 2009, pp. 765–78.

The syllabus that accompanies this Course Design is available on the journal's website.

Casie Fedukovich is associate professor of English at North Carolina State University. Her research explores writing program administration, labor, and teacher preparation and has appeared in *WPA: Writing Program Administration, Composition Forum*, and *Workplace: A Journal of Academic Labor*. She teaches courses in composition theory and rhetorical studies.

Brooke Mulhollem is a senior lecturer with the First-Year Writing Program at North Carolina State University. She has been teaching first-year writing for twenty-four years.

ENGL 111L: Grammar and Writing Workshop

Megan J. Busch

If you're a professor at a small liberal arts college (SLAC), you know all too well that roles, timelines, and responsibilities don't necessarily carry on in expected or typical ways. A year ago, I found myself at my own SLAC, in my second year on the tenure track, plopped into the chairperson role for our department of fifteen faculty members, and the recipient of an email from our Vice President of Student Success asking for a remedy for our over-burdened, bulging Bridge Program. This class, ENGL 111L: Grammar and Writing Workshop, is the corequisite course that has provided that solution in a way that actively encourages students to focus on their writing practice while meeting a pressing institutional need that likely exists at other SLACs—and perhaps larger institutions, too—as trends in higher education push towards the reduction and elimination of developmental writing programs. This course design offers one potential revision of a traditional developmental writing course that blends and adjusts existing research in the field to Charleston Southern's specific institutional context.

Course Description

ENGL 111L: Grammar and Writing Workshop is a "credited" corequisite course to a first-semester, first-year composition and rhetoric course (ENGL 111) at a small liberal arts institution (Uehling 143). The one-credit-hour workshop focuses on the mechanical basics of writing for college composition, and it functions as a mid-level placement for students coming to college with low GPAs and standardized test scores. ENGL 111L students meet once per week for a short composition-focused lesson that supplements the learning occurring in their primary ENGL 111 course and designated time to write alone or in groups with the guidance of embedded writing tutors. In the 2023–24 academic year, ENGL 111L served approximately 95 incoming first-year students.

Institutional Context

Charleston Southern University is a small, religiously affiliated liberal arts institution in Charleston, South Carolina. Over 3,000 students are enrolled in the undergraduate program, and the student body is primarily white and consists mostly of in-state students ("At a Glance"). There is no dedicated first-year writing program, and the students' only composition-rhetoric course is ENGL 111, which is taken in most students' first year on campus to fulfill a liberal arts core requirement. ENGL 112: Composition with an Introduction to Literature and a 200-level literature course follow this first composition class for all undergraduate students. The majority of professors who teach ENGL 111 are trained as literature professors and do not have degrees in composition-rhetoric. Ninety percent of the ENGL 111 courses are taught by full-time faculty members rather than adjuncts or visiting professors.

For nearly twenty years, Charleston Southern has offered a small Bridge Program, allowing students with below-admission-level GPAs and test scores to still attend the university with the requirement of taking ENGL 099 and/or Math 099. ENGL 099 is a four-credit-hour course that includes one additional hour (beyond class time) of one-on-one tutoring weekly in our campus's writing center. Since the COVID-19 pandemic, students' secondary-school learning—especially those coming from the South Carolina public school system—has suffered, and by 2023, the Bridge Program had grown beyond what the university could handle academically, financially, and pragmatically. Students were arriving unprepared for success in ENGL 111, but our Bridge Program could not sustain the demand. Thus, I received the aforementioned email from our Vice President of Student Success seeking a way to help students do well in ENGL 111 *without* adding new students to the beyond-capacity Bridge Program.

The institution uses the WritePlacer test to determine student placement in ENGL 099 (a Bridge Program course), ENGL 111 with ENGL 111L, or ENGL 111. If a student's GPA and/or standardized test scores are lower than the minimum admissions standards or if a student applies under the university's "test optional" admissions policy, they are required to take the WritePlacer, which offers a score on a 1–8 scale. Students who score 1–4 enter ENGL 099, students who score 5–6 enter ENGL 111 with ENGL 111L, and students who score 7–8 enter ENGL 111 (table 2). This placement structure aided student success and relieved the Bridge Program's burden in two ways:

1. Before the creation of ENGL 111L, admissions placed students who scored a 5 in ENGL 099 (table 1). These students typically did well in ENGL 099 and went on to succeed in ENGL 111 the following semester. The new placement strategy allowed these top Bridge Program students to go ahead and matriculate into ENGL 111 and offered the support of ENGL 111L.
2. Before the creation of ENGL 111L, admissions placed students scoring a 6 in ENGL 111 (table 1), but by-and-large, these students struggled in this course. Requiring them to take ENGL 111L offered additional support to move many students from C/D-level work into B/C-level work.

Table 1
Bridge Program Placement Model before 2023

Old Placement Model (Pre-2023)	
WritePlacer Score	*English Placement*
1–5	ENGL 099
6–8	ENGL 111

Table 2
Bridge Program Placement Model after 2023

New Placement Model	
WritePlacer Score	*English Placement*
1–4	ENGL 099
5–6	ENGL 111 + ENGL 111L
7–8	ENGL 111

Institutional context, too, requires a consideration of the students in this position and the broader implications of students required to take developmental courses. While our Bridge Program has helped many students succeed, there are significant financial and psychological drawbacks to placement in ENGL 099. The four-credit-hour course does not count towards a degree, and the necessity to take ENGL 099 in the first year often hinders a timely graduation, as many majors on inflexible schedules using cohort models require a specific sequence of classes beginning first semester freshman year (for Charleston Southern, that includes the two most popular majors, nursing and aeronautics). Further, on our campus and on many others, categorization as a "Bridge Student" comes with a certain negative stigma that's been associated with developmental writing courses for over two decades. Denise M. Crews and Steven R. Aragon explain (in 2004), "It appears to be more acceptable by the student to be informed that math is a need area rather than writing. Anecdotal evidence supports that many students believe that reading and writing are the most basic skills and are uncomfortable being informed that one is a need area for them" (10). For Crews and Aragon, identifying this need leads to a stigma that decreases participation in developmental writing courses, and the designation decreases a student's confidence in their ability to succeed in a college environment (15).

For these reasons, many colleges are considering a shift away from developmental writing courses—by redesign, reduction, or elimination—if they have not already moved in that direction (such as the University of Massachusetts Lowell experiencing this institutional push as far back as 2014—see Ann C. Dean's "Subsidizing Basic Writers"). In "Developmental Writing Reform at Onondaga Community College: From Corequisite to IRW, Eliminating Dev Ed While Supporting All Students," Choseed, DelConte, and O'Connor indicate that such a change in curriculum is necessary and successful for saving students "countless hours and thousands of dollars" (199). They further explain that such developmental programs "used up financial aid toward nondegree credits, took up an additional course slot in the student's first semester, and despite [their] best efforts, [were] still experienced as stigmatizing by many students" (205). While Charleston Southern is not yet ready to eliminate the developmental writing program altogether,[1] moving some students out of this program and into credit-bearing classes has had practical, financial, and psychological benefits. By allowing more students to test out of the Bridge Program, ENGL 111L serves to strengthen the writing of struggling students, removes financial hardship from some students, reduces the stigma associated with their writing placement, and lessens the burden on the institution's Bridge Program.

Theoretical Rationale

With this context in mind, I had several pedagogical goals for students in ENGL 111L. We needed to help students bypass the Bridge Program in a way that provided hands-on instruction and ample support for success in ENGL 111. To do this, I drew upon two areas of scholarly research in composition studies: corequisite courses and embedded writing tutors. The summer 2020 issue of *Composition Studies* proved to be invaluable in the creation of this course, and I'm confident that the work by the scholars in that issue directly led to a successful first iteration of ENGL 111L.

Corequisite course models have a long history of success in developmental writing contexts. Peter Adams indicates in "Giving Hope to the American Dream: Implementing a Corequisite Model of Developmental Writing" that a "corequisite approach to developmental education" has historically "improve[d] students' chances of success" in their future college semesters (24). Diane Kelly-Riley adds that corequisite courses are "viable model[s] to respond to instructional and curricular needs of developmental writers while also addressing external accountability mandates for increased retention, course and program completion" (35). However, the traditional models and guiding principles that Adams neatly outlines weren't just-right for our institutional context, and the ability to reshape current models to fit Charleston Southern's needs and resources shaped ENGL 111L.

ENGL 111L blends two of the approaches outlined by Adams: the Studio Model and the Tutoring Model. In the Studio Model, "[d]evelopmental students register for a three-credit college-level course . . . In addition, they register for a one-hour studio course with students from a variety of other courses requiring writing. At each studio session students present drafts, they are working on and receive feedback from other students, much as art students do in an art studio" (Adams 28). Alternatively, in the Tutoring Model, "[d]evelopmental support is offered through the Writing Center or a computer lab" (28). ENGL 111L draws from both of these tested structures by implementing a studio model with embedded tutors, essentially bringing the campus's writing center into the corequisite classroom.

While ENGL 111L implements many of Adams's recommendations (students are in a credit-bearing 100-level course, the course reduces the "stigma" that developmental students often feel, and students participate in hands-on instruction), it veers from Adams's framework for success in ways necessary for this specific institution (29–31):

1. **Large Class Size:** Adams indicates that the corequisite writing course should be small (fewer than 13 students as a benchmark) (33). However, Charleston Southern lacks the physical classroom space and composition-rhetoric-trained faculty to house multiple small sections of a one-hour course. Instead, we created a large course with a cap of 45 students, though actual enrollment ranged from 30–40 students in the 2023–24 academic year. (To note, this is not nearly as large as a "jumbo" class, as outlined by Kim Jaxon, Laura Sparks, and Chris Fosen (117)).

2. **Different Instructors for ENGL 111 and ENGL 111L:** Students may take ENGL 111 with any instructor. While Adams sees value in maintaining the same instructor for the lab and the primary course (33), we simply do not have the resources to make this happen from a scheduling perspective and a financial perspective, as the lab would increase all ENGL 111 professors' teaching contractual teaching load by one credit hour. Modifying Adams's recommendation in this way prevented overloads for our instructors (many of whom, quite honestly, would not have a desire to teach ENGL 111L).

3. **A Focus on Writing:** Adams indicates that a successful corequisite course should address issues of reading, writing, and "non-cognitive issues" (33). ENGL 111L only addresses writing issues. We do not currently have a reading-focused corequisite model of instruction available for students; however, non-cognitive issues are addressed in a general education course, which is recommended (but not required) for students who place in ENGL 111L.

Adams's research laid the foundation for this course and allowed me to think through the modifications necessary to fit our institutional context. Such modifications are significant as writing program administrators apply field research to their own institutions and student populations.

Further, research about embedded writing tutors informed the structure of the ENGL 111L class days. Kendon Kurzer, Anna Hayden, and Jennifer Nguyen praise the efficacy of embedded tutors in developmental writing, noting that—when compared to sending students to drop-in at a writing center—such a model leads to "gains in writing efficacy" and "normaliz[es] the interactions with students with tutors" by removing a stigma that meeting with a tutor is "somehow remedial" (37). To develop an embedded-tutor model at Charleston Southern, the University of Montana's "Sidecar Project" (described in Kelly Webster and Jake Hansen's "Vast Potential, Uneven Results: Unraveling the Factors that Influence Course-Embedded Tutoring Success") offered a framework by which we could bring tutors into the ENGL 111L classroom. As an adaptation of Candace Spigelman and Laurie Grobman's "classroom-based writing tutoring" (1), the Sidecar Project's model divides students into small groups led by tutors and encourages students to share their assignments and drafts with one another (Webster and Hansen 51). While the models of classroom-based writing tutoring presented in Spigelman and Grobman's full collection, *On Location: Theory and Practice in Classroom-Based Writing Tutoring,* are useful and varied, the Sidecar Project model aligned most with our institutional needs with one variation. The Sidecar Project model spreads tutors among various classes, in various departments, and with various instructors; tutors in ENGL 111L work with students in a single ENGL 111 class, in a single department, with a single instructor. Webster and Hansen report mixed success, but because of the narrower focus of ENGL 111L, we mitigated some of the larger challenges faced by the robust Sidecar Project, such as faculty buy-in, the logistics of managing a large number of faculty and tutors, and the relationships forming between many faculty members and tutors (and the complications that often brings) (54–56).

Significant to the success of ENGL 111L is the pedagogical structure of the daily grind in the classroom supported by the embedded tutors. Every week's meeting includes a 5–10 minute lecture on a focused element of academic writing (examples include college-level paragraph structure, integrating quotations, and synthesizing ideas) and 40–45 minutes of small group work with writing center tutors, similar to the Sidecar Project. The entire English department faculty assisted with choosing the topics addressed in ENGL 111L, providing input about (1) where students struggled the most in their writing and (2) the basic writing principles that most instructors were unable to address thoroughly during classroom instruction. A smaller committee focused on reviewing writing samples from ENGL 099 and ENGL 111 students to determine where students could use direct, writing-focused instruction. Table 3 lists the weekly topics for the 2023–2024 academic year.

Table 3

Instructional Topics by Week for the 2023-2024 Academic Year

Weekly Content for ENGL 111L	
Week 1	How to Interpret Assignments from Professors
Week 2	Writing Introductions and Thesis Statements
Week 3	Writing Body Paragraphs
Week 4	Writing Conclusion Paragraphs
Week 5	Writing in MLA Format
Week 6	Citing in MLA Format
Week 7	Analysis vs. Summary
Week 8	Integrating Quotes and Quote Sandwiches
Week 9	Paraphrasing without Plagiarizing
Week 10	Interpreting Professor Feedback on Writing Assignments
Week 11	Comma Splices and Fragments
Week 12	Passive Voice
Week 13	Sentence Structure and Academic Style
Week 14	Preparing and Revising a Final Research Paper

After the lesson, students have the opportunity to write and revise together in assigned groups (determined by their instructor for their primary ENGL 111 course) as they complete writing assignments. The instructor and writing center tutors remain busy the entire class period, answering individual questions from students, leading small group discussions about writing, and assisting students one-on-one with their writing. Students leave the class with a simple, printable reminder from the class's lesson that can live on their desk or writing space at home (example below). After a few weeks, the class atmosphere is vibrant as students get to know the instructor and tutors and lean on them for input on their assignments.

BODY PARAGRAPHS

A Beginning Template

Topic Sentence.
Further Explanation.
Example/Evidence.
Explanation of Evidence.
Repeat Example/Evidence.
Conclude and/or Transition.

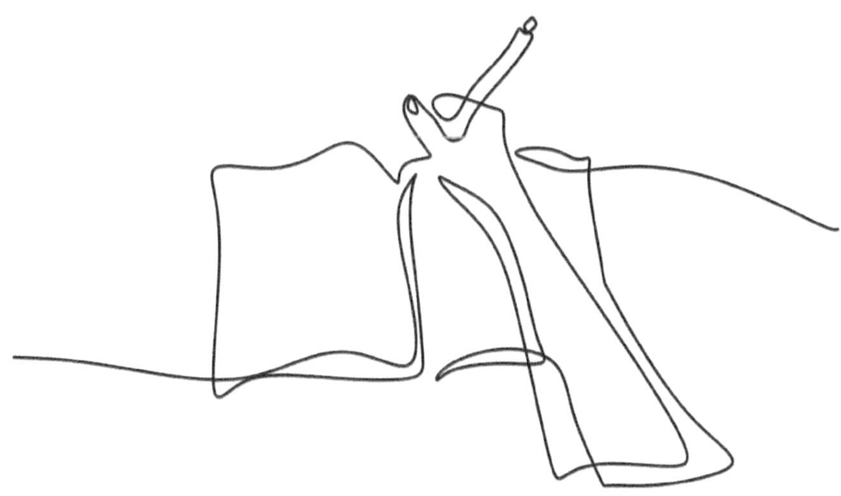

thesis statement
checklist

- ☐ I state my stance (or my conclusion).
- ☐ I can underline my topic.
- ☐ I tell my reader how I will reach my conclusion or support my stance.
- ☐ The statement is direct.
- ☐ The statement is specific.
- ☐ The statement is detailed.
- ☐ I've confirmed with my professor the appropriate length and met that requirement.
- ☐ I've confirmed with my professor if I can use "I" and met that requirement.
- ☐ My thesis statement is in the first paragraph.
- ☐ I've checked my spelling and grammar.

Figure 1. Printouts Easy for Students to Reference While Writing

Critical Reflection

In its first iteration, ENGL 111L provided ample support for students who would have otherwise struggled with writing in their ENGL 111 course. Data from the 2023–24 academic year support this model and instructional method (table 4). Ninety-four percent of students registered for ENGL 111L at the start of the term successfully completed the course (four students withdrew from ENGL 111 and ENGL 111L, and two students received a failure due to absences in both ENGL 111 and 111L). Eighty-eight percent of students who completed ENGL 111L passed their primary ENGL 111 course. This percentage is much higher if we remove those students who did not pass ENGL 111 for non-academic reasons (e.g., failure due to absences or withdrawal). If we remove these students from the data, only two percent of students enrolled in ENGL 111L failed ENGL 111 for academic performance.

Table 4

Pass Rates of ENGL 111 for Students Enrolled in ENGL 111L

ENGL 111L Success Rates	
Factor	*Percentage*
Completion Rate of ENGL 111L	94%
Overall Pass Rate of ENGL 111 of Students Enrolled in ENGL 111L	88%
Pass Rate of ENGL 111 of Students Enrolled in ENGL 111L (Removing Students who Failed due to Excessive Absences or Withdrew)	98%

In their anonymous course evaluations, students also indicated that they found the course's instructional material to be useful and supportive of their learning in ENGL 111. Many described the lab with comments like "The tutors really helped me throughout this class a lot" and "Reviewing my papers for English and even learning the proper MLA format really contributed to my English 111 grade." Some even requested that the class meet multiple times per week.[2] Because of its success in its first year, ENGL 111L will continue for the foreseeable future. However, despite this seeming initial success, the course still has much room for improvement.

The main revisions necessary for ENGL 111L aren't necessarily on a pedagogical level but on institutional and structural levels. Pedagogically, the course seems to work: students are passing ENGL 111, bypassing the Bridge Program and ENGL 099, and appreciating the class's purpose and learning outcomes. However, there is still a need for improvements to make the class even more functional:

1. **Standardizing the ENGL 111 Syllabus.** While the lessons taught in ENGL 111L are applicable to most stages in the writing process and most assignments planned for various ENGL 111 sections, having a standard syllabus, course calendar, and paper deadlines would make ENGL 111L flow more smoothly. In our department culture (literature-focused faculty able to teach ENGL 111 in their own way for over twenty years), I do not see this change happening in the near future. If a similar lab were implemented at an institution without these restraints, I believe it would be more successful if all students in ENGL 111 sections were learning from a standard syllabus.

2. **More Training for Tutors.** Our tutors are excellent writers, but they are not trained enough in classroom management or small-group tutoring. A more regular training schedule for these tutors would be ideal to strengthen not only their abilities but also their confidence in interacting with students. Many universities implement a practicum or internship program for tutor training, and such a program would likely serve embedded tutors well.

3. **More Professors Trained to Teach ENGL 111L.** In our literature-focused department, only a handful of professors are versed in composition-rhetoric research (myself and two other full-time faculty members). Ideally, all fifteen faculty members would be trained to teach ENGL 111L and mentor the embedded tutors.

4. **Better Placement Strategies.** Some top-performing students in ENGL 111L likely did not need the lab or the extra credit hour on their schedule. The WritePlacer test is not always precise in its scoring, which is completed by AI. Improved iterations of this course would likely include a more robust placement strategy, such as directed self-placement. At the time of this writing, our university does not have the resources necessary to overhaul our placement strategy.

5. **Accounting for the Institutional Unknown.** Because ENGL 111L is so connected to the current institutional structures, changes in those structures will impact the class. In the upcoming year, our writing center is moving from the full oversight of the English department and Bridge Program to the Office of Student Success, and there are whispers of eliminating the Bridge program altogether. Each of these institutional changes will impact ENGL 111L's place and function within the institution.

While I'm excited about the value this course brings to students matriculating into the university, it's also easy for me to see the numerous ways structures and institutional parameters could be improved upon. I hope to implement such changes in the future.

In the upcoming academic year, I expect ENGL 111L to serve nearly two hundred students as our incoming class continues to grow year after year (135 students completed ENGL 111L in Fall 2024). Its implementation has been an enjoyable practice in engaging with research in the field and applying it to our own institutional context to help students succeed in their first year and beyond. I see this course as a fresh, new opportunity to welcome students to academic writing through an engaging, hands-on learning experience geared toward their overall academic success. Such a privilege—to teach first-year students in such a way—is not lost on me.

Notes

1. Between the submission of this course design and its publication, the university's administration has created a task force (of which I am a part) to move towards the elimination of developmental writing courses altogether, though a plan is not yet in place. ENGL 111L remains a prominent part of the early drafts of this plan.

2. Just to note, there were three negative evaluation comments, which indicated that the students didn't feel they needed the class and which is perhaps a placement issue (and is discussed in the critical reflection).

Works Cited

Adams, Peter. "Giving Hope to the American Dream: Implementing a Corequisite Model of Developmental Writing." *Composition Studies,* vol. 48, no. 2, 2020, pp. 19–34.

"At a Glance: A Brief Look at CSU." *Charleston Southern University,* charlestonsouthern.edu/about/at-a-glance/. Accessed 23 April 2025.

Choseed, Malkiel, Matt DelConte, and Michael P. O'Connor. "Developmental Writing Reform at Onondaga Community College: From Corequisite to IRW, Eliminating Dev Ed while Supporting All Students." *Teaching English in the Two-Year College,* vol. 50, no. 3, 2023, pp. 199–223.

Crews, Denise M., and Steven R. Aragon. "Influence of a Community College Developmental Writing Course on Academic Performance." *Community College Review,* vol. 32, no. 2, 2004, pp. 1–18.

Dean, Ann C. "Subsidizing Basic Writers: Resources and Demands in Literacy Sponsorship." *Journal of Basic Writing,* vol. 38. no. 1, 2019, pp. 5–37, 10.37514/JBW-J.2019.38.2.02.

Jaxon, Kim, Laura Sparks, and Chris Fosen. "Epic Learning in a 'Jumbo' Writing Class." *Composition Studies,* vol. 48, no. 2, 2020, pp. 116–127.

Kelly-Riley, Diane. "Engaging Accountability: Faculty-led, Statewide Implementation of a Corequisite Model of First Year Writing across Two- and Four-Year Public Institutions." *Composition Studies,* vol. 48, no. 2, 2020, pp. 35–53, compstudiesjournal.com/wp-content/uploads/2020/08/kelly-riley.pdf.

Kurzer, Kendon, Anna Hayden, and Jennifer Nguyen. "Embedded vs. Drop-in Tutors in Developmental Writing Contexts: Course/Tutoring Perceptions and Impact on Student Writing Efficacy." *Writing Center Journal,* vol. 41, no. 2, 2023, pp. 26–41.

Spigelman, Candace, and Laurie Grobman. "Introduction: On Location in Classroom-Based Writing Tutoring." *On Location: Theory and Practice in Classroom-Based Writing Tutoring,* edited by Candance Spigelman and Laurie Grobman, Utah State UP, 2005, pp. 1–16.

Uehling, Karen S. "A Credited Support Course: Corequisite Writing Course at Boise State University." *Composition Studies,* vol. 48, no. 2, 2020, pp. 143–147, compstudiesjournal.com/wp-content/uploads/2020/08/uehling.pdf.

Webster, Kelly, and Jake Hansen. "Vast Potential, Uneven Results: Unraveling the Factors that Influence Course-Embedded Tutoring Success." *Praxis: A Writing Center Journal,* vol. 12, no. 1, 2014, pp. 51–56, repositories.lib.utexas.edu/server/api/core/bitstreams/6c2f31d4-a362-4bcd-b225-453d47e4bfb0/content.

The syllabus that accompanies this Course Design is available on the journal's website.

Megan J. Busch is chairperson of the English department and assistant professor of English at Charleston Southern University. She earned her PhD in Composition and Rhetoric at the University of South Carolina, where she served as the Assistant Director of the First-Year English Program. Her work has been published in *Peitho, Composition Studies*, and *Composition Forum*, and she is currently the managing editor of *College Composition and Communication*.

WRIT 400: Writing for Nonprofits

Meghan A. Sweeney

Course Description

WRIT 400: Writing for Nonprofits is a course offered by a newly formed independent Writing Studies Program at Saint Mary's College of California. The course fulfills an engaged learning (EL) core requirement, with three units for the class and one unit (20 hours) dedicated to indirect and direct service for a community partner (i.e. writing for a nonprofit). In this course, 18 students are grouped into teams of 3–4 and then partnered with one of five local nonprofit organizations. Working closely with an executive of the nonprofit, students produce written deliverables. These deliverables range in terms of genre—social media posts, grant proposals or research, website content creation, blog posts, annual reports, newsletters, donor letters—and skills required, with some projects only needing text-based writing, and others benefiting from additional skills, like journalistic interviewing, document design, and user-interface design.

Balancing the labor demands of deliverables across student groups is crucial. The nonprofit executive and professor meet the semester preceding the class to discuss the nonprofit's needs, determine deliverables based on those needs, and negotiate the size of the student team based on the size and number of deliverables. These pre-course conversations allow the professor to ensure that every team has a rich array and balanced set of deliverables. During the first week of class, the nonprofit partner attends class to describe the deliverables and define how collaboration, communication, and feedback will operate. After learning about the deliverables and how the nonprofit collaborates, students select their top three partners, and the professor distributes students into their teams based on those preferences. After these teams are made, the nonprofit partner acts as the teacher, editor, and client for the writing projects, while the professor operates as a supporting team member.

For the three-unit portion of the course, students complete three collaborative writing assignments. First, they write a project plan and community partner profile, so they can understand the nonprofit's community work while also planning the semester's nonprofit deliverables schedule. Then students conduct an analysis of the nonprofit genre(s) they are writing. Finally, they write a white paper about a social issue that affects their nonprofit's clients. Throughout the semester, students keep engaged learning logs, reflective low stakes writing that prompts students to connect the nonprofit writing with their classroom projects and their preconceived notions of community issues. These assignments augment and support the nonprofit deliverables that comprise the one-unit core requirement of engaged learning. See table 1 for an example of this assignment breakdown from one group.

Table 1
Overview of How These Projects Span the One- and Three-Unit Portions of This Engaged Learning Course

Collaborative course projects (3-units)	Nonprofit deliverables (example) (EL unit)
Project plan and partner profile	Report on accessibility of partner's website
Discourse community analysis	Mock-ups of proposed changes to website
White paper	Design template for partner's annual report
Partner project presentation	Copy for partner's annual report

Because this course stands alone in a newly independent writing program, with only a professional writing certificate and loose affiliations with other majors and minors across the university, it attracts a wide variety of students who are often learning about professional writing for the first time and have varying levels of writing confidence. As a result, this course and its revisions offer a useful examination for writing courses that can attract students from every discipline.

Institutional Context

An Hispanic Serving and Asian American and Native American Pacific Islander Serving Institution, Saint Mary's College of California is a small (~2500 students) private comprehensive university guided by a Lasallian mission of social justice and inclusive communities. In the Lasallian spirit, all undergraduate students must complete the Engaged Learning core requirement, similar to Service Learning. The Catholic Institute for Lasallian Social Action—a university office dedicated to supporting professors in the creation of Engaged Learning core-designated courses and students in the management of their 20-required hours of engaged learning—connects professors with community partners and manages insurance and student travel costs.

Despite its deep importance to the university mission, the Engaged Learning requirement can be difficult for many students to complete, especially for those in large, heavily structured majors that do not include an Engaged Learning designated course among its major requirements. For that reason, in 2017, I created Writing for Nonprofits as a version of the English Department's Advanced Composition course. It was the first Engaged Learning designated course in the English major, so most students who enrolled in Writing for Nonprofits were English majors or minors. At that time, I included foundational rhetorical theories, like rhetorical situation, context, audience, purpose, and genre because students had little to no foundation in rhetoric. There were no other professional writing courses taught at the university, aside from a business communication writing in the disciplines course in marketing.

In 2023, after the English department was broken into three separate units—Creative Writing, English, and Writing Studies—the course Writing for Nonprofits relocated to the Writing Studies Program. It remained an Engaged Learning course, but it also became part of a vertical professional writing curriculum and became more interdisciplinary; it attracted Creative Writing majors and minors, English majors and minors, Law and Society minors, and any student looking to fulfill their Engaged Learning core requirement. The vertical curriculum was part of a newly developed Professional Writing Certificate—a three-course certificate designed to augment any major. The certificate includes an introductory course WRIT 300 Theories and Practices of Professional Writing, an experiential course WRIT 400 Writing for Nonprofits or WRIT 495 Writing Internship, and a choice of many electives from across the university, like Multimedia Writing in the Media Productions Program and Sports Journalism in the Communications Department.

Because WRIT 400 reaches across disciplinary boundaries, it is institutionally important but curricularly complicated. First, students often discover professional writing through this course, drawn to the course because it fulfills a core requirement. Second, while before WRIT 400 was one class in the English major, now it is a foundational course in a professional writing certificate. For these two reasons, I revised the course to introduce students to not just rhetorical theories but also professional and technical writing theory, and, in particular, the social justice turn, which aligns with the college's mission and best practices in the field. However, because the course was still one of only two professional writing courses for students who span the curriculum, I had to consider the depth of that theoretical underpinning and how to use it to support students with varied experiences and writing confidence levels.

Students' disciplinary experience in this course typically includes English literature, creative writing, art, sociology, politics, and communications and then expands out from the humanities and social sciences to business majors—often economics and marketing. This range means that students are coming to the class with little to no knowledge of professional writing, but the dimensions of this disciplinary diversity can also be an intriguing asset to the curriculum as students bring identities as designers and writers and knowledge of visual rhetoric, marketing, social issues, economics, and systemic problems. These varied dimensions and this range of experience are important for the curriculum of the course—as students work closely with each other and the nonprofit, using their diverse experience and knowledge from other classes to support the nonprofit deliverables. As a result, I revised the course to be a heavily scaffolded professional writing class, with a series of projects that support the varied and often changing community partners' writing projects.

Theoretical Rationales

As a community-based engaged learning course and high-impact practice ("High Impact"), WRIT 400 operates as a support system for the writing projects students complete with their nonprofit partner, which vary and sometimes change mid-semester. These changes are a major source of risk in most community-based writing courses, as the professor has little to no control over the student experience and how that experience may or may not clash with a student's personal worldview (Holmes 51). The variety of projects and risk that they may change means I cannot structure the class to teach nonprofit genres generally. Instead, the course takes three threads of theory that support the varied experiences of each student group and provide them with the resilience and agility to adjust to new rhetorical contexts: (1) The concept of discourse communities to introduce students to client work preparation; (2) Asset-based inquiry to embrace the social justice turn in professional and technical writing; and (3) Critical reflection to mitigate risk.

Discourse Community

"Discourse community" is a concept that I introduce at the start of the semester and reinforce throughout. Discourse communities have their own values, norms, and lexis, and those unique qualities are communicated through accepted means to its members, members who vary according to expertise within the community (Swales). Discourse community, as a concept, plays a key role in this course: students recognize the nonprofit as a discourse community that they are seeking to understand better, as relative outsiders. When students view the classwork and dynamics through this lens, it releases a great deal of pressure—they see their lack of familiarity with new genres as normal and their writing as something that needs to be adapted to the norms and values of a discourse community. This process relaxes students who do not identify as writers.

With the first project, a nonprofit profile and project plan, students position themselves in a new discourse community, by learning everything they can about its communicative norms. This theory guides students to understand why they need to understand how a nonprofit organization defines its terms and references the communities and people they serve. For example, students discover that some nonprofits only use people-first language—some avoid negative diction. Framing the class with this theory establishes that students are apprentice writers entering a community that they must take the time to understand first, building a healthy respect for the nonprofit community's unique discursive practice.

In the second project, a discourse community analysis, students deepen their understanding with Dan Melzer's "Understanding Discourse Communities," which describes his process of becoming a new member of a discourse community, while also extending John Swales' work by including document-based questions (DBQs), or questions one might ask about a text to better understand a new discourse community. After students read Melzer's work, the projects they complete in class have more purpose, such as a voice chart created through DBQ to understand the lexis of the nonprofit, a nonprofit profile of the organization's values, and a genre analysis (e.g., if writing an annual report for their nonprofit, they analyze a few annual reports from other nonprofits).

Asset-Based Inquiry

In professional and technical communication, the social justice turn encourages scholars and writers to "adopt an intersectional, coalitional approach to problem solving" (Walton et al. 12). At risk is social justice work that further marginalizes groups, when it fails to value everyone's contributions and to preserve difference, instead demanding assimilation into problematic white, patriarchal structures (Walton et al. 9). In response to Walton, Moore, and Jones's call for change, Lucía Durá offers a methodological approach to technical and professional writers working in community called asset-based thinking. According to Durá, technical communicators are faced with "micro-decision points" when problem solving where they have opportunities to turn deficit-thinking to asset-based thinking (24). For example, when studying issues with college student writing, Durá advocated that the team look at students who are doing well with their writing as opposed to struggling writers (24). Since their students are often first generation—with demands of work, family, and school competing with their time—she wanted to understand the strengths of these students who are doing well: what could her team learn from those students? This method is an asset-based inquiry approach that "expands the solution space" by showing writers how to (1) ask questions that move away from deficit-based thinking and (2) legitimize local ways of knowing by encouraging discussion with group members (Durá 25).

By integrating Durá's work on asset-based inquiry, I invite students to see nonprofit writing as problem-solving. These nonprofits seek to solve homelessness, food insecurity, sex trafficking, and more, as part of a community with many strengths—and it's those strengths that should be examined and it's the diverse viewpoints of those community members that should be preserved. The nonprofits' attention to asset-based thinking quickly becomes apparent to the students: one nonprofit only employs people who have experienced homelessness in the past; another avoids the word victim in their description of sex trafficking survivors; and another foregrounds the voices of young black girls in their program instead of high school graduation statistics. Using Durá's asset-based thinking as a lens of inquiry, students reflect on and understand the nonprofits' rhetorical, asset-based choices. As writers, students understand the community and write from their perspective, from their experiences. In doing so, they are able to meet Walton et. al's call for writing that preserves difference.

Critical Reflective Practice

Reflection is often a foundational practice in writing classes to promote transfer (Taczak and Robertson; Wardle) and self-efficacy (Yancey). The practice promotes a self-awareness among writers that encourages them to understand themselves, their writing, their learning, and their ever-changing writing situations (Taczak and Robertson). Many scholars have asserted that this self-awareness helps writers develop an understanding that new contexts require new writing genres and styles, and helps them develop the facility to repurpose writing practices to new rhetorical situations (Wardle; Yancey). While Saint Mary's College of California's Writing Studies Program integrates reflective practice throughout its curriculum, in this community-based engaged learning course, reflective practice provides an additional pedagogical benefit. Community-based writing classes are "emotionally demanding" and risky for students (Holmes 48.). The emotional risks stem from the professor not being able to control what happens between the student and community partner and how the student experiences the partnership. To mitigate the risk in these classes, Holmes advocates for a feminist pedagogy that includes reciprocal care based on classroom transparency and continual shifting of teacher and learner roles (61). To establish this transparent classroom at the outset, I tell students that, while I plan the projects with the partners, contexts change and so may their projects, their relationships with their partners, and their relationships with their group members. To frame the shifting teacher and learner roles, I define the role of the community partner as co-teacher. For the students, I frame their dual role as learner with the partner and as teacher to me and their colleagues. My role, which would traditionally be teacher, becomes both teacher and learner about their projects.

To frame this transparency and these shifting roles throughout the remainder of the semester, two acts that shift the loci of power and authority for a feminist pedagogy, I use critical reflection to foster the reciprocity of care among student, professor, and partner, for which Holmes advocates. First, students reflect on the discourse community, asset-based thinking, and collaborative practices with every writing project. Using a portfolio assessment method that requires a robust reflective cover letter, I frame the cover letter as a document that students can use to explain to me the rhetorical choices in the project, the collaborative process (how it went and who took on what roles; how those roles shifted), problems that arose, and their desired feedback. As frames for their projects, these reflections shift the student into the role of teacher, as they explain the rhetorical and leadership choices made during the project, thereby establishing the professor as the learner and partner in responding to student issues with care.

Second, students write six engaged learning logs throughout the semester to reflect on the reciprocal process of engaged learning, the connections between their projects and the classroom-based work, their emotional connection to the community-based partner, their difficulties with their partners or group members, and their development as writers and citizens. For example, one log asks students to reflect on how their writing helped the community partner, what they learned from the community partner, and how they developed through the process. These learning logs also allow the professor to participate in the community partners' projects when asked to, and to identify risks or issues with partners. Almost exclusively, students work in their groups and with their partners on those projects, with the professor only participating when necessary.

Overall, these reflective practices allow for transparency from student and professor, highlight the shifting roles of teacher and learner, decenter professor authority, and create opportunity for reciprocal care from professor and student, by providing an outlet for the professor to identify any issues that arise in this risky course and to give students space to explore the transformative aspects of community-based learning. The rewards of community-based writing classes continue to outweigh these risks: students are more deeply engaged in writing projects (Holmes) and that deep engagement leads to long-term transfer (Tuomi-Gröhn and Engeström).

Critical Reflection

When WRIT 400: Writing for Nonprofits was first created, many advisors saw it as an opportunity for students across the curriculum to fulfill their engaged learning core requirement. Now with an independent writing program and a developing curriculum in professional writing, the course has necessarily shifted its goals to also introducing students to the discipline of professional writing. With this change come challenges. Specifically, the course needs to provide students with engaged learning opportunities, introduce them to the discipline, and ensure nonprofit organizations experience the partnership as useful, and not a burden. Students typically work with the executive director or fund development manager—typically busy, overworked individuals. As a result, when I consider how to improve the course for student learning, I feel an equal commitment to improve the utility of the course for the nonprofit. These intersecting needs inform my analysis of three primary issues: missing project management instruction, inconsistent engagement from nonprofits, and reflection expanding beyond the classroom.

I identified these issues by looking at data that I gathered from students' hourly logs (see table 2). Each hour that a student works, indirectly or directly, with the nonprofit gets logged into a database with a brief description of the task. Table 2 divides those entries among hours spent in their group of 3–4 students, with their nonprofit, and with themselves working on the nonprofit's projects. In the following sections, I explore how this data along with anecdotal experiences with students guided my critical reflection on course improvements.

Table 2
Student Hourly Logs

Group Meetings / Collaborative Time in Their Group	Number of Entries
Planning projects (e.g. outlining the project; planning the process)	48
Managing the project and collaboration (e.g. establishing roles)	43
Communicating with nonprofit organization via email	22
Reading or researching together / Discussing research	18
Writing collaboratively (i.e. meeting in the library to write together)	17
Editing or revising (i.e. sitting together and changing the piece)	17
Meetings with the Nonprofit Organization Representative	
Discussing the plans for the project (e.g. parameters of assignment)	55
Sharing work in progress and receiving feedback	45
Touring facilities, learning about the organization	19
Reflecting together on the process	4

Group Meetings / Collaborative Time in Their Group	Number of Entries
Individual Work on the Projects	
Writing / Designing / Creating	67
Reading or researching (e.g. finding data; analyzing a new genre)	39
Editing or revising	33
Planning projects	12

Define Project Management

The data from hourly logs shows that students are spending the most time planning these projects in groups (48 hours) and with their nonprofit (55 hours). They also pay a lot of attention to project management—defining roles in the groups, establishing tasks, and planning deliverable dates (43 hours). This data indicates course design strengths and opportunities for improvement.

A course design strength is that the theories used supported collaborative planning and project management. First, students read "Teamwork and Collaborative Writing" (Beilfuss et. al) and identified the different roles to share among the members of each team. I encouraged them to switch roles with each project, so they could all experience being a project manager, communications manager, and copy editor. Second, the theoretical frame of discourse communities established a classroom environment that privileged discovery. With each new writing assignment, students worked together in their groups to ask DBQs (Melzer). For example, when learning how to write in their nonprofit's voice, they created voice charts (Gonzalez) so they could analyze the vocabulary, verbosity, grammar, punctuation, and capitalization. When studying genres, they conducted in-depth rhetorical genre analyses (Bawarshi and Reiff). Third, asset-based inquiry garnered an unexpected focus from the students. After reading Durá's work, their planning conversations often focused on the assets of the team—who is a good artist, who has experience from other professional writing courses, who is a strong editor. They looked to each other for assets. At the same time, when given an assignment from their nonprofit, many groups also tried to figure out how to build long-term assets for the nonprofit. For example, a group that was asked to provide social media posts for four different platforms decided to take the project one step further and build a platform-based guide and templates that could be used by the fund development manager after the semester ended. The asset-based inquiry frame shifted project management and planning in surprising ways.

Despite these generative twists on asset-based inquiry and discourse community, I found that students felt adrift with these project roles, especially project manager. Beilfuss, Bettes, and Peterson describe these many roles well and address potential problems and conflicts. However, in the classroom, I found it difficult to prepare students for all the risks of collaborative writing and show them how to be effective, inclusive project managers. I introduced them to Gantt charts (a project management tool) and discussed my own professional experience with project management. However, failing to integrate project management theory into the course felt like a missed opportunity especially after the logs showed how much time was dedicated to project management and planning. In revisions to this course, I plan to define project management more purposefully by integrating parts of a resource like *Fundamentals of Project Management* by Joseph Heagney, which covers topics like the role of the project manager, planning the project, developing objectives for the project, identifying project risks, building a schedule, and managing the team. These selected issues would help students immensely in communicating with each other (managing the team), the nonprofit (building a schedule; identifying risks), and other participants, like interviewees. By identifying, naming, and providing tools for managing these project management issues, the students will be more successful in the course overall.

Issues with Nonprofit Communication Consistency

Sharing work with and receiving feedback from the nonprofit partner was an activity on which students collectively spent 45 hours (see table 2). For most groups, the process of sharing work and receiving feedback was positive, the feedback received ranging from instant approval to feedback that corresponded with the voice charts they completed, like changing the point of view to "we." Some students offered their nonprofit partners three designs for their projects before adding copy, allowing them to triangulate the needs of the nonprofit. Overall, hours spent on sharing work and receiving feedback were useful for students as they learned how to work as professional writers in a client-like relationship.

However, the data does not tell the whole story. A few groups did not have positive experiences with sharing work and receiving feedback. One group lost all communication with their nonprofit partner by mid-semester, so they became unsure of how to revise projects. They were able to work with a volunteer, but not the nonprofit executive with whom they started. Another group found that their nonprofit did not have enough writing projects to complete because the nonprofit kept completing them before giving the students a chance to write them. For both these nonprofits, the issues are understandable. The first nonprofit was fairly new and did not realize how little time they would have to dedicate to mentoring students. The second nonprofit found themselves having to meet grant proposal deadlines that could not wait for the pace of the course.

Reflecting on Holmes's accounting of risk in community-based projects, I found that students needed space to process the emotions that come from a change in expectations. For many groups, the nonprofit partner maintained the semester's project plan, providing stability. In the groups in which the nonprofit partner changed the plan, the students felt unstable, unsure if they could complete their 20 hours, and disappointed that their experience was not as seamless as the other groups. These emotions could be expressed through their reflective logs and cover letters. However, the feminist pedagogy framework supports the processing of these emotions as part of reciprocal care (Holmes 61). Since I established early in the semester that I do not have full control over their experience or their relationship with their community partner, nor am I the authority on what and how they write for the community partner, the center of authority is displaced, making it clear that these are not matters that I can fix. Instead, we can work together on improving them. Students' critical reflection allows for the processing of disappointment, but feminist pedagogy empowers students to be self-reliant rather than professor-or partner-reliant.

Two features of this class supported this self-reliance. By designing the classroom projects as potential deliverables to the nonprofit organization, I found that groups who had a change of plans could repurpose those internal projects as external deliverables. This adjustment mitigated the risk (not earning enough hours) and the emotions (not experiencing professional writing). Every in-class project was capable of being repurposed to become a deliverable: nonprofit profiles were repurposed as brochures, discourse community analyses were repurposed as style guides for marketing, and white papers worked as deliverables on their own. By having internal classroom projects that could also work as deliverables, we found a way to assuage student and professor concerns.

Asset-based thinking also encouraged student resilience as these groups brainstormed what assets they could create to help the nonprofit complete the planned projects when they did have the time. For example, the group that lost all contact created speech templates for high school students preparing to accept awards, even though the original plan was for them to workshop the speeches with the students. Asset-based thinking and the repositioning of students as teachers can encourage resilience among students when risks common in community-based writing affect the classroom. The students creating new projects—just as the teacher and partners did before the semester began—is an example of this resilience.

Reflective Practice Needs to be More Expansive

As I have described, reflective writing is an integral part of this course through portfolio assessment and engaged learning logs. This reflection was centered in the classroom. However, one nonprofit executive invited her team of students to also reflect with her. In table 2, there are four hours logged for reflection. This number comes from one group, the group who worked with a sex trafficking survivors nonprofit. They spent an hour at the end of the semester in deep reflection with their nonprofit partner, reflecting on how the projects changed them, how they experienced the projects, and how the nonprofit experienced it. The students highly valued this interaction with the nonprofit and shared the impactful experience with the class during their final presentation.

Before the nonprofit executive integrated reflection into her work with students, I had viewed the parameters of reflection exclusively within the confines of the classroom. However, this executive's choice to reflect with the students expanded my view and pointed to the possibilities for critical, reciprocal self-reflection. In revisions to this course, I plan to integrate reflection with the nonprofit organization if possible. It is potentially a stronger model, one that I believe should receive more exploration.

Works Cited

Allen, Danielle. "We need tech and government help with contact tracing. That doesn't have to mean Big Brother." *Washington Post,* 3 April 2020, www.washingtonpost. com/opinions/2020/04/03/we-need-tech-government-help-with-contact-tracing-that-doesnt-have-mean-big-brother/?outputType=amp.

Bawarshi, Anis S., and Mary Jo Reiff. *Genre: An Introduction to History, Theory, Research, and Pedagogy.* Parlor P, 2010.

Beilfuss, Michael J., Staci Bettes, and Katrina Peterson. *Technical and Professional Writing Genres: A Study in Theory and Practice.* Oklahoma State University, 2019, dx.doi.org/10.22488/okstate.19.000001.

Bickmore, Lisa. "Genre in the Wild: Understanding Genre within Rhetorical (Eco) Systems." Open English SLCC, 2016, pressbooks.pub/openenglishatslcc/chapter/genre-in-the-wild-understanding-genre-within-rhetorical-ecosystems/.

Bloomstone, Joshua A., Aubrey Florom-Smith, Christopher Barsotti, Bruce Kingsley, Patrick Velliky, Tania Haddad, George Semien, Richard Sanders, Sara Champoux, and Ron Wood. "Firearm Injury Prevention." *Envision Healthcare,* 2023 www.envisionhealth.com/firearm-injury-prevention-white-paper.pdf.

Durá, Lucía. "Expanding Inventional and Solution Spaces: How Asset-based Inquiry Can Support Advocacy in Technical Communication." *Citizenship and Advocacy in Technical Communication,* 2018, pp. 23–39.

Gonzalez, Elissa. "How I Made My First UC Writing Voice Chart." Medium, 2023 bootcamp.uxdesign.cc/how-i-made-my-first-ux-writing-voice-chart-106a4cab3867.

Hart, Vi, Divya Siddarth, Bethan Cantrell, Lila Tretikov, Peter Eckersley, John Langford, Scott Leibrand, Sham Kakade, Steve Latta, Dana Lewis, Stefano Tessaro, and Glen Wey. "Outpacing the Virus: Digital Response to Containing the Spread of

COVID-19 while Mitigating Privacy Risks." *Edmond J. Safra Center for Ethics,* 2020, projects.iq.harvard.edu/files/kakade/files/white_paper_5_outpacing_the_virus-2020.pdf

Heagney, Joseph. *Fundamentals of Project Management.* 5th ed., AMACOM Division of American Management Association International, 2016.

"High-Impact Practices." AAC&U, www.aacu.org/trending-topics/high-impact.

Holmes, Ashley J. "Transformative Learning, Affect, and Reciprocal Care in Community Engagement." *Community Literacy Journal,* vol. 9 no. 2, 2015, pp. 48–67.

"Vaccine Hesitancy in South Asia White Paper." International Vaccine Access Center, 2024 publichealth.jhu.edu/sites/default/files/2024-02/savi-vaccine-hesitancy-in-south-a ia-white-paperax.pdf.

Melzer, Dan. "Understanding Discourse Communities." *Writing Spaces: Readings on Writing Volume 3,* edited by Dana Driscoll, Mary Stewart, and Matthew Vetter, Parlor P, 2020, pp. 100–15.

Strom, Stephanie. "Does Service Learning Really Help?" *New York Times,* 3 Jan. 2010, pp. 26.

Swales, John. "The Concept of Discourse Community: Some Recent Personal History." *Composition Forum,* vol. 37, 2017, pp. 215–27.

Taczak, Kara, and Liane Robertson. "Metacognition and the Reflective Writing Practitioner: An Integrated Knowledge Approach." *Contemporary Perspectives on Cognition and Writing,* edited by Patricia Portanova, J. Michael Rifenburg, and Duane Roen, UP of Colorado, 2017, pp. 211–29.

Tuomi-Gröhn, Terttu, and Yrjö Engeström. "Conceptualizing Transfer: From Standard Notions to Developmental Perspectives." *Between School and Work: New Perspectives on Transfer and Boundary-crossing,* edited by Terttu Tuomi-Gröhn and Yrjö Engeström, Pergamon, 2003, pp. 19–38.

Walton, Rebecca, Kristen Moore, and Natasha Jones. *Technical Communication After the Social Justice Turn: Building Coalitions for Action.* Routledge, 2019.

Wardle, Elizabeth. "Creative Repurposing for Expansive Learning: Considering 'Problem-Exploring' and 'Answer-Getting' Dispositions in Individuals and Fields." *Composition Forum,* vol. 26, no. 1, 2012.

Yancey, Kathleen Blake. *Reflection in the Writing Classroom.* Utah State UP, 1998.

The syllabus that accompanies this Course Design is available on the journal's website.

Meghan A. Sweeney is associate professor and director of writing studies at Saint Mary's College of California, where she studies postsecondary literacies and writing program administration. Her work has been published in *Research in the Teaching of English, College Composition and Communication, Teaching English in the Two-Year College, Journal of Writing Assessment, Journal of Basic Writing,* and *WPA: Writing Program Administration.*

Where We Are: The Present and Future of Academic Conferences

Nimble and Sustainable: The Future of Feminisms and Rhetorics and Coalitional Conferencing

Cristy Beemer and Rebecca S. Richards[1]

There are highly structured and professionalized conferences in rhetoric and composition studies that offer corporate hotels, fancy receptions and events, and large book exhibits. But such conferences are expensive to run and require institutional structures that some find exclusionary, rigid, and bureaucratic (Kynard; Hassel; Hubrig and Osorio). If scholar-teachers are going to continue to use our finite energy and financial resources to gather together, we see the future of academic conferencing as sustainable and nimble, allowing for shifting priorities.

With around 400 attendees, Feminisms and Rhetorics (FemRhets), a biennial conference sponsored by the Coalition of Feminist Scholars in the History of Rhetoric and Composition (CFSHRC), practices an ethics of care—a tenet of feminist activism and scholarship, emerging from Carol Gilligan's research that values relationships, care, and responsiveness to community needs—that moves beyond a singular theme or structure to welcome a broad range of topics and provide mentoring and coalition-building opportunities. FemRhets operates on a limited budget that doesn't allow for all the frills; the conference only works when people show up, help out, and engage. We can conference in Mankato, MN or Palo Alto, CA. We can conference under the summer skies of New Hampshire, even after several years of holding a conference in the fall. In other words, we see the future of FemRhets changing and adapting to the needs of our members and changing site hosts.

We try to strike a balance between institutional knowledge and sustainable consistency, which comes from the CFSHRC, and a productive polyvocality and nimbleness that come from changing the site hosts. In the end, FemRhets and the CFSHRC focus on disseminating knowledge but also foreground community-building, mentorship, and meaningful engagement for our attendees and the larger communities that support the conference.

To be clear, as a smaller and biennial conference, FemRhets has always had to be nimble. However, more recently, we've been making changes to create sustainable structures that build upon our best practices and imagine a changeable future. Because the CFSHRC is a volunteer-based coalition and doesn't employ any staff, full-time or otherwise, we rely on members pitching in when they can to ensure the conference continues to be a welcoming and generative event. And each instantiation of the conference has a different ethos and structure because of the autonomy of the site hosts. We write this "Where We Are" as the current CFSHRC President (Richards) and Vice President (Beemer), the latter who happens to also serve as the upcoming site host for FemRhets 2025 at the University of New Hampshire (UNH), thus offering a glimpse into how the organization as well as hosts see the "future of conferencing" for our fields.

New site hosts for each conference means that the CFSHRC needs to provide more sustainable support for the volunteer site organizers. To this end, the CFSHRC created a standing committee, "Conference Planning Committee" (CPC), to provide sustainable structures and practices, as well as an archive, that allows site hosts to be nimble while responsive to the CFSHRC's mission. For example, the CPC continues to refine and restructure its call for hosts. A carefully constructed call-for-site-hosts releases several years before the conference, allowing the CFSHRC to vet applicants based on evolving and improving criteria. During our hiatus in 2021, the Coalition took the opportunity to honestly confront the CFSHRC's history of centering whiteness: specifically, the CPC re-imagined anti-racist and more inclusive guidelines for site hosts that are attentive to barriers for BIPOC, disabled, and/or LGBTQIA+ members. We now explicitly call for potential hosts to articulate how they would (non-exhaustive)

- "front themes of antiracist activism and center the work of feminists of color . . .
- identify ways to amplify the voices of disabled scholars and emerging scholars
- articulate possibilities for antiracist, inclusive conferencing practices through conference planning, featured events, conference themes, and programming
- address how conference organizers will engage the complexity of their conference location . . .
- describe strategies to ensure accessibility for all conference participants
- discuss steps to promote affordability . . ." ("2027 Call for Site Hosts")

Once the site host has been selected and approved by the Advisory Board, the CFSHRC provides some financial and advisory support of FemRhets but leaves the final programming decision to the site hosts. This decision-making structure allows each host team to make locally-informed decisions while cognizant of the CFSHRC's mission to encourage "inquiry in feminist histories, theories, and pedagogies of rhetoric and composition. As a network of diverse teachers and scholars, the Coalition promotes intersectionality, collaboration, and communication" ("Mission"). This combination of a sustainable structure, through a sponsoring organization, and nimble evolution, through a locally-informed site host, might be one future for conferencing.

After 2020, the CFSHRC took steps to implement practices that would share labor beyond the host institution and craft sustainable documents that could be used, updated, and implemented for each iteration of FemRhets. Most institutional site hosts receive little to no compensation or support from their home institutions to organize FemRhets. Therefore, lightening the workload of the host increases the likelihood that others will volunteer as hosts. As noted earlier, the CPC provides consistency as the conference host changes. This committee handles issues like crafting a call for site hosts, vetting those proposals, providing the structural support of website hosting, proposal submission, proposal reader recruitment and training, and brings a wealth of knowledge and experience from previous conference hosts.

Moreover, after each conference, the CPC archives the good work of organizers, allowing for continuing best practices moving forward. Documents like the conference accessibility guide can be updated and used as a basis for the next iteration. To ensure that all site hosts foreground anti-racist practices, the CPC developed and implemented a training video for anti-racist proposal reviewing that all site hosts share with external proposal reviewers. This video pairs with the collaboratively written and widely-circulated "Anti-Racist Scholarly Reviewing Practices" from 2021. This training video is archived and edited so that it isn't site-specific; we have again offered it to all reviewers for our 2025 conference. We have truly benefited from the generous contributions of our members that have served on these committees providing institutional memory and experiential knowledge.

Complementing and extending the CFSHRC's anti-racist proposal review practices, the 2023 FemRhets at Spelman College hosted restorative circles "as one part of the constructive reckonings that the conference organizers hope[d] to facilitate," where they invited "all BIPOC attendees to participate in a dedicated restorative circle process during our time together" ("Restorative..."). Professional facilitators led these circles, and feedback from attendees was overwhelmingly positive. FemRhets 2025 will continue this practice and host facilitated restorative circles for BIPOC attendees. The conference hosts at UNH, a predominantly white institution, will also offer a complementary session where white attendees, with the assistance of professional facilitators, can work to address their role in structures that have harmed others and work toward better practices moving forward.

While building upon the thoughtful work of previous conferences, a major issue requiring a nimble structure is the continued erosion of institutional funding and support for conference travel and planning. With continued higher education budgets cuts across the United States, conference funding for scholars from their home institutions has suffered. People simply don't have the budget to travel, and of course this affects our most vulnerable members—our contingent faculty and graduate students—precisely the members that can benefit most from in-person mentoring and networking. Although there are significant cost savings with virtual conferencing options, we still believe that the shared experience of gathering every other year in person is valuable to our members and our field's sustainability. We have kept these rising costs to our members at the forefront of our planning and have committed ourselves to keeping costs down as much as possible.

In order to reduce costs and offer an accessible location, FemRhets 2025 will be held in the summer rather than the traditional fall timeframe. During the school year, UNH cannot provide an ample selection of centrally-located and accessible rooms for conference panels. During the summer, FemRhets can practically take over one of the newly renovated, modern, and more accessible buildings at UNH. This year's change to a summer conference also enables UNH to offer very affordable dorm housing options. Dorm housing will likely appeal to our large group of graduate student attendees, as hotel options are limited locally and expensive during tourist season. Switching to the summer, however, means that our members must give up some of their well-deserved time off from teaching, and this is a risky endeavor. It's additionally risky considering that many institutions begin their fiscal years on July 1, which makes securing travel funding more onerous if not completely impractical for those who have travel funding.

Feedback gathered from previous conferences suggested that four days was a long time to be away at an academic conference. In consultation with the CPC, the UNH hosts reduced the in-person meeting time to three days. With a shortened meeting time, UNH plans to provide food during each day to keep the overall cost of attendance low and have better audience turnout for panels.

Still, this nimble sustainability we're using for FemRhets 2025 doesn't address the ongoing challenges of gathering for in-person conferences. We haven't reckoned with the environmental and public health impacts of people traveling great distances; using exceptional resources; and sharing air, food, water, and shelter. Many members enjoy gathering in-person because we can hug, laugh, and cry together in a way that helps sustain us in our lives, and yet we cannot deny the environmental and public health impacts of such events. Environmental studies and disability justice scholars have been speaking and writing about these harms for over a decade (Leochico et al; Manivannan). The future of conferencing must earnestly engage in these critiques about environmental impact and ableism.

Moreover, FemRhets and the CFSHRC haven't yet come up with a way to address the anti-diversity, equity, and inclusion (DEI) legislation that deems conferences with gender, race, and sexuality—like FemRhets—in the title can't be funded by state institutions. There are countless examples of this type of legislation. The laws are evolving and changing, making it difficult to cite one specific instance. That said, *The Chronicle of Higher Education* attempts to track institutions that are "dismantling of diversity, equity, and inclusion efforts" (Gretzinger et al). At the time of writing (January 2025), there have been 215 campuses in 32 states facing anti-DEI legislation. Future FemRhets might take place in a city center, conference center, or hotel to avoid these laws, but such shifts increase the cost burden.

In line with anti-DEI legislation regarding higher education, we must also grapple with how this oppressive and damaging legislation moves beyond the confines of campuses, impacting communities and states that put trans, queer, BIPOC, and/or disabled members at additional risk. We've started addressing this issue with our CFP for site hosts applications, asking them to address potential threats and challenges. However, a more sustained and cross-conference conversation must take place, so that this burden doesn't continue to prevent entire communities of colleagues from participating. We see this "Where We Are" section of *Composition Studies* as an urgent exigence for continued conversations.

Some see these issues as mandating a move to fully digital or virtual conferences. Virtual conferences may be the future of conferencing and sharing knowledge, but we are mindful that virtual doesn't necessarily mean accessible. In Spring 2024, the CFSHRC hosted a powerful webinar, "Scaling Collective Access: From Your Presentation to Our Field" by Ada Hubrig, who reminded attendees to make accessibility changes but that there is no singular, universal "accessible for everyone" format. Using Hubrig's work, we wonder about continuing to evolve the format of FemRhets into different formats like: small regional meet ups in lieu of a centralized conference with Zoom keynote events; "working conferences" where people propose co-working on projects; write-ins and teach-ins; fully virtual conferences every few years or in rotation with in-person conferences, etc. We hope the future of conferences "scales access" by imaging practices that don't continually foreground ableism and a single manner of engagement.

Finally, as busy teacher-scholars ourselves, we know that leading smaller orgs and conferences on a volunteer basis, like our own, is just not feasible for many people. Our home institutions don't provide financial or time support for the work we do for the CFSHRC and FemRhets, and this is the case for all of the volunteer labor that we rely upon, and are so grateful to have, to continue this work. This service model means that only those of us who have private support and privileges (extended community/family, personal finance, health status, housing, etc) can lead in this manner. This isn't equitable nor accessible.

We offer this scant history and insight to our current conference organizing and planning, in hopes that it makes transparent some behind the scenes work we do to offer FemRhets and earnestly names some of the shortcomings we still see in our own work. Octavia Butler once wrote that "the very act of trying to look ahead and discern possibilities and offer warnings is in itself an act of hope" (165). We offer our critiques of our own practices—not as a censure of past conferences and shortcomings—but as a way to help us all look forward and practice hope.

Note

1. Author names are listed in alphabetical order to convey shared first-author roles in composing this piece.

Works Cited

"2027 Call for Site Hosts." *Coalition of Feminist Scholars in the History of Rhetoric and Composition.* cfshrc.org/cfp-for-site-hosts-2027-and-2029/. Accessed 5 Feb. 2025.

"Anti-Racist Scholarly Reviewing Practices: A Heuristic for Editors, Reviewers, and Authors." 2021, tinyurl.com/reviewheuristic.

Butler, Octavia E. "A Few Rules for Predicting the Future." *Essence*, May 2000, pp. 165–66, 264.

Gilligan, Carol. *In a Different Voice: Psychological Theory and Women's Development.* Harvard UP, 1982.

Gretzinger, Erin, Maggie Hicks, Crista Dutton, and Jasper Smith. "Tracking Higher Ed's Dismantling of DEI." *Chronicle of Higher Education,* 20 Dec. 2024, www.chronicle.com/article/tracking-higher-eds-dismantling-of-dei. Accessed 24 Jan. 2025.

Hassel, Holly. "Afterward: People Always Clap for the Wrong Things, Or, Labor, Time, and Writing Have Always Been a Feminist Issue." *Recollections for an Uncommon Time: 4C20 Documentarian Tales*, edited by Julie Lindquist, Bree Straayer, and Bump Halbritter. WAC Clearinghouse, 2023, pp. 235–42.

Hubrig, Ada. "Scaling Collective Access: From Your Presentation to Our Field." *Cheryl Glenn Advancing the Agenda Webinar,* 15 Mar. 2024, cfshrc.org/cheryl-glenn-webinar-series-for-advancing-the-agenda-dr-ada-hubrig-scaling-collective-access-from-your-presentation-to-our-field-friday-march-15/.

Hubrig, Ada, and Ruth Osorio, editors. "Symposium: Enacting a Culture of Access in Our Conference Spaces." *College Composition & Communication*, Vol. 72, no. 1, 2020, pp. 87–117.

Kynard, Carmen. "Trigger Warning: This Post is about Academia and Its "Professional" Conferencing." *Carmenkynard.org*, Apr. 12, 2016, carmenkynard.org/professional-conferencing/.

Leochico, Carl Froilan, Melina Logoni DiGiuso, and Ramino Mitre. "Impact of Scientific Conferences on Climate Change and How to Make Them Eco-friendly and Inclusive: A Scoping Review." *Journal of Climate Change and Health*, vol. 4, 2021, 1–9.

"Mission." *Coalition of Feminist Scholars in the History of Rhetoric and Composition*, cfshrc.org/about-us/#mission. Accessed 24 Jan. 2025.

Manivannan, Vyshali. "The Successful Text is Not Always the One That Murders Me to Protect You." *Bodies of Knowledge: Embodied Rhetorics in Theory and Practice*, edited by A. Abby Knoblauch and Marie E. Moeller, Utah State UP, 2022, pp. 183–98.

"Restorative Circles: A 3-part Series for BIPOC Attendees by Honeycomb Justice." *Feminisms and Rhetorics 2023*, femrhet2023.cfshrc.org/special-events/249-2/. Accessed 24 Jan. 2025.

Cristy Beemer is Vice President of the CFSHRC (2024–2026) and associate professor of English at the University of New Hampshire. Her research focuses on feminist rhetoric in classical, early modern, and contemporary contexts. She has published articles in *Peitho, Rhetoric Review, and Teaching English at a Two-Year College,* among others. She is currently working on her book project, *It Ain't Pretty in Pink: Gen X and the Online Breast Cancer Community.* This work is a deeply personal exploration of a unique rhetorical space where first-hand accounts of cancer treatment form an instructive avenue of inquiry in medical care and create a virtual, global community of women writers contributing to wellness through shared experience, language, support, advice, and humor.

Rebecca S. Richards is President of the CFSHRC (2024–2026) and associate professor of English at the University of Massachusetts Lowell. Her research and teaching explore the intersections of rhetoric, gender, sexuality, and media. Her first book, *Transnational Feminist Rhetorics and Gendered Leadership in Global Politics* (Lexington Books 2015) analyzes how gendered concepts circulate among women who have been world leaders. Her most recent book, *Not Playing Around: Feminist and Queer Rhetorics in Videogames* (Parlor Press 2024) examines how playing videogames has a resistant rhetorical impact that allows for nuanced engagement with gender and sexuality. Her work also appears in journals like *Feminist Formations, Feminist Teacher,* and *Kairos,* as well as in edited collections like *The Routledge Handbook of Contemporary Feminist Rhetoric* and *Hillary Rodham Clinton and the 2016 Election.*

Reimagining Academic Conferences and Professional Volunteerism in a World of Academic Precarity

Genie Nicole Giaimo

I walk into the lobby of a nondescript megahotel in Chicago for the Modern Language Association (MLA), the flagship conference in my field. Around me, graduate students and adjuncts—harried as I am—scurry around the periphery of the room running between conference sessions, job interviews, and meetings. They check their folders, consult the hotel map, adjust their black suits, silent and a little grim.

In the center of the lobby sit the elicit few—senior professors—sipping cocktails and glasses of wine, laughing loudly with one another. They are not hurried. They are neither silent nor grim. They are positionally where they are figuratively: at the center, commanding the room.

This illustration of spatial layout and affective difference between academic workers is useful for imagining how the future of academic conferences might function in a profession with an ever-shrinking set of tenure stream faculty and a growing number of contingent workers. There is still a center and a periphery but over time these groups have become even more disproportionate and out of balance. The elect are few; the aspiring, many. Conferences, then, are the freighted space of the economic marketplace. Prestige (Wapman et al.), not meritocracy, networking, or any of the other outcomes that conferences promise, is the main mitigating factor in who gets a tenure track position. Yet, year in and year out, many of us still attend increasingly expensive conferences, or engage in academic volunteerism for our professional organizations, for varied reasons, notably among them the hope of the brass ring of tenure. How then, as a profession, might we rethink the future not only of conferences but of our professional organizations as our profession's marketplace dramatically shifts around us?

In the early days of my career, conferences represented a kind of homage or tithing I had to pay. I attended these events out of obligation rather than excitement or personal desire. However, after graduate school, I entered the field of rhetoric and composition and became part of the writing center and writing studies communities. And it was in the affiliate associations of International Writing Centers Association (IWCA) like Northeast Writing Centers Association (NEWCA) and East Central Writing Centers Association (ECWCA) that I found my people. Here, there weren't hotel bars with tenured professors holding court while everyone scurried around them. Instead, like marching band competition, mixed groups of peer and graduate tutors, as well as administrators, descended on conferences as teams. Here was *Land Grant University A* or *Liberal Arts College B*. They didn't wear uniforms or matching colors, but they projected pride in their centers and shared traditions and practices. The community and the pride were far more apparent at these conferences. The class divisions between workers were less prominent, though these material fault lines continued to exist.

Before I could afford IWCA, I began attending regional conferences in 2014. I chaired the ECWCA conference in 2018. I co-chaired the IWCA Collaborative (2019–2021) and the IWCA Summer Institute (2022). I was NEWCA Co-President (2021–2022). For most of this work, I was not compensated. For some (IWCA SI and NEWCA), I was given an honorarium that came out to about $15 an hour for my work.

Times have changed in the decade since I received my PhD. MLA is now trying to reckon with both its large adjunct contingent and writing instructor contingent. The profession has changed in significant ways over the last 20 years that make alt-ac careers far more prominent even at such flagship conferences. And since COVID-19, conferences like Conference on College Composition and Communication (CCCC) and IWCA are offering virtual options to members. The conference as a signifier, however, still holds even if the conditions under which conferences are hosted has dramatically changed over the past several years.

As writing center conferences have become more professionalized over the last few decades, the responsibilities and job duties related to conference organizing have also grown (like all paid and unpaid work under the neoliberal model of higher education, the cut costs from the top produce additional labor for those who are left holding the organizational pieces at the bottom of the organizational chart). Before I entered the profession, it seemed common for universities to host these events which cut down on cost immensely. But by the time that I started attending IWCA, they were hosted in megahotels in mid-sized cities. The contracts, which included catering, AV, Wi-Fi, and room blocks, cost hundreds of thousands of dollars. If conferences didn't generate enough revenue from registration fees the association would be on the hook for paying for the unrealized costs. Our associations, then, can often be one bad conference away from bankruptcy.

Since 2020, many academic associations have rethought their conference structure. Forced online for many events by COVID-19, IWCA rearranged itself into a semi-annual in-person conference. In the off-years, it holds an online conference, which just happened in 2024. The IWCA affiliates have mostly followed suit, switching between in-person and online conference formats every other year.

Prior to these changes, however, there was a reckoning that COVID-19 brought about where affiliates and IWCA, alike, grappled with what our associations do and what we provide. As President of NEWCA during CO-VID-19, I continuously asked whether affiliates should be conference-focused organizations. The labor and cost of a signature event prevents small grassroots organizations from taking on anything additional, like in-region assessment, advocacy work, or mutual aid support for struggling centers and colleagues.

NEWCA, however, did originally form to run an annual conference; this was written into the original mission and bylaws. Yet, as President I argued that we had grown beyond this mission and needed to look towards other ways of supporting our regional needs and our profession because of the material realities in which so many of our colleagues labor. The center and the periphery image at MLA has stayed with me all these years later. I wanted to bring contingent workers and non-tenure track workers into our organization and on more equal footing.

The pandemic taught us that academic volunteerism and conferencing—among many other things like the stability of the university—were not only precarious but were being held together by free and unrecognized labor. Here, the conference became a metaphor for all that heavy service lifting people in writing center work perform year in and year out with little recognition and no compensation. To say I was sick of doing this work is an understatement, especially at a time of worldwide crisis. So, instead, we offered a series of free workshops on labor hosted by compensated outsider speakers. These events were very well attended, and they provided a novel take on the conference structure. Instead of a fee-based event, we offered it freely to writing center practitioners. Instead of asking speakers to simply share their intellectual ideas and labor, we paid for it.

While extremely productive, the money we used for the NEWCA speaker series came from prior conference fees. This, then, is the challenge of offering free programming and support to the profession—the labor costs do not simply go away, they are transferred from a conference committee or conference organizers to a speaker series committee or something similar . . .

How then, as a profession, might we rethink the future not only of conferences but of our professional organizations?

In addition to moving away from a focus on an annual conference, might we consider fairly supporting the work of those who take on leadership roles in our organizations? Could better funded writing centers contribute a membership fee to our organizations that covers the costs of its services for underfunded centers? Or, could better funded centers and others put money into a stable full-time position, such as a members' liaison position, that conducts outreach, engages in events planning, and raises money through grants and other initiatives? Our organizations could also reimagine their work centralizing not around a conference or signature annual event, but activities like lobbying, accreditation, and activism.

Our professional organizations are money-making entities, despite their nonprofit status, grown on volunteer and free labor. And while conferences are one major way in which the coffers of our associations are sustained, there are other ways that nonprofits support their missions. The labor that goes into creating a conference is immense—it is a full-time job that many other disciplines either outsource to event planning companies or pay someone full time to arrange. Yet, the regionals, like NEWCA or ECWCA, as well as IWCA usually recruit people to do this work for free. Our institutions offer varying levels of support. Mine offered next to nothing in terms of administrative or financial support. Some institutions might give people course releases or additional compensation to run such events, but I imagine most were in a similar position to me—doing this work as part of my day-to-day job duties or working well into evenings and on weekends to carry it out.

Such concerns don't typically matter to the average conference participant, but for organizers and leaders, these kinds of monetary issues keep us up at night. When I organized ECWCA, I struggled to find a hotel big enough to fit 200 guests that was also close enough to campus. Driving along Olentangy Road, I saw a half-built hotel that I thought could suit our needs. I walked through the site wearing a hard-hat and booked the space with a hope and a prayer that it would be ready by the spring conference.

So many things could have gone wrong, but we needed the space and our university could not provide the housing or the large venues. Planning conferences can often feel like working with businesses regardless of choosing a hotel venue or a university venue because these institutions are not all that different. They both own real estate. They both rent out space. They both book up over a year in advance. They both charge a lot of money.

It is in these monetary challenges that, I think, the futures of conferences lay. And when I write about monetary challenges, I do not only mean honoring a conference contract or making sure hotel rooms book. I also mean the labor costs of such endeavors and the ways in which higher education has been contracting over the last several decades. The upstart, grassroots nature of many early writing center conferences has given way to more corporatized conferences which include, at times, paying for the very thing that universities and colleges used to provide for free, which is access to their on-campus facilities, or relying on third party vendors that offer incredibly expensive corporate-style venues. Yet we still work as if we are grassroots organizations—rolling up our sleeves and doing second or even third jobs for free.

I am unsure that higher education will be able to sustain the cost of more expensive professionalized conferences given that such contracts can wipe out an association's funding if the conference isn't well attended for one reason or another. I also know that it can be a struggle to secure conference hosts because of the rising precarity of people in our field—the majority of whom do not hold tenure stream positions—and the high levels of uncompensated labor associated with such work.

And, even now, there are the additional hidden costs of in-person academic conferences. For those of us who are disabled or who are caretakers or who struggle with travel and other anxiety, in-person conferences are either entirely prohibitive or immensely draining. Many of us struggle to keep pace with 12-hour days, multiple time-zone travel, and week-long commitments. Those of us with health concerns or with immunocompromised family members face additional risks to in-person events as COVID-19 and other respiratory diseases circulate in high numbers throughout the year.

This is what COVID-19, my stint at MLA, and all my service work has made me realize: academic conferences are experienced very differently from those in the center and those on the periphery. For those of us in precarious positions, or with health concerns or caretaking responsibilities, conferences can be financially and physically burdensome and time-prohibitive to attend. For those of us on the tenure track, who are not disabled, who are not caretakers, conferences can be an excellent break from the quotidian. And, of course, these boundaries are porous. We can shift between the center and the periphery several times, even annually, depending on what is going on in our lives and in our careers.

IWCA's move to a semi-annual online conference, or CCCC's move to offering participants the option to present online, speaks to the material realities of our profession. Some of us simply cannot afford—one way or another—to "get away" and conference for four to six days. The costs are too high, the benefits perhaps not high enough.

In many ways, conferences reflect the job market and lines of our members. Are we simply organizations that hold conferences or do we provide other services and support to our community? Are our organizations built to stand-in for the lack of professionalizing elsewhere in our field? I hope our academic organizations will do some soul searching, returning to that grassroots and more inclusive work of the early days alongside fair and more equitable compensation for those who lead us and advocacy for those who cannot.

Work Cited

Wapman, K. Hunter, Sam Zhang, Aaron Clauset, and Daniel B. Larremore. "Quantifying Hierarchy and Dynamics in US Faculty Hiring and Retention." *Nature*, vol. 610, 2022, 120–27.

Genie Nicole Giaimo is associate professor of writing studies and rhetoric and writing center director at Hofstra University. They are the co-editor of *Writing Assessment at Small Liberal Arts Colleges* with Megan O'Neill (2025), the co-author, with Dan Lawson, of *Storying Writing Center Labor for Anti-Capitalist Futures* (2024); the author of *Unwell Writing Centers: Searching for Wellness in Neoliberal Educational Institutions and Beyond* (2023), and the editor of *Wellness and Care in Writing Center Work* (2021). Giaimo is also professional editor of *The Peer Review*, an IWCA sponsored writing center studies journal. Their current research utilizes quantitative models to answer a range of questions about behaviors and practices in and around writing centers and writing programs. Their research has appeared in many peer reviewed journals in the field of rhetoric and composition.

What's the Future for Academic Conferences? What Should Be Their Future?

Kofi J. Adisa and Frankie Condon

Attending and participating in academic conferences has been a staple in Kofi's academic life since undergrad. Frankie attended her first academic conference as a graduate student but remembers well the pressure to get on the program of national conferences, to present well, and to publish articles or chapters built from conference papers. Membership in professional and educational organizations informs our teaching and research interests. Of course, sharing findings, ideas, and theories—not to mention hanging out with colleagues, old friends, and new ones—has made conferencing a delightful experience for both of us as well as for other academics . . . who are able and can afford to travel.

The truth is that whenever we attended a conference, it was because we had the privilege to do so. Not everyone is as fortunate, and some may never get to participate in any kind of conference. Professional development is relegated to whatever any given college or university is willing to spend. Too often, some of our administrators sound like characters from *Games of Thrones*, shouting "winter is coming" even as new administrative positions are created and filled and ground is broken for yet another building and some new pet project is initiated absent much or any consultation with faculty.

When some college or university officials give their States of the Union at the end of the fall or the beginning of the spring, they expect faculty and staff to understand why and how tightening the proverbial belt will benefit the college or university's future. However, some administrators may look at any savings as part of a blooming coffer to be used on yet another consulting firm that will tell them again that they have to make cuts. We believe that college and university leadership teams need to (re)learn the significance of ongoing faculty professional development to the quality of education their institutions are able to offer students.

We also recognize that the fiscal (and political) challenges facing higher education at this historical moment seem like the real thing. We don't know what education will look like a year or three years from now. We're just starting to see students entering college whose middle school years were spent on Zoom. What will teaching and learning look like if there is no U.S. Department of Education? If states can restructure curricula to fit increasingly nationalist, white supremacist, and cis–heteronormative ideology? If school funding shifts away—again—from under-resourced communities to more affluent communities? If the children of poor, working class, and communities of color continue to be increasingly denied educational access and opportunity?

Sounds gloomy, we know. Frankly, we don't know the future at all. What we do know is that when college and university higher-ups see trends or headwinds, having money becomes either the solution or the problem. And when cuts eventually come, they almost always impact those in the most precarious employment and student statuses: adjuncts and non-tenured faculty, graduate students, first generation and working class college attenders, and students of color. But no one is untouched, including full-time, tenured faculty. We have been through hard times before. Frankie attended her first Conference on College Composition and Communication (CCCC) by ridesharing and then sleeping in a hotel many miles from the convention in a room shared by eight other graduate students. Even though Kofi had gone to conferences as a student, he didn't necessarily have all the funding to support those trips. In fact, he was able to present at his first CCCC in 2017 after he received support from the Assistance Fund for Contingent Faculty. To be honest, though, this time feels worse, more gloomy, and the future darker and more uncertain.

The funding available to members from academic and professional organizations isn't limitless, and not all such groups can provide means to offset the costs faculty and graduate students must shoulder to attend a three or four-day conference. Add the conference site, which may be farther from their home institutions, families, and students, and we can see how costly conferences are for tenure-line faculty, still more so for contingent faculty, and particularly for graduate students. Many of us have disabilities that complicate our ability to travel. Many are caregivers, have children, or have aging parents. Many of us have other financial responsibilities within and beyond our families that prevent us from attending large, convention-style conferences.

Even if we omit the fears of what this second term of President Trump might do and be, the problems with how conferences are constructed, marketed, and delivered reinforce existing inequities within various privileged and marginalized communities. Those who cannot afford these conferences and work at institutions where travel funding is limited or non-existent are marginalized from their profession. This is especially true for community college professors whose labor in and outside the classroom is undervalued. It is also particularly true for graduate students. There are wonderful conferences led by and designed for two-year college faculty (TYCA, for example) as well as conferences led by and designed for graduate students. Yet no conference is without cost, and financial constraints are hurting all academic constituents from accessing the kind and quality of professional development that academic conferences provide.

We believe the time has come to radically reimagine academic conferences for *all* professors, regardless of rank or institution type, and for graduate students. We recognize that this reimagining will require that we also reimagine the professional organizations of which we have long been a part and that have so profoundly shaped our working lives. As CCCC officers, we know we must consider our fiscal responsibilities while supporting our vulnerable constituents. However, we cannot be fiscally responsible if we burden our members with travel costs. Likewise, we cannot help our members by merely funding them. As mentioned, funds are not limitless. So, perhaps the future of academic conferences needs to be more creative.

The following suggestions are meant to help us start thinking differently about conferences. We want all of our colleagues to have access and opportunities to learn from one another, to share insights on teaching and learning, and to develop and maintain a strong professional identity. We also want academic organizations to be financially solvent. This is a tricky dance, but here's what we are thinking:

- **Sponsoring conferences:** What would it look like if CCCC or National Council of Teachers of English (NCTE) lent their names to on-campus conferences? What if members of CCCC pitched a day-long conference on their campus or, better yet, collaborated with nearby two-year or four-year colleges to showcase, workshop, and/or present their theories, assignment designs, strategies for inclusion, etc.? So, instead of or in addition to having one large annual gathering, we have a number of smaller gatherings and have participants provide short 30-minute or less videos about a specific topic for the larger audience to view. This idea isn't new. Bedford/ St. Martins Macmillan does something similar, except they have participants create their videos, and then Macmillan posts them after their Writing Program Administrators Workshop. In this situation, Macmillan pays the participants. Now, we're not advocating that, but as an example, this can be done locally with the NCTE or CCCC stamp of approval. No money will be generated for the organization; however, participants who live nearby can still have their professional identity validated in ways that are different from being at an enormous conference.
- **Localized or regional conferencing:** The Two-Year College Association (TYCA), Council for Writing Program Administrators (CWPA), and the International Teaching Learning Cooperative (ITLC) are models of smaller regional conferences. Though travel costs still impact participants, smaller conferences may reach more people closer to the venue than a more prominent annual convention.

- **Pop-up Conferencing:** Academic organizations might sponsor these pop-ups to generate interest in a particular idea, theory, approach to teaching and learning, or trend impacting student engagement. Like the pop-up shops from the late 1990s to the early aughts, participants can utilize the space available, i.e., their campuses. Academic organizations could market these pop-ups to inspire others to do similarly for their educational community. These pop-ups could bring in new members to the organization, especially faculty who want to learn from other peers but haven't the time or money to travel.
- **Freestanding Conferencing:** Using YouTube, Substack, Bluesky, or other free-ish platforms, participants can invite and post the conversations for an audience's consumption.

Some or all of these suggestions may have hidden costs for professional academic organizations. Clearly, organizations have to be fiscally nimble while supporting their members, especially those in contingency positions where funding for conference registration, travel, and lodging is limited or unavailable for them. Even those of us in ranked positions may find challenges to securing money for conferences. Yet, if organizations take on more of sponsorship role that could enable smaller, focused conferences in particular regions or localities where community college and university faculty can collaborate on issues and topics pertinent to their community and their specific student population, there might be a chance to remix, reimagine what professional academic conferences can look like. Though we don't know what the future will bring to national organizations like NCTE, CCCC, or Modern Languages Association (MLA), we must start thinking differently about conferences so they do not further reinforce privileges and marginalizations of our colleagues and friends.

Kofi J. Adisa is associate professor of English at Howard Community College and the associate chair to CCCC. His fiction has appeared in *The Mandala Journal*. His journalism has appeared in *The Washington Post* under J. A. Kelly. He is a contributing member of MLA/CCCC AI Task Force.

Frankie Condon is associate professor in the Department of English language and literature at the University of Waterloo. Her books include *CounterStories from the Writing Center*; *I Hope I Join the Band*; *Performing Anti-Racist Pedagogy in Rhetoric, Writing, and Communication*; and *The Everyday Writing Center*. She is the recipient of the Federation of Students Excellence in Undergraduate Teaching Award (Ontario Undergraduate Student Alliance) and the Outstanding Performance Award (for excellence in teaching and scholarship) from the University of Waterloo.

Cohesion, Community, and Belonging: The Emergence of the TYCA National Conference as an Open-Access Advocacy Space

Joanne Baird Giordano and Charissa Che

Introduction: Origins of the TYCA National Conference

The Two-Year College English Association (TYCA) was formally established as an association of the National Council of Teachers of English in 1996 (Andelora "Professionalization"). However, the idea of a national conference for two-year college faculty originated in 1965 when NCTE began to sponsor conferences for TYCA regional organizations (Andelora, Giordano, and Smith). Because community college instructors often have limited travel funding, TYCA members met for more than half a century in smaller regional conferences instead of holding a national gathering (McPherson). Regional conferences provided participants with professional development centered on the unique challenges of community college teaching. Although some regions offered publications, newsletters, and other member benefits, the main function of TYCA regions before the COVID-19 pandemic was to hold in-person professional development conferences. At the national level, TYCA served as an organization that brought together representatives from regional groups to create a structure for supporting members, provide advocacy for two-year college faculty within NCTE and CCCC, generate guidelines (e.g., Calhoon-Dillahunt et al.; Madden; Klausman et al.) and initiate research on important issues for open-access literacy educators (e.g., Sullivan; Roberts). TYCA's primary method for disseminating information and engaging in scholarship at the national level was the journal *Teaching English in the Two-Year College.*

The first TYCA National Conference didn't take place until 2019 in connection with the annual CCCC Convention in Pittsburgh. The initial exigency for a national conference was to generate revenue to offset the cost to NCTE for sponsoring TYCA, including staff time and travel for elected national officers to visit regional conferences. The TYCA National Conference helps to pay for conference rooms on the Wednesday before CCCC, but the purpose of the conference has shifted away from cost to creating a way for open-access literacy educators to make connections with peers. TYCA needs a national conference because most other national conferences provide limited or no opportunities for members to engage in conversations about the challenges of teaching-intensive work at community colleges and the complex knowledge and labor required for teaching students who are excluded from institutions with admissions standards. Creating and preparing for the first national conference became an opportunity for TYCA to reexamine the organization and its mission in promoting open-access education and supporting instructors who teach the most widely diverse student populations in higher education.

The 2019 TYCA National Conference Planning Committee, chaired by Giordano, chose the theme "Starting the Conversation: Teaching Scholarship and Activism at Two-Year Colleges" to emphasize that the purpose of the conference (and TYCA itself) is to create a space for teacher-scholars to share best practices and provide practical learning that attendees could apply directly to their professional work. The committee worked with TYCA leaders to create proposal review criteria that deliberately distinguished the TYCA Conference from other English and writing studies conferences (for example, "Contributes to important national conversations about teaching English at two-year colleges or in the first two years" and "Provides attendees with effective strategies for taking action after the conference and/or enhancing their work as teacher-scholars").

The proposal guidelines helped TYCA articulate not only expectations for what the conference might become (a practical learning space for sharing scholarship directly connected to open-access teaching and labor) but also put into writing the evolving nature of TYCA as an organization that was moving toward creating a structure that would connect members at the national level. A national conference became the catalyst for TYCA to move beyond a support structure for regional organizations to a more fully developed organization with opportunities for members to engage in committee work and activities beyond the conference, including networks (special interest groups), monthly seminars, and virtual gatherings. The birth of the TYCA National Conference demonstrates that conferences can become a sustaining force within organizations even while funding sources and professional realities are shifting in ways that impact an organization's approach to serving its members.

Locating Ourselves Online: Reinvention and Recovery at the 2022 TYCA National Conference

Suffice it to say, a lot changed between the 2019 inaugural and the 2022 TYCA National conferences. The 2020 conference became a set of asynchronous online presentations. The effects of the COVID-19 pandemic, a contentious presidential election, and accelerating racial violence laid bare the extent to which our marginalized and underserved student populations were disproportionately affected. Many two-year college faculty found themselves learning how to teach online for the first time, while developing culturally-inclusive pedagogies that accounted for their students' lived experiences.

Themed "Recovery and Reinvention in our Profession: Emerging from a Recent Time of Crisis," the 2022 TYCA National Conference picked up where the previous year left off: In 2021, attendees considered how they have adjusted their teaching at the two-year college amid a time of exceptional social and political tumult. This installation looked ahead—at what lessons we can recover from this time, and what previously overlooked perspectives we can bring to the fore of our teaching of our diverse student bodies. "What is the significance of non-dominant narratives—and what happens when, after centuries of learning about the same events, through the same perspectives, the microphone is flipped around?" asked Conference Chair Charissa Che in her opening talk. "If this mic is passed, between teacher and teacher, teacher and student, and student and student, could we witness the construction of a new paradigm in higher education?" (Che 89).

Presentations looked at how we can integrate social justice conversations in the classroom ("Teaching Students to Enter Social Justice Conversations"; "Revisiting literature amid social tensions"); others considered students' mental and emotional well-being ("Creating Recovery: Leveraging Creativity to Address Non-Cognitive Issues"; "Writing as the Safe Space: Discussing the Trauma Spectrum and Our Classroom's Culture for Two-Year Colleges"); yet others urged attendees to expand what "writing instruction" can look like in composition's multimodal and digital turn ("Adapting innovative teaching strategies in a post-pandemic world"; "Undoing Traditional Practice: Revising Pedagogy for Post-Crisis Teaching"; "Transitioning to Online Learning: Experimenting with Digital Tools to Reach Students in a Pandemic").

In the conference's fourth year and as TYCA National's second online conference, attendees took part in the usual conference fare: concurrent panels, special sessions, and poster presentations. Tara Westover, author of the memoir *Educated*, was the keynote. Perhaps due to the affordances of the online space, and the desire for greater community at a time when instructors were speaking to student avatars for hours on end, the conversations that emerged from the sessions were extremely generative, as evidenced by the Closing Session discussion. The future of conferencing (as well as so many aspects of our profession) is trending online, and while it can't quite replace the intimacy of in-person interaction, there is something to be said about the unique affordances of an online conference: attendees can choose which sessions to attend immediately and which to view later; closed captioning and the ability to rewind recordings made following speakers easier; the ability to be off-camera, and the option to interact verbally and via chat welcomed greater participation from attendees who prefer to engage in different ways. As our organization moves forward with future in-person and online opportunities to bring TYC faculty together in conversation and community, we will no doubt continue to observe the affordances and constraints that these modalities pose for our members.

Bridging the "Great Divide": The TYCA Taskforce on Engaging Members with CCCC

When the conference wrapped, the TYCA Taskforce on Engaging Members with CCCC began its work of learning how CCCC can be more supportive of the interests and needs of two-year college faculty. Within professional development contexts, a disconnect between TYC faculty and their colleagues at four-year colleges has long been observed. Jeff Andelora notes in "The Professionalization of Two-Year College English Faculty: 1950–1990" that many TYC faculty feel professionally "tied more closely to their local communities than to the disciplinary communities or professional organizations of their university colleagues" (6). Additionally, geography, heavy teaching loads, and lack of support for professional development have deterred their involvement in TYCA and similar organizations (8). Practical factors aside, TYC faculty described CCCC as "'cold and uninviting'" (14), feeling as though "there was no place for us" (15).

The two-year college community is one of constant collaboration, and in true form, when we sent out a national survey, over 140 two-year college faculty responded. Questions sought to understand TYC faculty's attitudes towards the CCCC convention, the organization's governance, academic publishing, and the CCCC community. The taskforce was heartened by the volume of responses it received yet sobered to find that not much has changed since Andelora's report. Wrote one respondent, "2YC teachers at my institution are, by and large, unconcerned with Cs." Referencing the institutional disconnect, they attributed this lack of concern to "lingering Great Divide sentiments," and the perception that CCCC aligned more with theory than practice (Taskforce 8). Some respondents attributed their lack of engagement to feelings of being judged for not having a PhD, and they were therefore seen by their CCCC colleagues as not being "scholarly" enough. The emotional labor involved in navigating predominantly four-year college spaces was enough to deter some from attending, with one respondent admitting, "Having to justify or prove my intelligence because I'm a prof at a community college is tiresome." In contrast, respondents found a sense of community and camaraderie at their TYCA regional meetings, using words like "home," "welcoming," and "cohesive" to describe their local professional communities. These conferences were easier and less costly to travel to, smaller and felt less intimidating, featured more familiar faces, and felt more relevant to their immediate professional interests.

At the point that the Taskforce's work began, the TYCA National Conference was still in its nascent years, having only had one in-person meeting prior to the pandemic. However, the attendance and participation at our two online conferences and professional development webinar series, "Teaching in Times of Change," gave us a glimpse into how much more participative TYC faculty can be when there are accessible spaces dedicated to TYC faculty concerns that consider their material realities. The move to online conferencing forced many of us to consider factors in our faculty's lives that perhaps should have been in our conference planning all along: the impact of disabilities, family and life obligations, financial challenges, and attendees' overall feelings of dis/comfort within conferencing culture.

As TYCA grows in scope, the need for recognition from, and collaboration with, four-year college faculty becomes paramount in our collective professional development. Hassel and Giordano write, "Our professional organizations and the most privileged groups in writing studies (i.e., those who work at high-status, high-resource institutions) have an intellectual, scholarly, and moral obligation to work toward creating an inclusive profession that fully accounts for the diverse range of teaching and learning experiences in postsecondary writing" (127). TYCA National continues to work with CCCC to build stronger ties among its two- and four-year college faculty, and to have this reflected not just at our respective conference but also in our publications. In establishing a culture of mutual respect and recognition, we see TYCA National as having the potential to broaden how we discuss writing studies, mobilize diverse student literacies, and develop inclusive classroom pedagogies.

TYCA Today: Post-Pandemic Challenges and Affordances

In the aftermath of the pandemic, the experiences of TYCA leaders at the regional and national levels illustrate both the challenges of maintaining sustainable organizations in the absence of in-person conferences and the benefits of reimagining participation in professional organizations. The TYCA National Conference returned to a 2023 in-person gathering held in connection with CCCC in Chicago. However, some of the TYCA regionals are still struggling to rebuild their organizations after losing funding through cancelled conferences because regional revenue comes primarily from conference fees. For example, TYCA Southeast (Colorado, New Mexico, Texas, Oklahoma, Arkansas, and Louisiana) has moved to a virtual format for the foreseeable future, which creates challenges for organizing a regional community of educators but also widens the pool of potential participants. During the pandemic, the Pacific Coast region (California) disappeared as an organization, and TYCA is in the process of joining it with neighboring states after pandemic disruptions made it difficult for TYCA West (Arizona, Hawaii, Southern Idaho, and Utah) to hold elections. Bringing those two regions together, preventing the disappearance of TYCA at a regional level in the West, and organizing a virtual conference to launch the new region requires support from the national TYCA Executive Committee. TYCA's work with regions shows that the absence of a conference could potentially mean that an organization will no longer exist.

The move to an online national conference and some regional conferences helped English studies faculty increase awareness of TYCA and the benefits that it offers members of NCTE. Graduate students and faculty at teaching-intensive institutions are increasingly participating in the conference, TYCA committees, and other events. TYCA permanent committees and taskforces now have more diversity in their memberships, and faculty who aren't part of regional organizations are now identifying TYCA as a group that helps create a sense of belonging for them within NCTE. TYCA has more constraints than most organizations in organizing virtual events outside of the conference because all of its activities at the national level are sponsored by NCTE and require staff support. However, the regions have more autonomy in organizing virtual events (similar to the flexibility of special interest groups within CCCC), and some of them are moving toward offering more virtual events with invitations sent out nationally to other community college faculty through the TYCA listserv.

The story of the TYCA National Conference shows that conferences have a crucial role in providing a sense of community and creating sustainability for professional organizations. The story of TYCA regional conferences provides a perhaps more important lesson about the role that conferences play in sustaining organizations. For sixty years, TYCA regional conferences have provided professional development for faculty from underfunded two-year colleges, and they continue to serve an important role in bringing people together around issues of open-access education, even in the era of a national conference and virtual gatherings. Instructors who can't afford to attend a national conference can make connections through regional meetings that are often within driving distance of their campuses. They have opportunities to serve in and belong to a smaller organization within TYCA and NCTE, which leads to small-scale participation in service work and professional learning that sometimes becomes the starting point for national service. The TYCA regional and national conferences create a sense of belonging to a community of teacher-scholars for writing instructors and other literacy educators who often feel marginalized and excluded within larger professional organizations.

Works Cited

Andelora, Jeffrey. "Forging a National Identity: TYCA and the Two-Year College Teacher-Scholar." *Teaching English in the Two-Year College*, vol. 35, 2008, pp. 350–62.

—. "The Professionalization of Two-Year College English Faculty: 1950–1990." *Teaching English in the Two-Year College*, vol. 35, no. 1, 2007, pp. 6–19.

—, Joanne Baird Giordano, and Cheryl Hogue Smith. "Starting the Conversation: The Origin, Execution, and Future of TYCA's First National Conference." *Teaching English in the Two-Year College*, vol. 47, no. 1, 2019, pp. 8–17.

Calhoon-Dillahunt, Carolyn, Darin L. Jensen, Sarah Z. Johnson, Howard Tinberg, and Christie Toth. "TYCA Guidelines for Preparing Teachers of English in the Two-Year College." *College English*, vol. 79, no. 6, 2017, pp. 550–60.

Che, Charissa. "Feature: To Tell and to Teach What Is Rightfully Relevant: TYCA 2022 National Conference Chair's Opening Talk." *Teaching English in the Two-Year College*, vol. 50, no. 1, 2022, pp. 88–91.

Che, Charissa, Sarah Z. Johnson, Jamey Gallagher, Erin Doran, Jessica Kubiak, Taija Noel, and Sharon Mitchler. "Taskforce on Engaging TYC Faculty in CCCC: Final Report with Extended Rationales." 2023.

Frank Madden, John Lovas, Susan Miller, Mark Reynolds, Alabama Peter Sotiriou, Howard Tinberg, and Marilyn Valentino. *Research and Scholarship in the Two-Year College*. TYCA, 2010.

Hassel, Holly, and Joanne Baird Giordano. "Occupy Writing Studies: Rethinking College Composition for the Needs of the Teaching Majority." *College Composition and Communication*, vol. 65, no. 1, 2013 117–39.

Klausman, Jeffrey, Judith Angona, Holly Pappas, and Shane Wilson. "Characteristics of the Highly Effective Two-Year College Instructor in English." TYCA, 2012.

McPherson, Elisabeth. "Remembering, Regretting, and Rejoicing: A History of the Two-Year Regionals." *College Composition and Communication*, vol. 41, no. 2, 1990, pp. 137–50.

Roberts, Leslie. "An Analysis of the National TYCA Research Initiative Survey Section IV: Writing Across the Curriculum and Writing Centers in Two-Year College English Programs." *Teaching English in the Two-Year College*, vol. 36, no. 2, 2008, pp. 138–152.

Sullivan, Patrick. "An Analysis of the National TYCA Research Initiative Survey, Section II: Assessment Practices in Two-Year College English Programs." *Teaching English in the Two-Year College*, vol. 36, no. 7, 2008, pp. 7–26.

Joanne Baird Giordano is associate professor of English, linguistics, and writing studies at Salt Lake Community College. She chairs the Two-Year College English Association. She is a co-author of *Reaching All Writers: A Pedagogical Guide for Evolving College Writing Classrooms* and *A Faculty Guidebook for Effective Shared Governance and Service in Higher Education*.

Charissa Che is assistant professor of English at John Jay College of Criminal Justice, CUNY. She is associate editor of the *Journal of Basic Writing*, associate chair of the Two-Year College Association, and book review editor of *Teaching English at the Two-Year College*. She is the incoming co-editor of *TETYC*.

Living Our Principles: Designing an Accessible and Inclusive Virtual Conference

Theresa Evans, Kevin E. DePew, Amy Cicchino, and Cat Mahaffey

Much like online classes and remote work, many believe virtual conferences are poor imitations of "the real thing," and conversations about these virtual environments often begin and end with their limitations or absences. But as an organization whose work focuses on effective online interaction, the Global Society of Online Literacy Educators (GSOLE) has designed its virtual conference to be a digitally engaging experience. Founded in 2016, GSOLE supports and models digital online collaborations across a global community through synchronous/asynchronous interactions and a robust website (gsole.org/) that serves as our virtual headquarters. We take the "Global" part of our name seriously and have strategized to schedule meetings and events, including our annual virtual conference, so that members located in Africa, Australia, Europe, and the Americas can engage and contribute their voices to conversations around online literacy instruction (OLI). In the sections that follow, we further discuss how global participation and other aspects of access and accessibility are considered in conference planning.

First held in 2018, the GSOLE virtual conference is delivered by a volunteer conference committee led by two co-chairs, one of which is the Vice President. While considered small, with an average of around 140 attendees, the value of this event is its ability to recruit new members, offer a personable gathering space for those who can't or don't want to travel to onsite conferences, and overcome digital/online barriers like screen fatigue, lagging connectivity, and accessibility. Virtual presentations include synchronous and asynchronous offerings. In February 2025, GSOLE hosted its eighth conference—eight years of successfully delivering a completely virtual conference hosted by a completely virtual organization. While we do not claim to have fully addressed all challenges, we can say that our conference serves as a model, and we do believe that access to high-quality virtual professional development for underrepresented and underserved administrators, teachers, and tutors should become more common across writing studies.

Accessibility and Access as Conference Goals

GSOLE is guided by its OLI Principles and Tenets, the first of which is "to make OLI universally accessible and inclusive" ("Online Literacy Instruction Principles and Tenets"). While the work is never done, this principle serves as a heuristic for conference decisions. With regards to the conference, accessibility and access are approached from two perspectives: One is to consider the accessibility of virtual conference materials, presentation sessions, and engagement, so all GSOLE members can enter and engage with the virtual conference. The second perspective, the one that relates most directly to the anti-racist initiatives proposed by Genie Nicole Giamo, Nicole I. Caswell, Marilee Brooks-Gillies, Elise Dixon, and Wonderful Faison, is access to the conference event that affirms for GSOLE members a sense of safety and belonging—regardless of funding, rank, background, or professional status or experience. This definition reminds us access is "communal, fluid, and transformative" and works to "dismantl[e] and rebuil[d] exclusionary" practices and spaces (Hubrig and Osorio 91). In the sections below, we want to explain how we enact these goals in GSOLE's conference planning and implementation.

Accessibility

GSOLE defines accessibility in ways that shape who is able to participate in an event. Before we consider the accessibility of virtual spaces once a participant *arrives* at a conference event, we have to get them there. Travel expenses, registration fees, and membership fees have become increasingly expensive, while expense budgets are shrinking; however, conference costs have always been prohibitively expensive for the most precarious members, particularly non-tenure-track and contingent instructors and instructors at two-year colleges and other teaching-focused institutions. The intellectual cost to writing studies is profound if we consider all the voices lost and knowledge-making ignored. Holly Hassel asks, "what would it mean to make space for—virtual or otherwise—the work of instructors whose primary activity is talking with, writing with, and reading work by the first-year student writers whose labor props up the entire field of writing and rhetoric" (241). GSOLE is actively working to answer that question with a virtual conference that keeps costs down so that more voices can be heard, expanding that reach beyond first-year writing to include literacy educators from a range of disciplines in K–12 and higher education. The GSOLE conference registration fee is $10–$20 for members (depending on their rank as full-time or contingent/student/ emeritus professionals) with membership costs ranging from $20–$50 annually. Our Inclusion, Diversity, Equity, and Accessibility (IDEA) committee offers support for professionals unable to pay conference or membership fees as IDEA funding allows.

GSOLE can keep conference costs down because its executive board and virtual conference are volunteer-run, providing a welcome option for those who tend to be excluded from more expensive professional organizations and on-site conferences. Main expenses in running the conference include membership management software, website hosting, and a videoconferencing account used for all virtual events GSOLE hosts, including its meetings. GSOLE needs these services to manage day-to-day operations, so, in reality, the conference makes it possible for us to generate the income to keep the lights on. We recognize that virtual overhead costs are much less than on-site conference events and are grateful a virtual event fits the larger goals, mission, and identity of GSOLE.

Access to even a virtual conference can be affected by participants' physical locations, particularly time zones. To ensure progress towards the goal of living the "Global" part of our name, GSOLE refines the conference schedule and reimagines participation modalities to widen reach. We offer both synchronous and asynchronous options to fit a range of time zones, schedules, and preferences. The asynchronous presentations open a week before the live event, and we have expanded the live event to two days to offer breaks and limit screen fatigue. GSOLE asks presenters for day and time preferences as we map the synchronous schedule. We also have an archival process, which allows members to watch and revisit synchronous sessions while providing GSOLE with transparent and accessible documentation of conference history.

Further, GSOLE makes deliberate decisions to advance an accessible conference experience. Aside from its virtual format, which allows presenters—especially those with little-to-no travel budget—to contribute their knowledge to OLI, accessibility extends to digital accessibility practices. The conference accessibility guide was created in 2020 and is updated each year; it sets standards for slide and handout design, resource sharing, virtual presenting, and engagement (GSOLE, "Conference Guide"). Presenters are strongly encouraged to review and apply the guide, and they are given access to liaisons (committee members) who are available to meet with them throughout the conference presentation development window should they have any questions. Each presentation uses embedded auto-transcription captioning (which is a free feature in our video conferencing platform), and a presentation moderator and a technical moderator are present in every synchronous session to describe images in the chat, type out links and resources that are displayed visually, monitor time and chat conversations, and address technical issues as they arise. Our website management team delivers the conference program in multiple formats, using digital practices like the marking of headings, alt text, and embedded descriptive hyperlinks in addition to providing a printable/downloadable PDF. This sustained support for both presenters and attendees might sound daunting, but we have found it to be highly effective and can build towards accessibility by making advances each year.

Access

These accessibility practices described above feed into the larger goal to create access and equity for GSOLE membership. GSOLE defines access in ways that shape who feels welcome to participate in our conference. We do this by providing an inclusive environment for conference participants from proposal submission through the conference experience. GSOLE is aligned with Giaimo, Caswell, Brooks-Gillies, Dixon, and Faison, who stated, "taking action is not simply about doing something—it's also about acknowledging that one has the power and responsibility to do something" (258).

Access begins as the conference committee is recruited and built "through layered storying and actions of the members of that community, for better or worse" (Giaimo, Caswell, Brooks-Gillies, Dixon, and Faison 257). GSOLE is determined to build better. From the start of planning for the 2018 conference, we found that the committee builds camaraderie in ways that might be surprising. This shared sense of ownership and pride is visible throughout the planning process. Each summer, the two co-chairs send an open call to membership. Volunteers sign up for specific subcommittees (e.g., CFP, proposal review, IDEA, plenary speaker), so they can choose the amount of time they can commit to the process. Each year, new volunteers join the committee; working with the established volunteers who bring wisdom from past GSOLE conferences, they create a synergy that results in developing new and exciting ideas for creating a welcoming and appealing experience. The conference is designed by volunteers invested in a virtual meeting of the minds that is mutually beneficial to presenters and their audience.

We do our best to connect conference design to our audience, recognizing the diverse roles and experience levels of conference presenters and attendees. We understand that the individuals tasked with teaching and administrating online literacy courses and our target constituency range from graduate students to contingent faculty—who may have limited resources and time—to instructional designers and support staff—who often prefer practical, hands-on knowledge—to seasoned scholars—who seek intellectual exchange and networking opportunities. This understanding directly informs our conference design in several key ways.

First, our audience interaction tends to be pedagogical and informational, reflecting the needs of both newer and more experienced members of the writing studies broadly and the field of OLI specifically. We mentor and support participants through the proposal review process. Like some other conferences, we provide proposers with feedback and give those who have not articulated a clear understanding of OLI or demonstrated an understanding of their audience the opportunity to revise with a mentor who teaches them about disciplinary expectations—strategies that can be applied to future academic contributions.

Then, as they are accepted, a liaison communicates regularly to support them in meeting deadlines and answering any questions that arise while preparing presentation materials. And just as a traditional conference presenter wants to enter their room with little concern about the external logistics, GSOLE demonstrates its investment in presenter/audience interaction by giving each panel a presentation moderator and a technical moderator. Through oral and written interactions (i.e., group chat and DMs) with synchronous presenters and opportunities to interact with asynchronous presenters (i.e., comment discussion boards), we facilitate access between presenters and attendees, fostering the collaborative community our organization values.

Finally, after the conference, we survey participants to find out what worked, what needs work, and what they would like to see at future conferences. At this time, GSOLE also further reaches out to participants who have expressed interest in becoming more involved with OLI and the organization. Presenters are encouraged to submit their work to our journals, *Research In Online Literacy Education (ROLE)* and *Online Literacy Open Resources (OLOR) Effective Practices*. Conference attendees are introduced to certification courses, webinars, research grants, and awards. And because some simply want their participation acknowledged, we provide certificates presenters can use for review or promotion. Arguably though, the best post-conference impact is inspiring attendees to volunteer for the conference committee in subsequent years. GSOLE's goal is to help members to connect with others, find a place to share their expertise and ideas, learn from each other, and expand their influence through organizations beyond GSOLE, including our affiliates.

In Closing

As this article has argued, professional organizations *can* deliver engaging and community-building events virtually post-pandemic. In fact, the authors believe virtual options for professional development—including virtual conferences—*must* remain viable options for accessibility, inclusion, and to make professional development more equitable regardless of access to institutional travel funding, caregiving support, workload flexibility, or the normative physical standards that enable one to travel long distances, sit in uncomfortable chairs for hours on end, and walk back-and-forth repeatedly across a convention center, hotel wing, or campus. Virtual conferencing aligns with our purpose and audience as a professional organization. Virtual conferencing is also more practical than an on-site conference, given the financial and logistical challenges. Professional organizations benefit from virtual events that include more voices and perspectives. For GSOLE, virtual conferences have allowed a greater diversity in participants and membership across rank, institutional affinity, and nationality, leading to richer conversations and research about what it means to teach and tutor literacy well in online, hybrid, and digitally enhanced spaces.

That said, we want to avoid any pretense that GSOLE has figured it all out. Rather, as an organization, GSOLE, too, is constantly reflecting on what we can do better through annual assessment by our conference committee and feedback from membership. For example, we have shifted to a two-day conference model to create more accessibility across time zones but would love to develop a robust enough international presenter and attendee presence that the conference can "roll around the world" in a continuous 24-to-36-hour window. This is all to say good virtual conference design does not happen overnight and relies on a clear understanding of the organization's purpose and values and a plan for achieving short- and long-term goals.

Works Cited

Giaimo, Genie Nicole, Nicole I. Caswell, Marilee Brooks-Gillies, Elise Dixon, and Wonderful Faison. "Remaking IWCA: A Call for Sustained Anti-Racist Change." *Writing Centers and Racial Justice: A Guidebook for Critical Praxis,* edited by Talisha Haltiwanger Morrison and Deidre Anne Evans Garriott, Utah State UP, 2023, pp. 87–117.

Global Society of Online Literacy Educators. "Online Literacy Instruction Principles and Tenets." *Global Society of Online Literacy Educators,* 13 June 2019, gsole.org/oliresources/oliprinciples.

Global Society of Online Literacy Educators. "Conference Guide: Designing for Accessibility and Inclusion." *Global Society of Online Literacy Educators,* 2020, gsole.org/conference/presenterguide.

Hassel, Holly. "'People Always Clap for the Wrong Things,' Or, Labor, Time, and Writing Have Always Been a Feminist Issue." *Recollections from an Uncommon Time: 4C20 Documentarian Tales,* edited by Julie Lindquist, Bree Straayer, and Bump Halbritter, National Council of Teachers of English; WAC Clearinghouse, 2023, pp. 235–42. wac.colostate.edu/docs/books/documentarian/afterword1.pdf

Hubrig, Ada, and Ruth Osorio. "Enacting a Culture of Access in Our Conference Spaces." *College Composition and Communication,* vol. 72, no. 1, 2020, pp. 87–117. doi.org/10.58680/ccc202030892.

Theresa (Tess) Evans is associate teaching professor in the Department of English at Miami University (Ohio), where she teaches professional and technical writing courses in face-to-face, online, and hybrid environments. A founding member of the Global Society of Online Literacy Educators (GSOLE), she has served as conference co-chair since 2021.

Kevin E. DePew is associate professor of English at Old Dominion University, where he studies and teaches courses about online literacy instruction, digital literacy, and linguistic justice. He is the Vice-President of the Global Society of Online Literacy Educators and administrates its Certification course with Amy Cicchino and Nitya Panday. He co-edited *Foundational Principles of Online Writing Instruction* with Beth Hewett.

Amy Cicchino is associate director for the Center for Teaching and Learning Excellence at Embry-Riddle Aeronautical University in Daytona Beach, Florida. She is president of the Global Society of Online Literacy Educators (GSOLE) and former conference committee co-chair.

Cat Mahaffey is a teaching professor of writing, rhetoric and digital studies at the University of North Carolina Charlotte. She serves on the Executive Board of the Global Society of Online Literacy Educators. She researches AI, accessibility, and technical and professional writing. She co-wrote *ACCESS: Accessible Course Construction for Every Student's Success.*

Retracing Our (Mis)steps: The Purpose and Value of Our CWPA Conference

Erin Lehman, Kelly Blewett, Callie F. Kostelich, Amanda Presswood, and Mary Lourdes Silva

Introduction

Conferences have been a staple for academic communities for decades, a kairotic space, to use Margaret Price's phrasing, that includes the "pairing of spontaneity with high levels of professional/academic impact" (61). As a professional organization, the Council for Writing Program Administrators (CWPA) has sponsored conferences as an avenue for cultivating academic discourse, community, and support for writing program administrators. It has, like many organizations, viewed conferences as key components for professional development and scholarly contributions; however, conferences are not inherently accessible or appealing to all, as they often perpetuate ableist, classist, and elitist notions of successful engagement (Price; Kynard). CWPA must contend with how its sponsored conferences both serve member needs and reinforce systemic barriers. The authors of this piece, all Conference Planning Committee volunteers for CWPA's 2025 national conference, have, in part, taken up this task through 2025 conference planning and in this Where We Are reflection.[1]

We trace CWPA conferences from their 1986 origins to the pivotal changes of the 2020s, reflecting on challenges such as access, organizational disarray and rebuilding, and evolving membership. We have much to learn from our past experiences and how our conferences have—to varying levels of success—provided opportunities for participant engagement across modalities, locations, and contexts. It is with this grounding that we envision future conferences, including our 2025 virtual conference, in ways that honor CWPA conference legacy, while also creating more accessible and inclusive spaces that respond to and reflect CWPA's organizational goals and shifting membership needs.

CWPA Conferences 1986–2019: Rethinking Access and Inclusion

CWPA began hosting annual conferences in 1986. Until the late 2010s, the conference and WPA Workshop were connected, with participants coming early for the workshop and staying for the conference. Costs were relatively reasonable, because both events happened on a host campus. Early hosts included Miami University of Ohio (which hosted the conference every other year as CWPA's institutional home), Utah State, Portland State, and Purdue.

As CWPA grew, its annual events were based in hotels. Sites included Chattanooga, Tennessee (2006); Tempe, Arizona (2007); and, more recently, Baltimore, Maryland (2019) and Reno, Nevada (2023). Hotels, however, created complications. They generally require a minimum number of room reservations for favorable rates; the cost of meeting rooms can be excessive unless the convention meets a certain catering threshold and/or sleeping room quota; and AV expenses can be prohibitive. Moreover, WPAs who have large institutional service loads often become event planners, a situation parodied in a recent humor piece: "My outside service consists of organizing conferences for my field's main society. Recently, my brother-in-law pointed out that I was basically being an event planner for free" (McNulty).

As McNulty highlights, this is uncompensated work, and hotels don't necessarily work well. CWPA lost money on the 2019 and 2023 hotel-hosted conferences. More importantly, attending an in-person event at a hotel is inaccessible for many. As Holly Hassel explains, analyzing CCCC:

> [G]oing "to a place" has always been highly inaccessible for many . . . graduate students, contingent faculty, and independent scholars who have minimal or no academic funding; academics from under-resourced institutions like two-year colleges and some HBCUs and tribal colleges; disabled colleagues with needs that make travel uncomfortable, exhausting, or nearly impossible; parents of children at nearly any ages whose care must be considered; caregivers of any loved one who simply cannot be abandoned for four days to the care of others. (240)

As we reflect on CWPA's history of in-person conferences, we also remember events such as the WPA Breakfast, a longstanding CWPA tradition at CCCC where the overpriced eggs were a running "joke" for attendees. We consider the many people who could not afford to join such breakfasts (including an author of this piece) or travel to national conferences, and the jokes aren't funny, as overpriced eggs are representative of exclusionary practices. CWPA conferences during this era were similar to how Giamo et al. describe IWCA: "Our professional organization, then, seems to be organized for a far less complex—and a much whiter, abled, and privileged—set of members" (250).

To this point, CWPA in-person conferences seemed to mostly appeal to white members as well. Black scholars Collin Craig and Staci Perryman Clark attended CWPA's conference as graduate students and later wrote: "Prolonged stares made for socially awkward moments with conference participants who did little to alleviate our uneasiness with being some of the few folks of color there" (50). Craig was later denied entrance to a conference dinner because the security guard assumed he was with a different group, demonstrating how the conference participants and extra-/para- conference actors (the security guard) were part of making the space exclusionary. Attempts at the conference to directly address the situation exacerbated it. A decade and a half after Craig and Perryman Clark published this account, we are reminded of the importance of working to make our conferences and organizations more welcoming, affirming, and diverse. Now, just as then, it is imperative that we consider the ways in which racism and white supremacy function within, alongside, and outside of organizations and organizational events.

The overlapping crises of the early 2020s—including the pandemic and the racial reckoning that rocked our country including higher education—offer a much-needed opportunity to rethink conferences as they relate to organizational values of inclusivity and accessibility. As Hassel wrote of conference norms due to the pandemic, "All of these have been turned upside down in ways that I think are needed" (240). We agree.

CWPA Conferences 2020–2024: How to Right a Wrong(s)

CWPA has undergone significant organizational disarray, which 2017–2019 CWPA president Dominic DelliCarpini referred to as "the troubles" in his 2023 conference keynote (55). The organizational turbulence, which had been present for years, shifted into a new gear with the public boycott of CWPA for participating in "white supremacy culture" (Inoue), which the authors of this piece acknowledge. The accusation of participation in white supremacy culture and subsequent public boycott came on the heels of a failed attempt to revise CWPA's Outcomes Statement for First Year Writing. For context on the 2021 boycott, CWPA response(s), and the evolution of the organization, we encourage you to read resources beyond this brief article.[2] In our view, while the boycott was preceded by a specific event, CWPA had been called out for years, yet it continued to reflect white supremacist norms and values (see "CWPA Executive Board Statement in Response to the Recent Call to Boycott the Organization"). We want to be both clear in what happened and, in alignment with this Where We Are section, direct our focus to CWPA conferences during these years of reckoning, rebuilding, and hopefully, reconciliation. As CWPA took an organizational pause in 2021 following the boycott, the fate of the annual conference seemed uncertain.

Since 2021, CWPA conferences have varied: a contentious and difficult online colloquium (2022); an in-person conference (2023); and regional conferences hosted by campuses (2024). CWPA has attempted to pivot and accommodate through various modalities and formats, be it to move online due to a global pandemic or in response to members' needs. We also recognize that widespread, rapid adoption of online modalities during this time inadvertently re-excluded marginalized populations, as access and accessibility were not adequately considered during the planning and delivery of virtual events (Doran et al.).

Initially, the 2022 conference was supposed to be held in Reno, Nevada. However, a member survey revealed that most did not have travel funding and/ or preferred not to travel. CWPA pivoted to an online conference. A small team wrote a CFP for an "Unconference" that featured listening sessions, active learning, coalition-building, and an anti-racist workshop. However, the organization received backlash for failing to explicitly acknowledge how work from scholars such as Natasha Jones and Miriam Williams, and much of the work cited in the CFP, was grounded in the lived experiences, as well as the cultural and intellectual traditions, of BIPOC scholars who have taken personal and professional risks to share their knowledge and expertise that the mostly white leadership of CWPA would never have to take. One might say of CWPA what Aruna D'Souza said of art institutions: "it is alarming the extent to which their good intentions often lead to the entrenchment of whiteness within their walls rather than the opposite" (56). Still, the organization persisted, and a revised Colloquium event was offered to all registrants free of charge featuring the first international keynote in CWPA history.

The next couple of years saw several pivots. In 2023, CWPA held an in-person conference at a casino hotel in Reno, Nevada: the fulfillment of the contract initially scheduled for 2020. While attendees welcomed the opportunity to convene in-person, organizers received negative feedback about the casino space. Because CWPA didn't book enough hotel rooms (per the contract), the organization also incurred additional costs.

In 2024, CWPA received no site proposals to host the national conference, which seemed attributable to shrinking budgets and rising burnout. CWPA leadership pivoted to offer regional, in-person events, organized and held by local committees at college campuses. Though the events were small, several campuses applied to host regional events, which allowed members to connect with local WPAs and reach back to CWPA's affiliate roots (see Thoune, Blewett, and O'Meara). CWPA has contended with the logistical and labor-related challenges of hosting conferences by attempting several different approaches due in part to organizational dysfunction, soul searching, and reflection that continues to take place.

Looking Forward: Clarifying Purpose and Value

We find ourselves struggling with the long (and heavy) history of past conferences and the organization's history. We see this moment as one of experimentation, with mixed results. For the 2025 conference, we continue our experimentation with a two-day virtual conference.

The option to organize a virtual event is a more manageable task that we thought would best meet the needs of the membership this year. The CO-VID-19 pandemic forced the transition from historically in-person events to virtual formats (Haji-Georgi et al.)—and for some of us, the transition was/is comfortable, as we believe in the effectiveness and value of online learning and connection. Offering an online conference fits CWPA's direction and trajectory to offer events and conferences that are reasonable, responsible, and reflect our organizational mission—including our past missteps. We are aware of the rising travel costs, environmental concerns (Haji-Georgi et al.; Spinellis and Louridas), and reduced travel funding due to budget cuts in higher education. We see that members often rely on personal budgets to attend in-person events critical to their academic and professional development. Therefore, we are actively trying to meet the demands of our present while pivoting to welcome the future.

Some trends that we anticipate for our organization and others:

- Virtual or hybrid conferences will be a consistent offering.
- In-person hotel conferences will be offered less frequently, perhaps every other year for CWPA, with a better understanding of their affordances and constraints.
- Multiple, shorter events will supplement the annual conference that used to sustain members all year. There will be increased demand for these shorter, less expensive events and opportunities to connect.
- Connection is and always has been vitally important, particularly for WPAs, and we anticipate that leaders in CWPA will stay with this challenge, because the benefits of connection are central to the mission of the organization.

Moving forward, we are nimbly reconsidering CWPA's future conference iterations, including 2026 plans for an in-person conference at the University of Wyoming. As WPAs and writing teachers, we are used to navigating a "shifting" field with diverse people, diverse ideas, and complex questions (Lehman et al.). We need organizations like CWPA to foster community and take action on issues affecting writing programs. For instance, how will writing programs be impacted by the widespread use of generative AI; address the pending enrollment cliff; respond to laws and policies that threaten DEI initiatives; and manage ever-shrinking budgets? These interconnected wicked problems are today's exigence for CWPA.

Conclusion

As CWPA sorts through opportunities and possibilities for gathering, we don't have easy answers. Through our conference organizing labor, we aim to include a wide variety of people, possibly attract new members, and share WPA ideas and scholarship in a meaningful way—while avoiding financial burdens for our small, nonprofit organization. The impulse to broaden who is invited to engage while staying true to the mission of uplifting and building community among WPAs drives us to continue trying to figure it out.

Notes

1. The authors of this piece volunteered as conference organizers because we care about CWPA as an organization and believe in its broader goals to support WPAs, writing faculty, and the writing students we teach. It also does not go unnoticed that the initial volunteer team was all women, though one man has recently joined us.

2. For more information, please see the CWPA Timeline 2021–2024 and the 2023 CWPA Cultural Assessment Report, which are available on the CWPA website wpacouncil.org/ under the resources tab. While this is certainly not an exhaustive list, we also recommend Brent Cameron's "The Power of Story: Analyzing the Call for a Boycott of the CWPA," which won the 2023 CWPA Graduate Research Award for Writing in WPA Studies.

Works Cited

Cameron, Brent. "The Power of Story: Rhetorical Empathy and Antiracist Organizational Change." *The ScholarShip: East Carolina Institutional Repository.* July 2022.

Craig, Collin Lamont, and Staci Maree Perryman-Clark. "Troubling the Boundaries: (De)Constructing WPA Identities at the Intersections of Race and Gender." *WPA: Writing Program Administration*, vol. 34, no. 2, 2011, pp. 37–58.

CWPA Executive Board. "CWPA Executive Board Statement in Response to the Recent Call to Boycott the Organization." 23 April 2021. wpacouncil.org/aws/CWPA/pt/sd/news_article/366395/_PARENT/layout_details/false.

DelliCarpini, Dominic. "2023 CWPA Conference Keynote: Students' Right to Their Own Language: The Gordian Knot of Social Justice for Writing Program Administrators." *WPA: Writing Program Administration*, vol. 47, no. 2, 2024, pp. 42–60.

Doran, Aileen L., Victoria Dutch, Bridget Warren, Robert A. Watson, Kevin Murphy, Angus Aldis, Isabelle Cooper, Charlotte Cockram, Dyess Harp, Morgane Desmau, and Lydia Keppler. "Planning Virtual and Hybrid Events: Steps to Improve Inclusion and Accessibility." *Geoscience Communication*, vol. 7, no. 4, 2024, pp. 227–44.

D'Souza, Aruna. "The Case for Museum Reparations." *On Whiteness*, edited by The Racial Imaginary Institute, SPBH, 2022, pp. 55–58.

Giaimo, Genie, Nicole I. Caswell, Marilee Brooks-Gillies, Elise Dixson, and Wonderful Faison. "Remaking IWCA: A Call for Sustained Anti-Racist Change." *Writing Centers and Racial Justice*, Utah State UP, 2023, pp. 249–63.

Haji-Georgi, Maria, Xinyun Xu, and Oxana Rosca. "Academic Conferencing in 2020: A Virtual Conference Model." *Human Behavior and Emerging Technologies*, vol. 3, no. 1, 2020, pp. 176–84. doi.org/10.1002/hbe2.235.

Hassel, Holly. "'People Always Clap for the Wrong Things': Labor, Time, and Writing Have Always Been a Feminist Issue." *Recollections from an Uncommon Time: 4C20 Documentarian Tales*, edited by Julie Lindquist, Bree Straayer, and Bump Halbritter, National Council of Teachers of English, 2023, pp. 235–42.

Inoue, Asao. "Why I Left the CWPA (Council of Writing Program Administrators)." *Asao B. Inoue's Infrequent Words*. 2021. asaobinoue.blogspot.com/2021/04/why-i-left-cwpa-council-of-writing.html.

Jones, Natasha, and Miriam Williams. "The Just Use of Imagination: A Call to Action." *Association of Teachers of Technical Writing*, 2020. attw.org/blog/the-just-use-of-imagination-a-call-to-action/.

Kynard, Carmen. "Trigger Warning: This Post is about Academia and Its 'Professional' Conferencing." *Education, Liberation & Black Radical Traditions for the 21st Century.* Carmen Kynard's Teaching & Research Site on Race, Writing, and the Classroom, 2016, carmenkynard.org/professional-conferencing/.

Lehman, Erin, Kelly Blewett, Daryl Lynn Dance, Callie Kostelich, Amanda Presswood, Christal Seahorn, and Mary Lourdes Silva. "Proposal Guidelines." CWPA's 2025 National Conference, www.wpacouncil.org/aws/CWPA/pt/sp/conference_proposals-25. Accessed 13 February 2025.

McNulty, B. "A Faculty Member's Self-Evaluation at the End of the Semester." *McSweeney's Internet Tendency*. 2024. www.mcsweeneys.net/articles/a-faculty-members-self-evaluation-at-the-end-of-the-semester.

Price, Margaret. *Mad at School: Rhetorics of Mental Disability and Academic Life*. U of Michigan P, 2011.

Spinellis, Diomidis, and Panos Louridas. "The Carbon Footprint of Conference Papers." *PLoS ONE*, vol. 8, no. 6. doi.org/10.1371/journal.pone.0066508.

Thoune, Darci, Kelly Blewett, and Kat O'Meara. "The Power of Small." *Bits Blog*. MacMillan Community. 2 December 2024. community.macmillanlearning.com/t5/bits-blog/the-power-of-the-small/ba-p/22778he Small.

Erin Lehman is professor and faculty lead for the online School of Arts, Sciences, & Education at Ivy Tech Community College. In her current role, she works with about 800 faculty members and oversees 40,000 student seats (duplicated headcount) each term. She serves as vice-president for CWPA (2025) and co-facilitated the CWPA Summer Workshop (2022–2023). She serves as a faculty advising editor for *Young Scholars in Writing*, and on the editorial board for *WPA: Writing Program Administration*. Her work has been published in the *Journal of Teaching Writing* and *Understanding WPA Readiness and Renewal* (2023).

Kelly Blewett is associate professor at Indiana University East, where she also directs the writing program and teaches courses in writing and writing pedagogy. She served as president of the Council of Writing Program Administrators from 2024–2025. Her research on the social contexts of editorial work and feedback has appeared in *College English, JAEPL, Prompt, Peitho* and various edited collections.

Callie F. Kostelich served as assistant professor and WPA at Texas Tech University from 2022–2025, and she joins Baylor University as assistant professor and WPA beginning in fall 2025. She teaches methods and theory courses in composition studies and researches first-year writing, writing program administration, rural literacies, and feminist rhetorics. Her work has appeared in *Peitho* and *Open Words,* and she has published and has forthcoming work in several edited collections.

Amanda Presswood is assistant professor of English composition at Southern New Hampshire University. Amanda previously served as coordinator of the Klooster Center for Writing Excellence. Presswood serves as the current secretary for the Council of Writing Program Administrators. Her current research is located at the intersection of writing center studies, writing program administration, and labor studies. She is particularly interested in the lived experiences of writing center administrators who occupy non-tenure track or contingent positions, specifically at small liberal arts colleges.

Mary Lourdes Silva is associate professor of writing and director of first-year writing at Ithaca College. Her past and current research examines the citation practices of first-year college writing students; pedagogical use of multimodal and multimedia technologies and practices; implementation of institutional ePortfolio assessment; gender/race bias in education; movement-touch literacy as a modality to teach reflective thinking in first-year writing; the psychological and financial implications of faculty compelled to review biased student evaluations of teaching; and critical AI literacy in first-year writing. She is also a community organizer and teaches Argentine tango at Cornell University.

Unintended Benefits: Conferencing Through and Beyond the COVID-19 Pandemic

Caleb González, Annie Halseth, Jesse McLain, and Mike Palmquist

We've learned about directing conferences in rhetoric and composition like most other conference directors: the hard way. In early 2019, Caleb joined Mike as planning began in earnest for the Fifteenth International Writing Across the Curriculum Conference (IWAC 2020). By January 2020, the review of conference proposals was complete, presenters had been notified, the program was in place, registration was underway, and we found ourselves hoping that the new virus that was circulating would not become as serious as we feared. Our hopes, of course, were dashed. But we remained optimistic, delaying the conference until summer 2021, when we thought it might be possible to meet in person. Again, we were disappointed, and we found ourselves hosting the conference on Zoom and Whova—this time with Annie and Jesse joining the team as conference directors. By all measures (except, of course, the hallway conversations and socializing that are characteristic of the best conferences), it was a successful conference, with more than 500 registrants and a robust line-up of workshops, plenary presentations, and concurrent presentations. Better yet, every session was recorded and later released through the WAC Clearinghouse (IWAC 2020 Archives).

In 2023, we had the opportunity to once again host a face-to-face conference in Colorado, and the four of us signed on to direct the Seventeenth International Writing Across the Curriculum Conference (IWAC 2025, now on an odd year rotation after IWAC 2020 was delayed by a year). "What could go wrong?" we asked ourselves (all the while wondering about Bird Flu, Ebola, and other potentially disastrous possibilities). Setting our concerns aside, we began both to revisit the issues we'd faced when we planned IWAC 2020 and to consider what we might do differently as a result of what we'd learned in the intervening years.

While planning any conference is a complex endeavor, we found ourselves most comfortable with the nuts and bolts of conference planning—developing a conference theme, creating and issuing a call for proposals, reviewing proposals and creating a program, marketing the event, and developing a budget, among other necessary activities—and less so with how best to understand and address evolving understandings of what it means to create an inclusive, equitable, accessible, and sustainable conference. In this article, we focus on the latter set of issues and reflect on the lessons we learned as we considered (and continue to consider) how best to address them.

Designing a conference cannot be divorced from the larger political, social, cultural, and economic forces that shape both our larger social spaces and the much smaller spaces of academic conferences. As Andrea Olinger, Caitlin Burns Allen, Michael Benjamin, and Alex Way have observed, conferences serve as "incubators of academic writers' personal and professional development—and of disciplines themselves" (1). While WAC celebrated the fiftieth anniversary of its founding (the WAC seminar led by Barbara Walvoord in 1969–1970 at Central College in Iowa; see Bazerman et al.), and while David Russell has chronicled several similar movements in higher education since the turn of the twentieth century, WAC is very much an evolving field, as Al Harahap, Federico Navarro, and Alisa Russell, who presented the closing plenary at IWAC 2020 have noted. In their essay in the edited collection emerging from the conference, they identified three key issues facing WAC as a field: the legacy of coloniality, the pursuit of linguistic justice (which they treat under the broader heading of ethics), and the challenge of ensuring sustainability not only for individual WAC programs but for the field as a whole. Harahap, Navarro, and Russell's work has been meaningful to envisioning not only the ways in which conference topics emerge for IWAC 2025 but also the ways in which we design spaces for disciplinary conversations.

Additionally, as we planned and prepared for IWAC 2025, our questions about how the conference would contribute to the growth of the field were shaped by the issues raised by these scholars, by our work with other members of the WAC community, by our work on IWAC 2020, and by our work on initiatives associated with the WAC Clearinghouse. These issues and experiences shaped the formation of the conference advisory board; the development of the conference theme and call for proposals; the development of statements and support materials addressing issues of inclusivity, accessibility, and linguistic justice; the development of a budget that reflected our commitment to equity; and the development of processes for supporting continued access to the work presented at the conference.

Forming an Inclusive Conference Theme and Call for Proposals

The advisory board for IWAC 2020 had been formed with attention to issues of representation. In addition to asking ourselves if a given member of the board would feel comfortable offering advice—even (and especially) in cases where their contributions diverged from the current state of a conversation— we had sought to represent differences in institutional type, job status, years working with WAC, gender, race, and nationality, among other factors. We began our formation of the IWAC 2025 advisory board with similar goals. We initially reached out to members of the IWAC 2020 board to ask if they would like to serve in that role again, and then we invited other members of the WAC and writing studies communities to join the board. Our board members range from graduate students to emeritus professors, from tenured faculty to faculty in contingent positions to staff members, and from those who are new to WAC to those who have decades of experience. Some do not focus primarily on WAC. Some serve in administrative positions. And, as a group, they represent a range of races, ethnicities, nationalities, and genders, among other markers of difference.

We felt, as a result, that our board as a whole could bring a wide range of perspectives and experiences to discussions of the conference theme and call for proposals. Following a few rounds of email discussion, we gained reasonably quick agreement on the theme — WAC and the Global Future: Flexibility, Action, Innovation. We found it challenging, however, for the board to come to consensus first on the broad outlines and then the details of a call for proposals (CFP). Our goal was to balance attention to recent challenges to equity and inclusiveness with long-standing concerns about designing, implementing, assessing, and sustaining WAC initiatives. The initial drafts of our CFP were heavily oriented to the former, an imbalance that led to a five-week email discussion involving more than 90 messages and numerous revisions to what at times was a rapidly changing document. The discussion was central to developing a CFP that resulted in more than 170 proposals for workshops, panels, roundtables, individual presentations, poster sessions, and teaching demonstrations.

The lessons we learned from the experience—and the advice we would offer to other conference directors—is to include as many voices and perspectives in these discussions as possible. This process should be transparent, equitable, and inclusive. For IWAC 2025, we believe it resulted in a strong theme and CFP. We suspect that will be the case for others.

Creating an Accessible Conference

The lessons we learned from shifting the IWAC 2020 conference from a fully in-person event to a virtual event have helped us view accessibility in a more comprehensive way than we did prior to the COVID-19 pandemic. With a face-to-face conference in mind, we had modeled our accessibility guide on the guide developed for the CCCC annual conference, which itself was informed by the principle that we should build a disciplinary culture of access and inclusion.

Shifting the IWAC 2020 conference from an in-person to an online event introduced new accessibility concerns—primarily technological. Our decision to use Whova, which allowed for live sessions, preserved some of the human-to-human interactions we valued. We also provided options for presenters who were unable to participate in real time (due to time-zone differences or unreliable network connections) to record their presentations in advance.

In 2021, we were unable to afford live-captioning. Fortunately, that is now well within the reach of most conference budgets. We invested instead in editing the closed captions created automatically by YouTube, recognizing that doing so would benefit both conference attendees and the larger WAC community. We also experimented with providing transcripts in advance of a session, as we did with our third plenary presentation by Al Harahap, Federico Navarro, and Alisa Russell.

For IWAC 2025, we have found the cost of live streaming each conference session prohibitive, but we are working with conference presenters to record as many sessions as possible so that we can make the sessions available after the conference. We are also working with presenters to ensure that presentation materials follow the latest guidelines for accessibility.

Promoting Equity

Our work on IWAC 2025 has been informed by a question posed by Antonio Byrd, Maria Novotny, Michael A. Pemberton, and Vershawn Ashanti Young: "How might we collectively evolve our disciplinary identity to integrate and support social justice work that sustains itself?" (41). That is, how can we ensure that access and inclusion are not just reactive considerations but are fundamental to the disciplinary identity of our field? We recognize, for example, the irony in supporting a session that is about WAC and linguistic justice at a conference presented only in English. With this in mind, we developed a website that offers a Spanish-language option and a Google Translate option for roughly 250 languages. While there are complexities in using language translation software, we found this integration meaningful to our design process even as we continued to ask how we could best support scholars who wished to present in a language other than English. In response, we developed a statement on language practices that is available on the IWAC 2025 website, a policy informed by what Vershawn Ashanti Young and Aja Martinez describe as language varieties that are fluid across formal and informal contexts (Young & Martinez, 2011).

The shift to a virtual format offered new opportunities, but it also exposed limitations—showing that the pursuit of equity is not a fixed goal, but a process of learning, adapting, and advocating for change. As we engaged in this process, we considered the interrelated issues of access and linguistic justice, labor conditions within the academy (which we addressed by keeping registration fees low and offering discounts for various groups), and our desire to generate funds to support the work of the Association for Writing Across the Curriculum.

Pursuing Sustainability

We find it meaningful to mention our decision to create a digital archive of the IWAC 2020 conference sessions because the archives allow researchers, teachers, and WAC administrators to continue leaning into disciplinary conversations and the complexities of WAC. In their introduction to the edited collection that emerged from IWAC 2020, Megan Kelly, Heather Falconer, Caleb González, and Jill Dahlman explain that "at least, the pandemic has demonstrated how truly complex and complicated WAC work is" (3). Through archived sessions, the discipline can continue to track the ways in which disciplinary conversations continue to evolve. For example, archiving sessions supports future research that seeks to identify the ways in which WAC is shaped by global contexts (like a worldwide pandemic).

Sustainability as it is more commonly understood has also been a key factor shaping our decisions about IWAC 2025. Sharing the program in digital form rather than in print, for example, has an impact on the waste stream. And while we cannot stream the full conference, offering options for presenting at a distance reduces the impact of travel. Even relying heavily on campus housing reduces the impact of travel to and from local hotels. While we recognize that any conference will have substantial impacts on the environment, even modest efforts like these can be beneficial.

Looking Ahead

As we write this article, we are nearly five months away from the start of WAC 2025. Our efforts to plan and host the conference are shaped by a sense that we must both adapt to the individual needs and circumstances of our presenters and attendees and remain committed to the values that have shaped—and, to some extent, been shaped by—our work as conference directors. IWAC 2025, as a result, is a work in progress. We know we will learn from participants, presenters, and each other as we continue to understand both how and what it means to consider inclusiveness, accessibility, equity, and sustainability as critical factors in the design and management of an academic conference.

Works Cited

Bazerman, Charles, Joseph Little, Lisa Bethel, Teri Chavkin, Danielle Fouquette, and Janet Garufis. *Reference Guide to Writing Across the Curriculum*. Parlor P/The WAC Clearinghouse, 2005. wac.colostate.edu/books/referenceguides/bazerman-wac/.

Byrd, Antonio, Maria Novotny, Michael A. Pemberton, and Vershawn Ashanti Young. "Social Justice Conference Planning for Writing Studies: Frameworks, Triumphs, and Challenges." *Writers: Craft & Context*, vol. 3, no. 1, 2022. doi.org/10.15763/issn.2688-9595.2022.3.1.28-44.

Harahap, Al, Federico Navarro, and Alisa Russell. " Imagining WAC's Future: Coloniality, Diversity, and Sustainability." Kelly et al., pp. 253–72. doi.org/10.37514/PER-B.2023.1947.2.17.

IWAC 2020 Conference Archives. The WAC Clearinghouse, 2021, wac.colostate.edu/repository/collections/conferences/iwac2020/.

Kelly, Megan J., Heather M. Falconer, Caleb L. González, & Jill Dahlman, editors. *Adapting the Past to Reimagine Possible Futures: Celebrating and Critiquing WAC at 50.* The WAC Clearinghouse/UP of Colorado, 2023. doi.org/10.37514/PER-B.2023.1947.1.3

Olinger, Andrea R., Michael J. Benjamin, Caitlin Burns Allen, and Alex Way. "Conferencing toward Antiracism: Reckoning with the Past, Reimagining the Present." *Writers: Craft & Context*, vol. 3, no. 1, 2022. doi.org/10.15763/issn.2688-9595.2022.3.1.1-7.

Russell, David R. *Writing in the Academic Disciplines: A Curricular History.* 2nd ed., Southern Illinois UP, 2002.

Young, Vershawn Ashanti, and Aja Y. Martinez. *Code-Meshing as World English: Pedagogy, Policy, Performance.* National Council of Teachers of English, 2011.

Caleb González is assistant professor of rhetoric, composition, and literacy studies at the University of Texas Rio Grande Valley. His research focuses on what it means for writing programs at Hispanic-Serving Institutions (HSIs) and Emerging Hispanic-Serving Institutions to make meaning of their designation through transformative practices of writing.

Annie Halseth is a composition instructor and a PhD student in the education, equity, and transformation program at Colorado State University. She is a director of the IWAC 2025 conference, which will be held at CSU in Fort Collins this summer.

Jesse McLain is a composition instructor at Colorado State University. She holds a Juris Doctorate and is a licensed attorney. Her interests focus on the intersection between free speech, social change, language, and justice.

Mike Palmquist is emeritus professor of English and emeritus associate provost at Colorado State University. He is the founding publisher of the WAC Clearinghouse (wac.colostate.edu), an open-access publishing collaborative. His scholarly interests include writing across the curriculum, the effects of computer and network technologies on writing instruction, and new approaches to scholarly publishing.

Reflexivity, Accountability, Relationships: Conferencing through the Lens of Watson 2021 and 2024

Andrea Olinger, Shayani Almeida, and Steve Shoop

The questions that this Where We Are section raises land forcefully with us; we—the 2021 and 2024 Watson Conference director (Andrea Olinger) and the 2024 Watson Conference assistant directors (Shayani Almeida and Steve Shoop)—have been grappling with the past, present, and future of the academic conference in our two most recent iterations. Our commitment to these questions, however, arose less because of exceptional courage or foresight on our parts than because history, both local and international, forced a confrontation. The 2021 Watson Conference (held on Zoom), "Toward the Antiracist Conference: Reckoning with the Past, Reimagining the Present," issued from a series of compounding harms perpetrated by conference organizers and fueled by and inflected with white supremacy. And the 2024 conference (in-person, hybrid, and virtual), "Create, Connect, Reflect: Launching Collaborations and (Re)building Community in Our Fields," sprang from the "fracturing" effects of multiple pandemics on the "professional networks and relationships that should form the bedrock of our work" ("Call for Proposals").

In these remarks, we share some of the lessons we have learned through interrogating our own roles in the racist, classist, ableist, and otherwise oppressive practices of conferences and through our attempts to intervene with our own conference planning. Toward that end, we offer two strategies that have guided our interventions: namely, engaging in reflexivity and accountability and fostering relationships, including across modalities. We also invite readers to consult past Watson presenters' own scholarship on conferences, which has been published in our online archive on antiracist conference design ("Resources"), a special issue on the same topic (Olinger et al., "Conferencing toward Antiracism"), and a forthcoming special issue exploring cross-institutional collaborations (Olinger et al., special issue of *WCC*).

Some background on the Watson Conference on Rhetoric and Composition may offer context on our resources and scale. The University of Louisville's Watson endowment was established in 1995, when Thomas Watson—a local doctor, banker, and entrepreneur—donated $1.2 million to the English department to develop a biennial International Conference in Rhetoric and Composition and a Visiting Distinguished Professorship in conjunction with our PhD program ("History"). Launched in 1996, the conference has run every two years. (The past two conferences, however, have been three years apart.)

These fourteen conferences, held over thirty years, have been directed by nine different faculty members in rhetoric and composition, each organizing one or two conferences apiece. Every conference has a theme and has generated a publication containing keynote speeches, an edited collection, or both ("Conference Archive"). The conference has traditionally been small, though it gradually increased in size through 2018, when around 450 attended. The 2021 Zoom conference had 344 registrants, although we estimate that only half attended, and the 2024 conference—which sponsored 14 projects across in-person, hybrid, and Zoom attendance—had 155 participants and 49 facilitators.

The 2021 Watson Conference: "Toward the Antiracist Conference: Reckoning with the Past, Reimagining the Present"

The theme of antiracism in conference design emerged from the 2018 Watson Conference—although, more accurately, one could say that its origins lie in the Watson Conference's imbrication in histories of white supremacy in the department, university, and field. During a white presenter's keynote in 2018, the presenter used the N-word in recounting a racist incident she witnessed as a child. The responses by Watson organizers, Andrea included, incited a series of harms that culminated in the resignations of most of the 2020 keynotes and the postponement of that conference. If not for inquiries by a Black scholar who was one of our invited keynotes—who had heard about what happened in 2018 and wanted to learn about our response—very little would have changed.

Our statement, "Watson and Anti–Black Racism," describes and analyzes the events and apologizes for the hurt we caused (Olinger). It also articulates commitments to fighting anti–Black racism at subsequent Watson events. In addition to creating and publishing the statement on our website, Andrea reached out to the scholars who had resigned and wished to be recontacted, inviting them to participate in the revised conference. Furthermore, for the Black scholars she invited who were at the greatest professional risk of affiliating with Watson, given the racial history of that particular slur, we were able to offer a smaller honorarium for the emotional and intellectual labor they had already engaged in. (More details on the repair work can be found in our final report [Olinger, "Watson Conference 2021"].) We also determined that a new conference would be an opportunity for other conference organizers and for us to study antiracism in conference design and execution; all speakers thus received an honorarium, serving, essentially, as consultants.

One of the primary lessons we learned from this experience, which was reiterated in 2024, was that conference organizing requires an appreciation of the emotional labor involved if BIPOC attendees—or other multiply marginalized attendees—are giving feedback to white organizers about problems with the conference (Evans and Moore). We have found Marcus Croom's discussion of the "practice of race theory" and "post–White"[1] conference design valuable, as they prompt conference organizers to exercise racial literacies and ask, "When are we ourselves (not) practicing race? And why? When is race (not) practiced in conference documents (written form) and discussions (unwritten form)? And to what effect?" (60). Alongside this reflection process, organizers must "[de/reconstruct] the priorities and practices" that perpetuate an anti–Black or post–racial orientation and create new structures that promote a "post–White" orientation (Croom 60).

This difficult work, of course, demands "collective accountability" (Johnston et al.). Our efforts toward reflection on race practice and accountability have involved practices like the following in 2021 and/or 2024:

- Asking facilitators who were proposing projects in 2024 to engage with essays by Croom and by Emily Rónay Johnston, Amanda Solomon Amorao, and Jonathan Kim and describe strategies they might use to foster an inclusive, accessible, "post–White" environment (Croom) founded in "intersectional collaboration, collective accountability, and radical care" (Johnston et al.). Accordingly, this aspect was one of several criteria we used to evaluate proposals.

- Developing and sharing commitments that include guidance on how to respond to microaggressions and address such practices as attending to power dynamics in participation and creating a culture of access (e.g., "2024 Watson Conference Commitments").

- Creating time for small- and whole-group reflection on how everyone did with the commitments. As Victor Del Hierro, Daisy Levy, and Margaret Price declare, "Allyship is not a state to be achieved, but a community-based process of making." Writing about the Cultural Rhetorics Conference, they argue that such gatherings "must include deliberate spaces for negotiating allyship, both the moments it fails and the moments it is re-made in our everyday encounters." These moments of collective reflection have been a productive way for attendees and organizers alike to process their experiences.

- Including questions in the anonymous post–conference survey about how well organizers, facilitators, and participants met the conference commitments.

- Developing and publicizing a policy of compensation for the emotional and intellectual labor involved when members with marginalized identities educate conference organizers. No policy like this could ever "fix" oppressive conference practices, but it is one small way organizers can acknowledge the effects of this feedback and its value.

- These practices can never prevent microaggressions, hate speech, or hurt—see, for example, two Indigenous scholars' reflections on the 2021 conference (Riley Mukavetz and Tekobbe)—but they can, hopefully, create space for reflection, cultivation of racial literacies, and accountability.

The 2024 Watson Conference: "Create, Connect, Reflect: Launching Collaborations and (Re)building Community in Our Fields"

Although some of the 2021 conference structures were nontraditional (e.g., honoraria to all speakers and no concurrent sessions) and more accessible (e.g., Zoom-only attendance and a sliding-scale registration fee), it was still very much a traditional conference, with 20–30 minute presentations and 90-minute workshops and, thus, more limited synchronous interaction between the speaker and attendees or attendees and one another. The attempts at accessibility and inclusion were, arguably, what Jay Dolmage calls a retrofit: "a component or accessory to something that has already been manufactured or built. This retrofit does not necessarily *make* the product function, does not necessarily fix a faulty product, but it acts as a sort of correction" (20). Retrofits, while helpful, are limited by their underlying "default" form. And what was untouched by this structure, we felt, was the fact that conferencing as usual—presenting to an often-minuscule group of people with limited interaction beyond the Q&A—did not live up to the promise of what conferences could be and did nothing to redress our isolation or the cracks in our professional networks. As our CFP read,

> The many pandemics afflicting our world have wrought and revealed new and longstanding harms; among these is the fracturing of the professional networks and relationships that should form the bedrock of our work. Although in-person conferences have resumed, few(er) of us, especially graduate students, have the resources—whether of health, time, or funds—to travel to conferences. With fewer occasions to interact with others around our common passions have come reduced opportunities to meet, connect, laugh, commiserate, and collaborate with people from different institutions, parts of the country, and parts of the world. ("Call for Proposals")

An effort to forge an inclusive, equitable, and antiracist conference, we thought, would entail a structure based on meaningful collaboration and access for all (or universal design). In asking "Who can access Watson?," we sought to consider structural barriers across identities and positionalities and design for maximally rich access. We shaped the three-day conference so it would foster collaborative projects that would launch at the conference itself, and, unlike collaborations that one might learn about only after, say, the book is published, participation would be open to anyone who demonstrated interest and commitment. The endowment paid for modest honoraria to the facilitation teams, and registration was on a sliding scale. Projects were held on Zoom in late February or in person at the university the following week; a few in-person projects were hybrid. Except for the keynote and optional social activities, attendees stayed with their projects for the duration of the conference (approximately 11–12 hours of work time).

This approach certainly enriched the Zoom conference experience, where, under a traditional model, a sense of isolation is common, and it eliminated the in-person experience of presenting to a small audience (Tellez-Trujillo). However, the downside of this three-day commitment was the intensity. Zoom facilitators, in particular, had to be especially thoughtful about designing for screen breaks or alternative means of communication. And while many participants found the experience meaningful, some surely found it too intense, and some did not participate at all because they could not commit for the duration (or did not find a project that interested them). By limiting participation to three-day-long collaborations, we excluded people who could not manage that level of commitment and/or might have preferred a more traditional presentation opportunity.

We also sought to facilitate relationship-building across modalities. Disability studies scholar Vyshali Manivannan, who is chronically ill, stressed to Andrea the importance of ensuring that the Zoom attendees were not treated as lesser than in-person attendees. Toward this end, we sought to encourage interaction between Zoom and in-person attendees in a few ways:

- a conference-wide pet-photo contest and social activities on Zoom (creative writing workshop, pub-trivia-style contest)
- bios that included hobbies posted on a private web page and a daily icebreaker posted on the conference-wide Slack (e.g., favorite pump-up song)
- an invitation to in-person and hybrid participants to attend the showcase of Zoom participants and vice versa
- a system for cross–modality feedback, which we called the "buddy system." Each in-person and hybrid project was asked to give feedback on the deliverable of a Zoom project, and vice versa—feedback that, problematically, was to begin once the deliverable had been presented at the Zoom showcase or, for the in-person and

> hybrid showcase, once the conference was over. Given that only
> 12 of 32 respondents to our anonymous attendee survey said they
> participated in this process, we would not recommend structuring
> feedback the way we did.

These activities may have felt like extra work for those who were already maxed out. Nonetheless, we hoped they would appeal to at least some of the participants. In our estimation, the collaborative projects—and these cross–modality activities—were important ways to develop one's "weak tie network" (Melcher) and build relationships beyond one's own institution.

Conclusion

Watson's endowment, at least for the time being, gives us ample resources; yet, paradoxically, we are operating within a college with a steep deficit. English salaries are woefully low, tenured faculty currently receive no travel funding, and even toner has become unaffordable. The Watson Conference is not insulated from this environment. We are each compensated through only one course release per year. With the college returning fewer and fewer lines for tenure-track hires, fewer faculty are available to direct the conference. Given the immense amount of intellectual and emotional labor required (Almjeld and Zimmerman), it is easy to question whether the role of conference director is worth it.

Yet in today's frightening political environment, where academic freedom is under attack—as is, for the most marginalized among us, simply the ability to live without fear—the urgency to gather is even greater. We need opportunities to challenge and heal from the legacy of white supremacy, strengthen our ties, strategize across institutions, and collectively battle state, federal, and local actions. Attending to reflexivity, accountability, and relationship-building can help shape experiences that nurture, rather than deplete, and thus fortify us for the fight ahead.

Note

1. Croom defines the "Post–White Orientation" as "rejecting—*in every way*—the false notion of White(ness), or the hyporaced[,] as above the hyperraced, or BIPOC(ness)" (60).

Works Cited

"2024 Watson Conference Commitments." *Watson Conference on Rhetoric and Composition*, U of Louisville English Department, louisville.edu/conference/watson/2024-watson-conference/2024-watson-conference-commitments.

Almjeld, Jen, and Traci Zimmerman. "Invaluable, but Invisible: Conference Hosting as Vital but Undervalued Intellectual Labor." *Journal of Multimodal Rhetorics*, vol.

4, no. 2, 2021, pp. 32–42, journalofmultimodalrhetorics.com/4-2-issue-almjeld-and-zimmerman.

"Call for Proposals: Create, Connect, Reflect: Launching Collaborations and (Re)building Community in Our Fields." *Watson Conference on Rhetoric and Composition,* U of Louisville English Department, louisville.edu/conference/watson/2024-watson-conference/call-for-proposals.

"Conference Archive." *Watson Conference on Rhetoric and Composition,* U of Louisville English Department, louisville.edu/conference/watson/history-and-conference-archive/conference-archive.

Croom, Marcus. "Peer-Reviewed Article: Conferencing toward Racial Literacies from the Post-White Orientation." *Writers: Craft and Context,* vol. 3, no. 1, 2022, pp. 58–64, journals.shareok.org/writersccjournal/ojs/writersccjournal/article/view/90.

Dolmage, Jay. "Mapping Composition: Inviting Disability in the Front Door." *Disability and the Teaching of Writing: A Critical Sourcebook*, edited by Cynthia Lewiecki-Wilson and Brenda Jo Brueggeman, Bedford/St. Martin's, 2008, pp. 14–27.

Del Hierro, Victor, Daisy Levy, and Margaret Price. "We Are Here: Negotiating Difference and Alliance in Spaces of Cultural Rhetorics." *enculturation: a journal of rhetoric, writing, and culture,* no. 21, 2016, enculturation.net/we-are-here.

Evans, Louwanda, and Wendy Leo Moore. "Impossible Burdens: White Institutions, Emotional Labor, and Micro-Resistance." *Social Problems,* vol. 62, no. 3, 2015, pp. 439–54. doi.org/10.1093/socpro/spv009.

"History of the Watson Endowment." *Watson Conference on Rhetoric and Composition*, U of Louisville English Department, louisville.edu/conference/watson/history-and-conference-archive/history-endowment.

Johnston, Emily Rónay, Amanda Solomon Amorao, and Jonathan Kim. "Sharing Lessons Learned: Intersectional Collaboration, Collective Accountability, and Radical Care in Antiracist Programming." *Writers: Craft and Context*, vol. 3, no. 1, 2022, pp. 13–23, journals.shareok.org/writersccjournal/ojs/writersccjournal/article/view/97.

Melcher, Michael Urtuzuástegui. *Your Invisible Network: How to Create, Maintain, and Leverage the Relationships That Will Transform Your Career.* Matt Holt/Benbella Books, 2023.

Olinger, Andrea. "Watson and Anti–Black Racism." *Watson Conference on Rhetoric and Composition*, U of Louisville English Department, 11 Oct. 2020, louisville.edu/conference/watson/commitments/watson-and-anti-black-racism.

—. *Watson Conference 2021: Racial Equity and Inclusion at the Conference.* U of Louisville English Department, louisville.edu/conference/watson/history-and-conference-archive/conference-archive/past-conferences/2021-watson-conference/2021-report-and-remarks.

Olinger, Andrea R., Caitlin Burns Allen, Michael J. Benjamin, and Alex Way, editors. *Conferencing toward Antiracism: Reckoning with the Past, Reimagining the Present,* special issue of *Writers: Craft and Context*, vol. 3, no. 1, 2022, journals.shareok.org/writersccjournal/issue/view/4.

Olinger, Andrea, Shayani Almeida, and Steve Shoop, editors. Special issue of *Writers: Craft and Context*, forthcoming.

"Resources for Antiracist Conference Design." *Watson Conference on Rhetoric and Composition*, U of Louisville English Department, louisville.edu/conference/watson/public-archive.

Riley Mukavetz, Andrea, and Cindy Tekobbe. "'If You Don't Want Us There, You Don't Get Us': A Statement on Indigenous Visibility and Reconciliation." *Present Tense,* vol. 9, no. 2, 2022, www.presenttensejournal.org/volume-9/if-you-dont-want-us-there-you-dont-get-us-a-statement-on-indigenous-visibility-and-reconciliation/.

Tellez-Trujillo, Karen. "What Am I Doing Here? When Conference Acceptance Doesn't Mean Conference Inclusion." *Writers: Craft and Context*, vol. 3, no. 1, 2022, pp. 8–12, journals.shareok.org/writersccjournal/ojs/writersccjournal/article/view/96.

Andrea R. Olinger is associate professor of English at the University of Louisville, where she directs the composition program and, from spring 2020 to spring 2025, served as the director of the Thomas R. Watson Endowment on Rhetoric and Composition.

Shayani Almeida is a PhD student in rhetoric and composition at the University of Louisville and an assistant director of the Watson Conference. Her research interests include writing transfer, empathy, inclusion and access, and second language acquisition.

Steve Shoop is a PhD student at the University of Louisville, where he studies rhetorics of disability, autism, and science as well as collaborative composition and screenwriting.

Book Reviews

The Black Box: Writing the Race, by Henry Louis Gates, Jr., Penguin Press, 2024. 262 pp.

Reviewed by Kimberly A. Bain, Palm Beach Atlantic University

Henry Louis Gates Jr. discusses the historical implications of what it means to be consciously Black in America through practices of writing and creating to shape identity in *The Black Box: Writing the Race.* This book looks at the power of words and how they have shaped the Black identity in America over time, from examining how words have been used to standardize and validate the Black experience to exploring how words have been used to marginalize and denigrate that experience. Gates provides readers with a tangible understanding of how these literary practices have shaped Black identity and humanity through various artistic and literary expressions.

The Black Box provides a clear map of the shaping of Black cultural expression throughout history. Chapter one, "Race, Reason, and Writing," explores anthropological concepts of Black identity established through English literacy and language practices. Chapter two, "What's in a Name?," takes a semiotic approach to the evolution of Black identity through the social and cultural implications of naming a race. Chapter three, "Who's Your Daddy?: Frederick Douglass and the Politics of Self-Representation," explores the patriarchal considerations of race and how they have shaped anthropological preconceptions of Black identity and its intellectual abilities. Chapter four, "Who's Your Mama?: The Politics of Disrespectability," examines the cultural stereotypes placed on women and how the perception of Black intelligence contributes to the stigmatization of those stereotypes. Chapter five, "The 'True Art of a Race's Past': Art Propaganda, and the New Negro," identifies the contentious ways Black artists and writers have sought to preserve and convey history and culture through expression. Chapter six, "Modernism and Its Discontents: Zora Neale Hurston and Richard Wright Play the Dozens," looks at new ways that Black culture has been explored and contended in schools and through modern culture, challenging previous notions of "right" expression among the Black community. Chapter seven, "Sellouts vs. Race Men: On the Concept of Passing," brings *The Black Box* to a close with a discussion on the struggle to establish a sense of being while being Black in America. In this chapter, Gates considers what it means to pass as another identity while contending with an ongoing sense of "double consciousness." Gates concludes this book with the chapter entitled "Policing the Color Line," in which he details the recent political consequences of the internal identity struggles that exist among the Black community.

In Chapter one, "Race, Reason, and Writing," Gates gives a historical account of enslaved authors whose works provide a context for understanding how Black individuals would establish their humanity through intelligible written works, aligning with Standard Written English practices and publishing English works with the support of their enslavers. Gates uses examples of young, enslaved authors who sought to be appreciated for their works but could only do so under the strict confines of a standardized culture and language. Gates points out, "As shocking as it sounds to us today, 'scholars' of the Enlightenment raised questions about what sort of beings sub-Saharan Africans actually were" (4–5). These preconceptions lead Gates to frame the context for questioning Black intelligence and its ability to demonstrate standardized literary practices.

Chapter two, "What's in a Name?" explores the evolution of naming the Black race and how the rhetorical aspects of naming have positioned Black individuals at different points in US history. For the Black individual, naming demonstrated a relationship with Africa and the diaspora. Gates explores the disputes surrounding naming Black people based on the barriers it would create by referencing a notable Black 19th-century abolitionist, Henry Highland Garnet, who opposed the idea of naming the Black individual for fear that it might cause contentions of identity, calling it a "terrible yoke" (qtd. in 78). Chapter two explores what it means to be labeled and a label's impact on Black identity, exemplifying the rhetorical power of the Black identity and its representative marks in written and spoken language practices in the US.

Chapter three, "Who's Your Daddy?: Frederick Douglass and the Politics of Self-Representation," focuses on the historical perceptions of Black identity and the nuanced consciousness of being mixed race, particularly when having a father who is an enslaver. Gates exemplifies Frederick Douglass's struggle of being of both races as detailed in Douglass's slave narratives. He references the famous line penned by Douglass, which states, "My father was my master; my master was my father" (qtd. in 96). The paternal consideration, along with Douglass's efforts to refute these claims to maintain the African identity within the "chain of being," is one that Gates considers when looking at the phenomena of Black intellect as "exceptions to the rule" (100, 105). Understanding the nuances of existing as a Black individual with white patronage highlights the deep-seated conflicts of intellect and its associations.

Chapter four, "Who's Your Mama?: The Politics of Disrespectability," looks at the maternal considerations of naming and identity through the lens of maternal heritage. Gates examines early 20th-century stereotypes of Black people, particularly Black women, which prompted a dissonance for those seen as exceptions who did not fit the general stereotype of a hot mamma or a mammy. These images became a contentious route of self-denial among the Black community, which led to questioning the efficacy of artistic expression of identity.

The struggle among Black individuals to articulate their identity through writing practices is shown through Gates's resonances of the rhetorical conflicts that existed during the Harlem Renaissance as detailed in chapter five, "The 'True Art of a Race's Past': Art Propaganda, and the New Negro." While the Harlem Renaissance may seem like a period of enlightenment and esteem of Black culture to the broader audience, opponents such as W.E.B. Dubois would come to question the rhetorical validity of the works featuring nonpolitical expressions. Gates notes, "The lofty goals of the Renaissance…had no chance. Art has never liberated a people" (143). The very style and composition of writing put out by the Harlem Renaissance is perceived as a political stance. Gates references Dubois by reflecting that "'[Black individuals] are hemmed in' by the choice of subject matter and language, and so 'our new young artists have got to fit their way to freedom'" (146). Gates reflects on what could be left out of history and its preservation if certain aspects of a culture are critiqued and seen as not rhetorically effective.

In Chapter six, "Modernism and Its Discontents: Zora Neale Hurston and Richard Wright Play the Dozens," Gates examines the questioning of one's own cultural practices and how that questioning can lead to self-hatred, alluding to the metaphor of "the Sunken Garden," which has been notably detailed in the film *Get Out* (165). Gates addresses what Dubois famously coins as "double consciousness," discussing the internal struggle of existing as one being but understanding the consequences of existing as that being by "looking at one's self through the eyes of others" (qtd. in 166). This chapter grapples with the ways that identity places the Black individual between existence as a person of African descent and as one identified as African American.

In Chapter seven, "Sellouts vs. Race Men: On the Concept of Passing," Gates exemplifies these concepts of internal struggle through a historical account of the conflicts among Black literary figures who accused each other of appealing to other audiences through the rhetorical elements in their artistic expressions. However, perceptions of "betraying the race" are a common theme when existing in a state of double consciousness (185). It's almost as if Gates is reminding his audience of what can be lost when false binaries exist to prohibit creative expression. Gates elaborates, "Concepts like passing [as another race] are dependent upon the fiction of the existence of races as discontinuous essences or entities" (189). This is particularly noted by Gates when he questions what it means to be an authentic Black individual and the ways that authentication practices of identity can "suppress [Black] individuality" (210). These limitations can also be seen as Black individuals struggle to express themselves through composition practices for fear of being perceived as an inauthentic representation of the Black experience.

The Black Box concludes with the chapter "Policing the Color Line." In this chapter, Gates looks to the historical context of Jim Crow in US school systems to address the present. As schools are now seeing changes in what can and can't be taught concerning Black history and culture, Gates wonders how that constraint will affect the preservation of culture being articulated through various lenses.

The strength of *The Black Box* is its thorough engagement with the historical and cultural contexts in which Black communication, writing, and discourse are situated. What Gates calls for is the continuation of a deep sense of wonder and engagement in the world through a multifaceted lens. Through *The Black Box,* it can be understood how language and writing practices have been used as cultural capital in American society and how restrictions on who is allowed to express themselves authentically, and in what context, have held Black culture and identity back. Acknowledging these contexts while practicing "more humility, and more humanity" is Gates's call to the reader (228).

For instructors, a lens into what identity and expression have historically meant for the Black community in America is invaluable for engaging with these communities through pedagogy. It is essential to the engagement and appreciation of Black individuals' strivings to express themselves, particularly in an academic setting where Standard Written English and identity practices are upheld. Furthermore, understanding the social and cultural context of Black rhetoric in American history can provide a better perspective on how to engage in pedagogies of humility through English composition instruction.

West Palm Beach, Florida

Kimberly A. Bain is assistant professor of English at Palm Beach Atlantic University. She teaches first-year and advanced-level rhetoric and composition. Her research focuses on multimodal implications for rhetorical argumentation. Her research as a writing center administrator has focused on issues of multiculturalism and language awareness.

Sanctuary: Exclusion, Violence, and Indigenous Migrants in the East Bay,
by Cruz Medina. The Ohio State University Press, 2024. 168 pp.

Reviewed by Katie Silvester, Indiana University Bloomington

Against the political backdrop of Trump's first presidency, Cruz Medina
investigates the intersections of race, language, and citizenship in the
lives of Indigenous Mayan Guatemalan immigrants residing in the East
Bay of Northern California, a populous and geographically diverse region
inclusive of the South Bay cities within Silicon Valley, Palo Alto, the East
Bay, Oakland, Berkeley, and Alameda. In the context of the Trump administration's draconian immigration policies, concepts of migrant "sanctuary"
as sacred, quiet places and places of refuge are upended in Medina's searing
account of an economy of exclusion that sets non-white immigrants apart
from white citizens through visa limitations on access to property, education,
and a livable wage. Detailing political and historical accounts of injustice
perpetuated by neocolonial, white supremacist forces shaping transnational
migration, specifically towards Indigenous peoples in Central America and
residing in the US, Medina poses a central question for readers: What does
it mean for migrants fleeing genocidal violence to seek and find sanctuary,
only to end up on the other side of xenophobic, white supremacist migration policies? Through tautly knit political and historical analysis of exclusion
and violence alongside ethnographic vignettes, Medina explores questions of
how discourse and policy have been used to exclude Indigenous people and
migrants from the rights of white citizens, provoking a reconceptualization of
home, belonging, and refuge amidst early 21st century logics of coloniality.

The book is organized into six chapters that work to create a synergistic
analytical and methodological framework for investigating race, language,
and citizenship in the context of a sanctuary city in the East Bay. Blending
Critical Race Theory (CRT) and decolonial analysis with grounded theory
methods, Medina links the formation of citizenship laws to the protection
of white property and how white supremacist policy impacts transnational
migration. Through this colonial matrix, Medina reads economies of exclusion
and violence in both US-based political rhetoric undergirding neocolonial
capitalism and migrant accounts of local racism. Once this theoretical and
analytical foundation is laid, Medina applies grounded theory methods (survey
data, interviews, and participant observation) to analyze linguistic and racial
differences in property ownership, leasing disputes, and literacy work at the
Sanctuary, a Spanish-speaking Church in the East Bay that provides English
classes and community support to the Mayan Guatemalan immigrants that
Medina encounters as a volunteer. In the book's concluding chapters, Medina

explores migrant counterstories, exposing the myth of literacy acquisition and the limitations on adult learning imposed by xenophobic educational policies.

In chapter one, "Citizenship, Economies of Exclusion, and Tech Money," we learn how an economy of exclusion plays out in the life of Antonio, a migrant from Guatemala, who asks how Medina's research and teaching, rooted in volunteerism at the Sanctuary, will make a difference. "How can you help me?" Antonio asks. Antonio's question becomes the basis of Medina's inquiry into the relationship of the Indigenous Mayan Guatemalan community to the East Bay and how historical and contemporary policies of exclusion in Central America and the US inform Antonio's pressing questions about how participating in Medina's analysis will help him. Chapter one sets the context for the following three chapters, which wind readers through the interconnections between violence as a motivating factor for the migration of Mayan Guatemalans, like Antonio, and the low wages and uncertain future that continue to exploit them once they arrive in the US. Medina reads this tension as part of the legacy of colonial genocide and settler colonial capitalism, which continues to this day in immigration policies that claim to provide sanctuary while continuing to exploit and exclude asylum seekers and migrants fleeing violence.

Chapter two and chapter three are titled "Decolonizing Immigration with Critical Race Theory" and "Violence and the Legacy of Colonial Genocide," respectively. These chapters work at unraveling the colonial logic that remains after colonialism by illustrating how white supremacist settler policy functions to constrain the mobility of US-based transnational Indigenous migrants impacted by genocide and the violence of exclusion following the creation of a US-backed Guatemalan government in the 1980s. Chapter two provides an analytical apparatus for exposing how coloniality shapes US-backed capitalist strategy in Latin America and how this strategy aggravated relations between the Guatemalan government and Indigenous communities, leading to policies of exclusion and violence. Sanctuary is a complex concept in this context. On the one hand, the US offers sanctuary for Indigenous migrants fleeing violence, while on the other, it is US-backed support for the Guatemalan government that reinforces genocide. These divisions become even more clear in the case of the Sanctuary, or the Spanish-speaking church where Medina volunteers during the early years of Trump's first administration. Set in relation to an English-speaking church that occupies the same property, the Sanctuary must learn how to mobilize its congregants in property disputes centered on language, race, and citizenship differences between the two churches.

The struggle of the property leasing agreement is the central focus of chapter four, "Sanctuary Struggle, Linguistic Discrimination, and Indigenous Displacement." Medina applies grounded theory to analyze how linguistic and racial differences are used to exclude Indigenous migrants from full civic and spiritual participation in community and church life. Chapter four presents a struggle over the lease with a predominantly white congregation; the white congregation renewed the lease without including the Latinx, Spanish-speaking congregation. Medina reads this as a property grab on the part of the white congregation and argues that the conflict over the lease demonstrates how settler-colonialism manifests in everyday disputes, with the white congregation using language and citizenship status as a rationalization for expropriating church property from migrant churchgoers.

Chapters five, "Volunteer Literacy Teacher Counterstory," and six, "Concluding a Story without an End," work to reinforce the previous chapters' examination of how the immigration system excludes non-white migrants through an analysis of language and literacy assumptions based on the singular privileging of English monolingualism. Chapter five uses counterstory methodology to present migrant perspectives on the motivation and desire to learn English set against stock stories that reproduce deficit-based narratives about Indigenous literacy and motivation. Medina explores the tensions between counterstories and stock stories around literacy work at Sanctuary, juxtaposing the perspective and experience of Jackie, a frustrated and under-resourced adult English as a Second Language (ESL) teacher, and Carlos, an adult learner at Sanctuary caught in a cycle of unending violence that follows him through pre- and post-migration locations in Guatemala and the US. Weaving these two counterstories together, Medina does not resolve the tensions among race, citizenship, and language but adeptly illustrates how ordinary people navigate these tensions in their everyday literacy work and learning. Jackie's and Carlos's stories compel us to unearth how the complexities of individuals' experience of race, citizenship, and language at Sanctuary resist reductive stereotypes around teaching and learning, desire and aspiration, in an immigrant ESL context. Chapter six offers an ending so far that addresses Medina's personal situatedness at Sanctuary and the (un)answered questions that remain in the space between Trump presidencies.

What does a more complex conceptual understanding of sanctuary provide scholars and critics in rhetoric and writing studies? Medina's reading of sanctuary provokes an articulation of agency, or in Medina's words, "pluriversal possibility," at the intersections of race, language, and citizenship, made possible and constrained by the violence of capitalism in the neocolonial context of Indigenous Mayan migration to the US. In addition, Medina provides new research methodologies within citizenship and education contexts that call attention to the persistence of racism and dominant ideology via grounded theory and migrant counterstories. While the lens is trained on detailing and exposing how an economy of exclusion works through intersectional injustices, I wonder about how socio-cultural and political practices of faith, refuge, and belonging contribute to the limits and possibilities of remaking citizenship in contexts of transnational migration and what these practices might mean for mobilizing more effective anti-racist, anti-violence coalitions in and with immigrant communities. Still, what this book achieves methodologically by bringing CRT and decolonial analysis together is a kind of local-global, transnational, intersectional analysis that is uniquely characteristic of US-based, neocolonial immigration policies and practices. This book offers a complex and holistic analytical lens for parsing US complicity in neocolonial acts of violence and exclusion to complicate our understanding of a colonial matrix of power and to deepen our understanding of what is at stake in English language teaching in migrant contexts. Both rhetorical scholars seeking to train their analytical lens on the US complicity in neocolonialism and its intersections with racism, genocide, and transnational economics of immigration and also teachers of English, especially in community contexts and in contexts of refugee and migrant adult education, will greatly benefit from *Sanctuary's* descriptions and analysis of the geopolitical dynamics at play in people's everyday motivations and experiences of transnational migration, English language learning, citizenship, and belonging.

Bloomington, Indiana

Katie Silvester is associate professor of English and director of composition at Indiana University Bloomington.

***The New Work of Writing Across the Curriculum: Diversity and Inclusion,
Collaborative Partnerships, and Faculty Development***, by Staci M. Perryman-
Clark. University Press of Colorado, 2023. 145 pp.

Reviewed by Gideon Kwashie Kwawukumey, Virginia Tech

Staci M. Perryman-Clark's book, *The New Work of Writing Across the Curriculum* adopts a holistic approach to examine how institutions can articulate culturally-sustained pedagogies around writing to address the needs
of writing across the curriculum (WAC) and inclusion and diversity initiatives. As emphasized by Jennifer Craig, a contribution to the conversion of
diversity and inclusion is needed, because racial diversity has not been much
focused on in WAC studies. Perryman-Clark's work responds to this exigence
by weaving theoretical and practical frameworks to illuminate the intersections of campus-wide diversity and inclusion initiatives with WAC programming. In so doing, her scholarly discussions on writing program administration, faculty development, and strong partnerships establishment between
institutions provide a comprehensive climate for recognizing and embracing
"intersectional identity" (76), thereby strengthening diversity and inclusion
within institutional spaces.

   The New Work of Writing Across the Curriculum contains five chapters,
each emphasizing the need for faculty development, diversity, inclusion, and
institutional transformation through WAC, while also offering useful strategies
for building strong partnerships. Perryman-Clark advocates for collaborative
work between WAC programs and faculty development centers to promote
inclusive higher education.

   The introductory chapter, "Committing to the New Work of Writing
Across the Curriculum: Diversity and Inclusion and Faculty Development,"
emphasizes the interconnected work of WAC, faculty development, and diversity and inclusion initiatives. In this chapter, the author captures how the
three areas intersect in creating an inclusive higher education. Drawing from
her emic perspectives, Perryman-Clark, a Writing Program Administrator
(WPA), argues that the operationalization of WAC goes beyond first-year
writing programs to broader faculty development initiatives. As part of this
expanded focus, Perryman-Clark develops workshops on linguistic justice and
pedagogies to promote diversity and inclusion programming, mentorship,
and support for faculty, particularly for faculty members who are women of
color. These workshops are designed to offer professional development opportunities and address issues such as workplace microaggressions faced by
faculty members. Perryman-Clark's introductory chapter, therefore, sees WAC

work as intersecting with instruction, faculty development, and diversity and inclusion initiatives.

In chapter one, "Faculty Development and Writing Across the Curriculum Initiatives: Enhancing Diversity in Twenty-First-Century Higher Education," Perryman-Clark highlights the historical connection between WAC and faculty development in higher education. She argues that aligning these efforts with broader social justice initiatives can improve diversity and inclusion. Building on the existing scholarship on faculty development and diversity, she highlights racial diversity gaps and emphasizes the urgent need for multicultural approaches in WAC and faculty development to support diversifying pedagogical practices and scholarly identities. As a result, she draws on Marchesani and Jackson's theory of Multicultural Organizational Development (MCOD), which provides a framework for aligning institutional diversity efforts with broader social justice initiatives. This theory emphasizes adapting teaching and learning practices to institutional diversity and inclusion initiatives, diversifying faculty development programs, and expanding efforts to include cross-cultural and social justice pedagogies to foster inclusivity. Building on this framework, Perryman-Clark suggests strategies such as international diversity training for faculty and staff, implementing diversity in first-year courses, and curricula to address such issues. For instance, such training should involve workshops on inclusive teaching practices and equitable assessment practices that enhance cultural inclusivity and support multicultural student populations. This chapter therefore emphasizes integrating multicultural initiatives into WAC and faculty development through frameworks like MCOD to foster diversity, inclusion, and pedagogical practices in higher education.

In her second chapter, "Fostering Partnerships Between WAC, Faculty Development, and Diversity and Inclusion in General Education Reform," Perryman-Clark provides a case for collaborative partnerships between WAC, faculty development, and diversity initiatives in shaping higher education reforms, emphasizing the importance of WAC and faculty development in these efforts. One example is her involvement in Western Michigan University's (WMU) general education reform. She contributed to creating a new curriculum called WMU's Essential Studies, which includes a sequence of four foundational skills-based courses—Writing, Communications (oral), Quantitative Literacy, and Inquiry and Engagement: Critical Thinking in the Humanities—applied to specialized areas of study. This design requires instructors to create at least one assignment that speaks to diversity and inclusion, with support provided through faculty training and workshops to address the needs of diverse student populations. This reform is valuable for WAC initiatives, because the new curriculum model calls for programmatic sharing of practices and pedagogical approaches through workshops and faculty development programs.

A significant aspect of this chapter is Perryman-Clark's advocacy for institutionalizing WAC through a teaching center to support first-year writing and develop learning outcomes that help students connect writing conventions across various courses and understand how those conventions differ across subject areas. Perryman-Clark argues that writing is a common learning outcome at WMU, and WAC should offer professional development by leveraging inclusive writing assessment and diversity initiatives to support faculty members who teach general education courses. In sum, the chapter highlights the potential of partnerships between WAC, faculty development, and diversity and inclusion initiatives to drive meaningful higher education reforms, as exemplified by the WMU Essential Studies program.

Her third chapter "The Work of Writing Never Ends: Writing Across the Curriculum and Diversity and Inclusion Professional Development Opportunities," indicates the pivotal role WAC programs can play in enhancing diversity and inclusion in higher education. The chapter identifies WAC initiatives such as the Office of Faculty Development (OFD) Teaching Inclusivity summer seminar, which provides a platform for faculty development workshops to promote culturally-responsive teaching practices and foster linguistic diversity. As part of WAC outreach efforts, the OFD's Teaching Inclusivity Series also offers workshops on topics such as creating inclusive pedagogical materials. OFD seminar plays a crucial role in educating faculty to honor students' writing practices and respond to their errors in ways that respect their core beliefs. One key strategy the WAC outreach offers is the use of inclusive rubrics that honor language rights and support diverse student writing. In this way, WAC initiatives like teaching inclusivity seminar become an essential platform for valuing the writing practices of speakers of other Englishes and promoting linguistic diversity.

Chapter four, "Toward an Institutional Transformation of WAC: A View Forward Despite Shrinking Operating Budgets," addresses issues of inadequate funds and resources to finance WAC operationalization. Situating financial challenges within the institutional landscape, the author shows that a budgetary model of resource and financial distribution limits the autonomy of WAC programs, particularly in contexts where institutions struggle to generate funds. To resolve this, she challenges institutions to shift from an incremental budget model, a top-down approach to a "responsible-centered budget model (RCM)" (100). This approach is beneficial for institutions, because they can control the revenue they generate while allocating funds to support activities like WAC. RCM can also help resource-limited institutions integrate WAC with faculty development programs to improve teaching and learning.

Additionally, Perryman-Clark indicates that low enrolment of people of color in post-secondary institutions has contributed to reduced funding for WAC programs. This revelation shows how limited funding for WAC can hinder efforts to admit more students of color. For the transformation of WAC, Perryman-Clark urges institutions to develop budgetary allocations that prioritize inclusion to increase enrollment and retention of students of color in higher education. This approach not only supports these goals but also enhances WAC's role in creating equitable educational opportunities for people of color.

In the final chapter, "Now What? Final Strategies of Forming Partnerships," Perryman-Clark offers concrete steps for building stronger collaborations with teaching and learning centers in the wake of budgetary constraints. The author emphasizes the importance of collaborations between WAC programs and teaching and learning centers to secure initiative-based funding and embed Diversity, Equity, and Inclusion (DEI) initiatives into WAC programs. Embedding these DEI initiatives into the curriculum requires WAC programs to prioritize the needs of shifting demographics, as Black and People of Color (BIPOCS) students continue to increase in higher education. When forming partnerships, WAC programs need to value diversity and inclusion in their practices, ensuring these values align with the institutional missions and goals of teaching and learning centers. This alignment is therefore crucial for sustaining students of color in higher education.

Building on the above recommendations, Perryman-Clark's work provides a new perspective on WAC within a broad-based landscape of faculty development and institutionalized strategies for promoting diversity and inclusion. Significantly, she advocates for expanding the conversation around linguistic diversity beyond writing programs, given that such programs often do not clearly extend this discussion about racial issues and the inclusion of BIPOC identities. In this regard, Perryman-Clark inspires me, a person of color, to advocate for supporting faculty and administrators of color, who will take on administrative roles in their future careers. Moreover, Perryman-Clark's work offers insights into WAC diversity and inclusion initiatives, suggesting practical solutions such as workshops on linguistic diversity and inclusive teaching practices to support faculty development. The book also emphasizes strategies such as integrating diversity training into faculty development programs and aligning WAC with initiatives, as described in multicultural organizational development (MCOD) framework. Ultimately, these strategies can help WAC scholars, administrators, and teachers to enhance inclusive educational and administrative environments that support both students and faculty, particularly those from BIPOC communities.

Work Cited

Craig, Jennifer Lynn. *Integrating Writing Strategies in EFL/ESL University Contexts: A Writing-Across-the-Curriculum Approach*. Routledge, 2012.

Blacksburg, Virginia

Gideon Kwashie Kwawukumey is a broadcast journalist, doctoral student of rhetoric and writing, and first-year writing instructor in the department of English at Virginia Tech. His research interests are linguistic justice in FYW, evaluating linguistic justice in technical communication, translingual rhetoric, rhetoric and language policy, and sports communication.

Rhetoric and Guns, edited by Lydia Wilkes, Nate Kreuter, and Ryan Skinnell. University Press of Colorado, 2022. 259 pp.

Reviewed by Sean Murray, Piedmont Virginia Community College

The editors of *Rhetoric and Guns* contend that rhetoricians must boost their analysis of gun violence, as the issue has not been "systematically" examined in the field (3). While scholarly volumes devoted to gun rhetoric do exist, the current reality of our gun impasse demands a fresh rhetorical examination, which the contributors cogently deliver here. "Race," "technology," "interventions in public discourse," and "embodied reactions to . . . gun violence" are identified by Wilkes et al. as the four fundamental "resonances" or themes spanning the volume's fourteen chapters (14). These resonances provide a helpful way to organize this review, though the book is not sequenced into discrete sections as such. Beyond the resonances, what unites the chapters is the contributors' concerted effort to curtail gun violence through rigorous research and analysis.

Race, the first resonance, covers three chapters. In chapter four, "The Gun as (Race/Gender) *Technê*," professor/activist Lisa M. Corrigan uses Heidegger's notion of "*technê*" to illuminate the racial and gendered dynamics of U.S. gun policy, particularly Stand Your Ground laws (71). Essentially, she argues that guns enable Caucasian males to manifest "themselves through a biopolitical erasure of Black people," concluding that white people's mounting fear of the diversifying population foreshadows a future of deadly, racialized violence (79). In the face of such racialized gun violence, Lydia Wilkes probes the "rhetorics of acquiescence," or societal numbness, that overcomes communities in chapter seven, "This Is America on Guns: Rhetorics of Acquiescence and Resistance to Privatized Gun Violence." However, she takes pains to emphasize that this stupor is only available to the privileged; Black mothers, in contrast, have rejected numbness and instead mobilized against racialized gun violence. Likewise, Wilkes highlights the "glimmering hope" embodied by March for Our Lives participants, who also repudiate paralysis (131–32). This optimism offers readers a respite from the sobering tone pervading much of the book. Chapter ten, Scott Gage's "National News Coverage of White Mass Shooters: Perpetuating White Supremacy through Strategic Rhetoric," is congruent with Wilkes' acquiescence critique. Gage examines the "apocalyptic sublime," a phenomenon by which media viewers become dazed from interminable shooting tragedies while media producers utilize language that ignores the systemic reality of anti-Black violence (170). He closes with a paradox: scholars want to help, but by "intellectualizing violence," they may inadvertently diminish the emotional pain with which people live (182). His caution is compelling, raising questions about how best to leverage academic work for maximum impact on public policy.

Next, the technology theme appears prominently in four chapters. For example, in chapter two, "Muzzle Velocity, Rhetorical Mass, and Rhetorical Force," Nate Kreuter presents the unique analogy that "the physics of how firearms actually operate also serve as metaphors through which we can understand the rhetorical forces that drive contemporary American gun policy debates" (32–33). A gun owner himself, Kreuter equates the velocity, mass, and force of a bullet exiting a gun to a message's delivery speed and effectiveness. Briefly, rhetorical velocity is the speed at which a message initially travels; rhetorical mass is a message's weight, often affected by the number and/or status of the speakers; finally, rhetorical force, drawing on the physics formula, $F = M \times A$ (force equals mass multiplied by acceleration), is produced by combining a message's velocity and mass. To illustrate, Kreuter relates his personal experience of publishing a piece on gun violence only to find himself facing a frenzied backlash from the anti-regulation crowd. While the finer points of the physics comparison may strike some as abstruse, Kreuter spurs readers to ask crucial questions: Why do some perceptions about guns spread faster and persist longer? And how can proponents of stronger gun laws mine the physics metaphor to achieve their goals? Charting a different course in chapter three, "Hunting Firearms: Rhetorical Pursuits of Range and Power," Brian Ballentine frames science not as metaphor but as the means for humans to "actualize the maximum potential" of their technological creations (49). He employs Kenneth Burke's work on "entelechy" (49) to argue that our collective craving for "technological advancement" (66) explains why we push firearms and projectile capabilities far beyond what hunters need to kill animals. His firsthand knowledge as a hunter, combined with the volume's only photographs, provides a basic education on bullets and rifles that can boost non-gun-owning readers' confidence to participate effectively in policy debate. In chapter six, "The Activism Gap and the Rhetoric of (Un)Certainty," Craig Rood applies his extensive scholarship on guns to the problem of rhetorical complexity and uncertainty obfuscating public discussion. He encourages reform advocates to progress by 1) emphasizing the "*certainty*" of their arguments, 2) highlighting the "*uncertainty*" of far-right claims, and 3) confronting the false expectation that legislation can eliminate gun violence (112–14; emphasis mine). Finally, in chapter twelve, "Hiding Guns in Schools: The Rhetoric of U.S. Mass Shootings," Nathalie Kuroiwa-Lewis touches on gun technology via a discussion of Parkland shooter Nikolas Cruz's legal purchase of an AR-15, though the chapter centers on a rhetorical analysis of an information sheet from the Civilian Marksmanship Program, an organization Cruz took part in as a student. Her astute examination, grounded in the notion that "language creates reality" (201), demonstrates how this youth-focused organization fabricates a false sense of safety around guns.

The third theme, "interventions in public discourse," surfaces in four chapters, each offering rhetorical strategies for gun reform advocates to reframe the debate. For instance, Patricia Roberts-Miller's chapter one, "The Only Thing That Stops a Bad Guy with Rhetoric Is a Good Guy with Rhetoric," elucidates the rhetorical, demagogic process by which discussion on guns is simplified to an existential struggle between "those who are anti-gun and gun owners," a distortion that negates the fact that many gun owners believe in some level of gun regulation (20). Bradley A. Serber, in chapter eight, "'The Last Mass Shooting': Anticipating the End of Mass Shootings, Yet Again," urges reform activists to focus their rhetorical efforts on pragmatism and perseverance rather than prevention, underscoring Rood's earlier cautioning about viewing legislation as a panacea. Matthew Boedy warns of the organization Turning Point USA's promotion of gun rights in schools via their appeals to Christian nationalism and female empowerment in chapter eleven, "Guns and Freedom: The Second Amendment Rhetoric of Turning Point USA." Eventually, he shares his personal story of landing on the group's "Professor Watchlist" as a propagandist against freedom for writing and speaking out against permissive campus carry laws (194). Echoing Kreuter's story in chapter two, Boedy's experience illustrates the political right's rhetorical strategy to paint outspoken academics as radicals intent on limiting people's liberties. Finally, chapter fourteen, "Talking Together About Guns: TTAG and Sustainable Publics," by Peter D. Buck, Bradley A. Serber, and Rosa A. Eberly, encapsulates an edifying conversation among key organizers of a Penn State series of public gun discussions that can serve as a blueprint for activists aiming to host similar forums.

"Embodied reactions to gun violence," the final resonance, includes chapters five, nine, and thirteen. Ian E.J. Hill's chapter five, "Rhetoric of Open Carry: Living with the Nonverbal Presence of Guns," illustrates how the government reacts differently depending on the race of people openly carrying firearms through comparisons of the Black Panthers' 1967 armed protest at California's state legislature, Ammon Bundy's 2014 clash with the Bureau of Land Management, and the 2014 police killing of Tamir Rice. In chapter nine, "Campus Carry, Academic Freedom, and Rhetorical Sensitivity," Kendall Gerdes links a Texas law permitting campus carry to white students' "racialized fears" and recaps the University of Texas at Austin faculty's unsuccessful challenge to the new law (153). This legal analysis will interest college professors, as it provides a case study on disputes over academic freedom. In chapter thirteen, "A Non-Defensive Gun: Violence, Climate Change, and Rhetorical Education," Ira J. Allen's discussion shines for the link he forges between gun deliberation and our environment— topics rarely connected in public discussion. He explains that his gun is not a so-called "defense gun," a dubious label given the murky line between self-protection and aggression; rather, it is "an-end-of-the-world gun," reserved for society's imminent disintegration should we fail to halt climate change (218). Allen dangles a modicum of hope via "rhetorical education," defined here as "a form of sense-making, constraint-negotiation on behalf of fuller political community, developed in and for contexts of frequent violence" (229). He paints rhetorical education as a way to live more honestly with the violence inherent to the "rhetorical tradition" and references helpful sources like Cheryl Glenn's "Rhetorical Education in America" (230).

Ultimately, *Rhetoric and Guns* is a substantial contribution to the ongoing conversation on gun violence, providing key knowledge and insights pertaining to history and policy, as well as a reminder that language shapes the reality in which we live—and die. As most contributors here specialize in rhetoric and composition, the volume will serve as a valuable resource for scholars in these fields, related disciplines such as communications and media studies, plus a variety of other areas including public policy, political science, and sociology. That several of the contributors are gun owners prevents the book from being pigeonholed as an echo chamber and makes it a springboard for productive discussion in advanced undergraduate and graduate courses. Beyond academia, activists seeking to change the way we talk about guns and lawmakers wanting to impact policy will find this collection useful. In the end, *Rhetoric and Guns* challenges readers of all backgrounds to educate themselves and work constructively to minimize the gun violence rife in America today.

Charlottesville, Virginia

Sean Murray teaches English composition at Piedmont Virginia Community College and science, technology, and society at the University of Virginia.

2024 Reviewers

Matthew Abraham
Courtney Adams Wooten
G. Edzordzi Agboza
Cydney Alexis
Ira Allen
Anthony Atkins
Hadi Banat
Joshua Barszczewski
Christopher Basgier
Logan Bearden
Tyler S. Branson
Beth L. Brunk
Antonio Byrd
Ellen Carillo
Sheila Carter-Tod
Chen Chen
Kirsti Cole
Lida Colón
Vanessa Cozza
Meghalee Das
Doug Downs
William Duffy
Casic J. Fedukovich
Maggie Fernandes
Amanda Fields
Melanie Gagich
Chris Gallagher
Anne Ruggles Gere
Jillian Grauman
Anuj Gupta
Susanne E. Hall
Matthew Halm
D. Alexis Hart
Carrie Byars Kilfoil

A. Abby Knoblauch
Eric Leake
Rory Lee
Jason Luther
Paula Mathieu
Stephen McElroy
Megan McIntyre
Heidi McKee
Annie S. Mendenhall
Laura R. Micciche
Lilian Mina
Casie Moreland
Jeff Naftzinger
Michael Neal
Maria Novotny
Stephen Parks
Stacey Pigg
Mya Poe
Nupoor Ranade
J. Michael Rifenburg
Iris D. Ruiz
Hannah J. Rule
Virginia Schwartz
David Slomp
Angela Sowa
Courtney Stanton
Mary K. Stewart
Melissa Stone
Alexis Teagarden
Darci Thoune
Megan Von Bergen
Stephanie West-Puckett
Melissa T. Yang
Vershawn Ashanti Young